ENOUGH IS ENOUGH

ENOUGH IS ENOUGH

Aboriginal Women Speak Out

AS TOLD TO

Janet Silman

women's
PRESS

First printing 1987
Second printing 1988
Third printing 1990
Fourth printing 1991
Fifth printing 1992
Sixth printing 1994

CANADIAN CATALOGUING IN PUBLICATION DATA

Enough is enough

ISBN 0-88961-119-X

1. Indians of North America — New Brunswick — Women-
Legal status, laws, etc. 2. Tobique Women's Group.
3. Indians of North America — New Brunswick —
Government relations. 4. Tobique Reserve (N.B.) —
Biography. I. Silman, Janet. II. Tobique Women's Group.

E98.W8E66 1987   323.3′4′0971553   C87-094999-3

Cover photo by Stephen Homer

This book was produced by
the collective effort of members of
Women's Press

Printed and bound in Canada

Published by
Women's Press
517 College Street No. 233
Toronto, Ontario, Canada M6G 4A2

Women's Press and Janet Silman gratefully
acknowledge financial support from The Canada Council
and the Ontario Arts Council.

CONTENTS

Dedicated to the memory of
Lilly Harris 1916–1989
and
Ida Paul 1914–1989

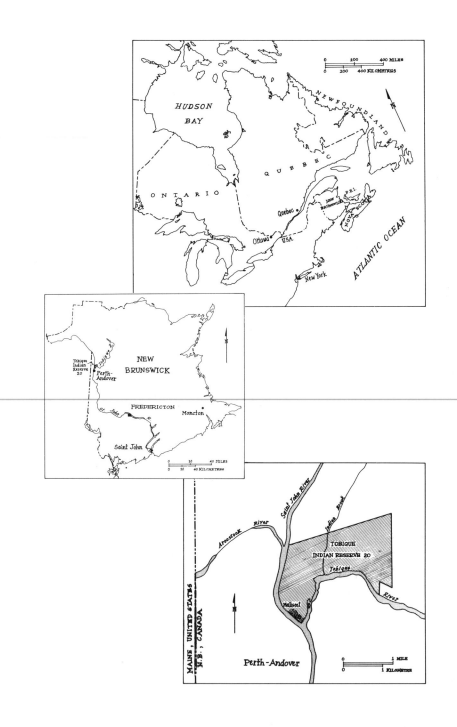

INTRODUCTION

We've had a long, hard struggle. I think what kept us going was our heritage and our sticking together. Maybe we didn't have all the same ideas, but we all had the one main goal in mind: equality for the women. We're just as good as the men. That was our one strive. I think what really kept us going is our determination to seek what is rightfully ours. And that *is* our heritage. We all knew that no government agency—be it white or be it Indian—was going to tell us we were no longer Indian, when we *know* we are Indian. Here the Canadian government was making instant Indians out of white women. You might as well say they were trying to make instant white women out of us Indians. And it cannot be, because being Indian is our heritage: it's in our blood. I think that is our determination right there—it's because we are Indian. We were fighting for our *birthright*.

Tobique woman, Mavis Goeres

In June of 1985 the Canadian Parliament passed a bill which ended over one hundred years of legislated sexual discrimination against Native Indian women. The passage of legislation to amend the Indian Act marked the culmination of a long campaign by Native women to regain their full Indian status, rights and identity. *Enough Is Enough: Aboriginal Women Speak Out* is the candid story of an extraordinary group of women from Tobique Reserve in New Brunswick who have been in the forefront of that struggle. The story is not about them, but rather, *by* them in that it is in their own words, beginning with memories of growing up on the reserve and moving into conversations about the tumultuous events of the past ten years.

The Tobique women actually began to form as an "entity" in the mid-1970s, not initially to change the Indian Act, but to improve local living conditions for women and children. Countless surveys and government reports have documented the formidable problems faced by Native women in Canada. For example, a federal study done in 1979 concluded that:

> Indian women likely rank among the most severely disadvantaged in Canadian society. They are worse off economically than both Indian men and Canadian women and although they live longer than Indian men, their life expectancy does not approach that of Canadian women generally.[1]

Furthermore, "About a third of the Indian deaths (irrespective of sex) are reported as being due to 'accidents, poisoning and violence' in comparison to about ten percent for the total population."[2]

There are approximately six hundred reserves in Canada. The reservation system is as old as Canada itself, "Lands reserved for the Indians" being defined in the Constitution Act of 1869. Since 1876 reserves have been governed by the Indian Act, a comprehensive piece of federal legislation which holds Indian land in trust by the Crown and regulates virtually every aspect of reserve life, including band politics. For example, the chief and band council are elected every two years, regardless of whatever traditional patterns may have existed. It also defines who is legally Indian.

An Indian self-government movement has gained in momentum in the past decade, seeking to gain greater decision-making powers for aboriginal people who see themselves as First Nations. However, legislative change has been approached with caution because, although the Indian Act has constrained aboriginal people, it also has defined their special status. This is one reason why Indian women seeking to eliminate sexual discrimination from the Indian Act met with resistance from some sectors of their own community. Prior to 1985, the last time the Indian Act was amended was in 1951, and even in 1951 the main aspects of the 1876 legislation remained unchanged:

> The new Indian Act did not differ in many respects from previous legislation, ie., protection of *Indian lands* from alienation and *Indian*

property from depredation, provision for a form of *local government*, methods of ending Indian status, were preserved intact.[3]

Indian reserves are "home" for over 200,000 aboriginal people in Canada. The social conditions for many bands are appalling, and even for those, such as Tobique, where conditions recently have improved somewhat, the scars may be less visible, but the wounds of over a hundred years of government regulation are still fresh.

Unemployment, suicide, school drop-out rates, health problems and housing shortages are at epidemic levels on most reserves, Tobique being no exception. While Native women long have endured the grim reality which underlies these statistics, in the mid-1970s the Tobique women decided they no longer were going to accept their situation without a struggle. Over the years more and more women were being thrown out of their homes by husbands. While the men then moved their girlfriends—often white— into the family home, the Indian women and children had to move into condemned houses or in with relatives who already were overcrowded. Since the Indian Act gave men sole ownership of property through *certificates of possession*, women had no housing rights or recourse to help through the law. Finally in 1977 when yet another woman was evicted from her home, two women, Eva Saulis and Glenna Perley, started to gather women together to protest against the situation.

In Chapter One, "Strong Women, Hard Times," individual women recall what growing up on the reserve was like for them. Their personal stories begin with the older women and move through to the youngest, so that a picture emerges of Tobique Reserve as it has changed over the years. Then Chapter Two, "We're Not Taking It Any More," traces the growing awareness women were gaining in the early to mid-1970s of the injustices they bore *as women*; and the subsequent movement from consciousness to action. Pain, anger, and compassion can be seen as motivating forces which drove the Tobique women to take drastic actions at considerable personal risk.

Because the chief and band council would not listen to the women's grievances, what began on August 30th, 1977, as a demonstration, turned into an occupation of the band office which lasted for nearly four months. The women's occupation was marked by episodes of violence and a polarization of the entire reserve into "supporters of the women" and "supporters of the band administration." In Chapter Three, "For Want of a Decent House," the women recall those emotionally-charged times.

The band office occupation received almost daily media coverage, and the Tobique women rapidly learned the value of publicizing their story. Also, as they sought (and received little) assistance from government officials, the multi-layered Indian Affairs bureaucracy came into sharper focus, and with it, that piece of legislation which governs virtually every aspect of reservation life: the Indian Act. Women were given various reasons for not receiving assistance, but the most unequivocal "no" was to those women who had lost their Indian status by "marrying out"; in other words, by marrying men who did not have Indian status.

The Indian Act not only governs the life of 350,000 Native Indians in Canada, it also has defined *who* is, and is not, legally an "Indian." From 1869 until 1985 the determination of Indian *status* was determined by a patrilineal system; that is, by a person's relationship to "a male person who is a direct descendent in the male line of a male person..."[4] When she married a non-status man, an Indian woman born with status lost it, unable to regain it even if she subsequently was divorced or widowed. Along with her status, the woman lost her band membership and with it, her property, inheritance, residency, burial, medical, educational and voting rights on the reserve. In direct contrast, an Indian man bestowed his status upon his white wife and their children, and could bestow it by adoption upon any other children. Consequently every Indian woman was dependent upon a man—first her father and then her husband—for her identity, rights and status under the Indian Act.

Maliseets were traditionally matrilineal, tracing ancestry through the woman. However, Indian tradition was irrelevant to the architects of the Indian Act, and regardless of traditional values and practices, the Act uniformly imposed the nineteenth century patrilineal European view of women as essentially the property of men. As on many other reserves, Tobique women were unaware of the far-reaching implications of "marrying out" until they later sought to move back to the reserve. A number of women who were either divorced or widowed from white husbands returned to Tobique in the mid-1970s. As women began to exchange stories and work more closely for better housing conditions, "the non-status issue" came to light as a specific instance of sexual discrimination. During the 1977 occupation, Tobique women decided to work towards raising the awareness of the Canadian public regarding Native women's problems by taking a case against Canada to the United Nations.

Actually, as early as the 1950s, Mary Two-Axe Early of Caugnawaga, Quebec, spoke out against "Section 12(1)(b)," the section of the Indian Act which stripped women of their rights if they married non-status men. In the early 1970s, Native women began to organize across Canada, 12(1)(b) being one of the issues they raised. In 1973 the Supreme Court of Canada heard the cases of Jeannette Lavell and Yvonne Bedard against Section 12(1)(b), and ruled in a five to four decision that the Indian Act was *exempt* from the Canadian Bill of Rights.

This 1973 ruling allowed the Act to remain in force, and left Native women with no avenue to challenge 12(1)(b) in Canada. Indian women who supported Lavell and Bedard were attacked by Indian leaders and labelled "white-washed women's libbers" who were undermining their Indian heritage. Organizations such as the National Indian Brotherhood mounted a lobbying campaign against Lavell and Bedard. Their argument was that the Indian Act must be kept intact for use as a bargaining lever with the federal government, and any tampering—such as amending 12(1)(b)—would play into the government's "1969 White Paper" plan of doing away with special Indian status. Although this argument was convoluted and not without holes, it continued to be employed well into the 1980s. It was used against the Tobique women when they entered the scene in 1977 by taking the case of Sandra Lovelace to the United Nations.

The reason the United Nations accepted the case as a legitimate complaint against Canada, was that, since the Supreme

Court ruling against Lavell and Bedard in 1973, Native women had no legal recourse left in Canada. The final decision of the U.N. Human Rights Committee was not made until 1981, and in the meantime, the Tobique women planned and implemented another major strategy to attract Canadian attention to the problems of Native women. In July of 1979 they held a one hundred mile Native Women's Walk from Oka Reserve near Montreal to Parliament Hill in Ottawa. The women and children's walk attracted tremendous national press coverage. Upon arrival in Ottawa they staged a large rally on Parliament Hill and met with the prime minister and several cabinet ministers. Chapter Four, "On To Ottawa: The Year of the Walk," covers the walk, the chain of events leading up to it, and the continuing protests continuing into 1980.

In 1981 the U.N. Human Rights Committee ruled in Sandra Lovelace's favour, finding Canada in breach of the International Covenant on Civil and Political Rights. The final ruling put additional pressure on the federal government to amend the Indian Act by "embarrassing" Canada—tarnishing the country's image—in the international community. Although the lobbying campaign to amend 12(1)(b) seemed on the verge of victory, four more years of concerted lobbying actually were necessary. During those subsequent years, Tobique women became seasoned lobbyists with an issue that had become "a political football." In Chapter Five, "Lobbying," the women most involved in lobbying recall the high and low points of their determined campaign to change the Indian Act.

Throughout their various campaigns, the women encountered tremendous opposition and persevered through countless frustrations and disappointments. As is evident in their testimonies, they never lost their marvellous sense of humour. Also evident throughout is a pure, strong spirituality which sometimes is expressed through Roman Catholicism, but which seems to retain powerful and life-giving undercurrents from the old traditional ways and values. The final chapter of *Enough is Enough*, "Looking Back," is a retrospective, now that a major hurdle has been crossed.

It is an assessment of where Native women are now, and a looking ahead at the challenges and hopes for the future.

Enough is Enough is the story of truly strong women who have survived hard times and overcome tremendous odds to regain their Indian birthrights. In so doing, this relatively small group of Indian women from one reserve in the hinterland of New Brunswick, have influenced the course of Native history in Canada. They would be the first to stress that they did not change the Indian Act alone; there were women before them such as Mary Two-Axe Early and the Quebec Native Women's Association, and others too numerous to mention. They would also make the disclaimer that they do not represent *all* Tobique women; they are known nationally as "the Tobique Women," but they have come to call themselves, "the Tobique Women's Group," or more formally, "the Tobique Women's Political Action Group."

The Tobique women do not share their testimony without risk, because they have been candid about a sometimes bitter struggle in their own community. However, they have felt that telling their story is worth the risks involved—not to settle any old scores, but to show people what life is like for Indian women in Canada, and to demonstrate how a group of women can work together to create a better future for themselves and their children.

When Glenna Perley first asked me to write this book with the Tobique women, she described what they wanted:

> We have been thinking about a book we do ourselves, with you to help us. Journalists and others have come in to do stories and films about us, but they leave and we never see them again. A book really telling our story would offer different things to different people. Indian women who read it would see, "Why, if they could do that—accomplish that—then we can, too." To white women and others, it would be an education: they would see what life on a reserve is like for women. They would see what all our protesting has been about.

When Glenna asked me to embark on this collective book project in September of 1984, I was a doctoral student in Christian social ethics and had been working informally as researcher and writer for the Tobique women for about a year. (Having some "Indian blood" myself—from a strong Scottish Metis grandmother —has led me to working with Indian people for a good part of my life.) I lived at Tobique for most of the next two years, travelling with the women who went out lobbying, doing the interviews for this book, and having a marvellous time becoming increasingly "at home" with the people at Tobique.

FOOTNOTES

1 Research Branch, P.R.E., Indian and Inuit Affairs Program, *A Demographic Profile of Registered Indian Women*, October, 1979, p. 31.

2 *Ibid.*, p. 28.

3 Canada, Department of Indian Affairs and Northern Development, *The Historical Development of the Indian Act* (Ottawa, 1978), p. 149. Quoted in *Indian Self-Government in Canada: Report of the Special Committee* (Ottawa, 1983), p. 19. (*Indian Self Government in Canada* is available from the Canadian Government Publishing Center, Supply and Services Canada, Ottawa, Canada K1A 0S9.)

4 *Indian Act*, R.S. 1978, s. 11(1)(c). See *Indian Women and the Law in Canada: Citizens Minus* by Kathleen Jamieson (Ottawa: Advisory Council on the Status of Women/Indian Rights for Indian Women, 1978) for an excellent history and analysis of sexual discrimination against Indian women in the Indian Act.

I
WOMEN OF TOBIQUE

CHAPTER ONE

STRONG WOMEN, HARD TIMES

Shirley Bear

LILLY HARRIS

WHEN I FIRST MET LILLY, she was living in a mobile
home trailer. I was with her neice, Caroline

Ennis, and since it was around supper time, we were expected as a matter-of-course to sit down to a wonderful traditional Saturday night meal of baked beans, cole slaw and home-made bread.

I wanted to interview Lilly not only because she is one of the elders on the reserve, but also because she has been a strong advocate of Indian womens' rights. When she returned to the reserve in the mid-1970s she discovered that she had lost her Indian status by "marrying out." As she told me later, "I knew what losing your status is like because it happened to me."

Lilly supported the women who occupied the band office in 1977 by cooking and baking for them. She walked the entire one hundred miles from Oka, Quebec to Ottawa in 1979. Indeed, she still attends Native womens' meetings when needed, and continues to keep informed and involved.

When I was growing up we always had hard times and hardly enough to eat. I was an orphan myself. My mother died when I was two so I stayed with my grandmother and shifted around, sometimes with my older sisters. One would take me for a while, and then another one, because they hardly had anything to eat either. I went to school till about fourth grade, but couldn't go to school in winter time—no shoes. My father was always in the woods working. When he came out he would drink and by the time he got home he had no money. My sister Ida and I couldn't go to school. We would have a pair of shoes until they were gone, and no rubbers or nothing. In the fall time you'd pick potatoes and buy yourself shoes, but you couldn't buy yourself everything because the wages were so low.

We used to get three cents, then it went up to three cents and a half for a barrel (about 200 pounds in a barrel). In the fall was the only time you could earn money so that you'd have clothes—a couple of dresses, underwear, stockings and shoes. That's about all you could buy, and when those shoes were gone, you couldn't go out in the snow without rubbers or thick stockings ... you'd have to stay home.

One day my girlfriend's father left the mother and the children. The mother got some help from the Indian agent, so that my little friend got a pair of rubber boots. She told me go down and ask the

Indian agent; she said, "He gave me a pair so I can go to school. You go down and ask him."

I went down early in the morning and sat there. Somebody asked me what I wanted and I said I wanted to see the Indian agent. I sat there all day while he was seeing everybody else. I was only about eight years old and already nervous when I went in.

I was real nervous now; I had to get back before dark. So I was the last one sitting there and he said, "Do you want to see me?" I was mad inside, but nervous too. I asked him, "I can't go to school. I need a pair of rubbers," and he said, "You've got a father. Let him buy you shoes." But my father was always in the woods all winter and when he came out in the spring he would have a little money but he would drink it up. So after all that the Indian agent wouldn't give me no shoes. He could have told me when I first went in, "You're not going to get anything."

In the spring we used to pick fiddleheads and sell them, and in the fall, blueberries, raspberries. We used to work hard so that we could get enough for underwear, stockings. Sometimes we had to go fourteen miles—seven miles there and seven miles back. We'd walk to Fort Fairfield to sell whatever we had—fiddleheads or berries.

When I was fourteen I left; I went to Houlton, Maine. The woman I had worked for here was from Houlton. She said, "Come over and I'll get you a job." I went with her and worked for $3.00 a week, but at least I had my meals and a warm place to stay. I did housework with white people who needed a mother's helper. They used to tell me what to do because I didn't know—they used to say, "Take the kids out, wash clothes, wash the floors...."

One day I was looking at help wanted's in the paper, the Bangor Daily News and it said the rates were $5.00 a week. I thought that was good—it was good for those days—about 1936. So I asked another Indian girl who was working, "Let's go down to Bangor, Maine." She said, "How are we going to get down there?" I said, "We'll hitch-hike," and that's what we did.

We got there in the afternoon, went down to the river and washed up. There were a bunch of young girls there who knew the town. One little girl said, "Come on over. You must be hungry.

I've got an uncle who owns a restaurant." We went with her and he fed us for nothing. Another girl said, "I know a woman who wants a housekeeper." We went there first and the woman said to me, "I'll take you." That was good—she paid $3.00 a week because she couldn't pay more. The other girl got a job that same day too, only about two houses away.

Then a hand-sewing job of making moccasins came along—a really good-paying job—because they didn't have any men. It was a men's job but the men had been drafted for service in World War II. So when the men went they hired women and I asked my boss if they would teach me too. That's how I made my living the rest of the time.

It was especially hard for orphaned children and for women who didn't have husbands. It makes me mad now thinking about the Indian agent because there was money all the time some-where for the Indians and he was so stingy. He wanted to keep it for himself, I guess.

When I came back to the reserve I didn't hate him but I didn't like him either. Once when I was twenty-one or twenty-two, I went into the store for something. He came up to me and said, "Don't I know you?" I felt like saying, "You refused to give me shoes one time," but I said, "I don't think so." He said, "I think I do. What's your father's name?" I said, "William Laporte." He said, "Oh yes, I remember you." But I didn't say anything. I figured, it's gone past. Still, you carry that around for a long time....

I think Molly had a worse time than me. I had married but I didn't have any children and she had small children plus no place to go. Nobody got help from the Indian agent. We didn't know that we had money somewhere. The old people including the chief didn't have any education. He didn't know how Indian Affairs worked and the Indian agent had a really good time with us because he knew we didn't know. Now when some of the younger people got educated they found out those things. That's why we got as far as we have now.

The nuns taught us. They had the school here. It was good, I didn't have anything against them.

My sister, Madeline, used to sew clothes. People would pay her with money, but it wasn't very much. Twenty-five cents, thirty-five cents, fifty cents. If you had an old coat and it was faded, she would turn it around and use the other side. It'd be just like new when she was finished, and no pattern.

Then we returned to Lilly's more recent story.

When the women first started protesting for better housing and for the non-status women, I was still working in the States. I came back about ten years ago—that was after my husband died—and had been gone since I was fourteen so I don't know too much about what was going on then.

Lilly's story continues in Chapter Two with her awareness that she no longer had status.

IDA PAUL

Born in 1914, Ida has seen the reserve go through tremendous changes. When she was little, there were only a few small houses scattered over the triangle-shaped field bordered on one side by the Tobique River, on the other by the St. John River. Now the houses are bigger and they cover that field—presently holding about 1,000 people—and are spilling up the single road which links the reserve with the outside world.

Through Ida and her sister, Lilly Harris, we are given a glimpse through children's eyes of reserve life in the 1920s; and as they grow up, a picture of what life was like for women in the ensuing years. What we see are "hard times" and yet, in the midst of much hardship, a strong, caring sense of *community*; of people depending on one another, sharing what little they had. In their isolation from the white outside world, they kept their Maliseet language, and with it, the deep Indian values that were either too intangible or pervasive for the Roman Catholic influence to erase.

Since Ida had eleven children, she usually had visitors—children, grandchildren, great-grandchildren, other relatives—home for holidays or dropping by.

Although Ida admits that she never got as actively involved in the women's campaigns as her sister Lilly—that she is not so "political" by nature; she told me, "I have always supported the women; always believed that it was wrong for women to lose their status. I would have gone on that women's walk to Ottawa, but even then I couldn't walk very well, on account of my bad foot." Indeed, Ida always has given her moral support and encouragement to the younger women in their endeavours to improve the lot of Indian women and children.

My mother died in 1918 in that flu epidemic. It must have been a very strong flu because so many people here died from it then. I was four and Lilly, my sister, two. My father was working in the woods where the men would be gone for two or three months in the winter trapping for furs. When my mother died, they couldn't reach him, and when he got back she was already buried.

When he found out he took off somewhere, but he left us with my sister, Madeline, and her husband, Madech (Louis Sappier). They had one child of their own and Madech kept saying, "I can't take care of you. I don't have enough to take care of my own family." They were so poor back then. Later my father came back and gave me away to an Indian man and his French wife in Edmundston, and Lilly to a family in Old Town, Maine.

One real early memory I have of the reserve was Christmas Eve. I was four, Lilly two, and we had an older sister, Mamie, who was six. I remember we could look through an upstairs window and see the big light of the train as it passed through the valley. My older sister, Mamie, was watching for that train because she said, "If our father is not on that train, we won't get anything for Christmas."

I said, "Our father has nothing to do with it. Santa Claus will bring us something." She was older and must have known about Santa Claus, but I didn't. We argued about it, and I must have said, "Let's put our stockings up anyway," even though our father wasn't on the train. Later that night the three of us did put our stockings up on a wall. By this time we were all real excited. (We went to bed and I couldn't sleep very well, thinking about Santa Claus!)

We woke up very early, it was still dark outside. We couldn't wait until it was light to see if we had gotten anything, so we all felt our way downstairs in the dark. I still remember running my hand along the wall to where the stockings were, over the stockings, and there was nothing in them. Nothing at all. By then I was so sure there would be something, but there was nothing. No candies, no nuts, no fruit. We were so disappointed, we all cried for a little while, and then went back to bed.

The couple I went to didn't have any kids when they took me. I stayed there a few years—long enough to go to school. Since they only spoke French to me, that is what I learned to speak. One day that French lady told me, "I've ordered a baby in the catalogue. I don't know if they're going to send a boy or a girl. If it's a boy, I will keep you here, but if it's a girl I'll have to send you away."

I didn't understand what she was talking about, but a few months later she must have gone to the hospital to have her baby. She came back with the baby and said to me, "They've sent me a girl, so you will have to go back to the reserve."

An older woman was visiting them from the reserve—from Tobique—and the French woman told her to take me back with her on the train. I remember it seemed I was crying all the way back. I don't know exactly what I was crying about. The Indian man had always been good to me, taken me with him in his horse and wagon. Perhaps that was what I was missing. When I got back to my grandmother's, Lilly was living there and my grandma looked after me too. It was very hard though, because by then I couldn't understand Indian or English. I could understand my grandmother because she was French, but nobody else. I couldn't understand the kids at school and when I tried to speak English or Indian they would laugh at me. I guess I pronounced words wrong and it sounded funny to them. But eventually I learned a little bit of English and Indian, and managed to get along.

I remember other Christmases after I returned to the reserve too. My grandmother only got old age welfare, so with raising us she couldn't afford to get us anything for Christmas. My aunt Monique had ten kids and this particular Christmas morning one of her sons ran over to my grandmother's place and said, "Come over to our house Santa Claus came over there for you and Lilly!"

We were so excited. We got a doll each. We were so happy. I must have been seven or eight and that was the first time we had ever got dolls.

We couldn't go to school in winter-time—no shoes—so we played with them every day. Then one of the boys was playing with a hammer. He threw it on the bed where I had covered up my china doll and it shattered. Oh, I cried and cried over that china doll. After that I had to use a little stick and wrap rags around it, so that I would have a doll when Lilly played with hers.

Another Christmas one of my aunt's boys came running over again. This time "Santa" had brought us a red sled with a Santa Claus face painted on it. Our aunt said, "You have to share it because Santa Claus is poor and he could only afford one sled for the two of you." We did share it, too. We got a paper bag of candies and an orange from her as well.

Lilly and I can't forget it now, that our Aunt Monique did all that for us when she didn't have much and with so many of her own children to think of. She was good to everybody, not just to her own family, such a good-hearted woman. She must be in heaven now. Maybe that is how you feel about a mother, because I never really knew my mother. I was too young when she died.

When I was fourteen my grandmother said to me, "Now that you are fourteen you have to go out and earn your own living." I said, "How can I, because I am going to school, and there are no jobs." She said, "Well, I can't afford to keep you. Your father doesn't help with your keep at all. You will have to get a job, something to pay your own way." She must have talked to an old woman who made baskets on the reserve, since she told me, "You go work for this woman and she will pay you fifty cents a week. That is the best I can do." So I worked for that old woman, and did I work! I scrubbed her floors, and washed her clothes on a washboard, cleaned her house.

I'd go from one place to another, staying with different people—for a while here, for a while there. I stayed with Madeline for a time, but her husband would say, "I've got kids of my own to feed. I can't afford to feed you." He went down to McPhail's store (McPhail was the Indian agent and owned the store) and asked him for some money for my keep, but McPhail refused, saying, "No, she's got a father. He has to look after her." But my father was drinking all the time, and he never did help us out.

I met Frank around that time and married him when I was seventeen. He was from the reserve at Kingsclear, but three of his sisters had married men from here and lived on this reserve. He had been living with one of his sisters when we got married. She already had a big family so had no room for us to live there. My grandmother had an upstairs she didn't use in the winter. Madeline gave me a bed and we were given a few blankets—that was all we had, and for the first while we lived upstairs at my grandmother's.

Then my sister, Marie (who is no longer living), had to go into the hospital to have a baby, and her husband was out in the woods working, so we moved in there for a couple of months to help look after her kids. They were crowded, as it was, though. We heard about an old, small log cabin a fellow had who was working in Red Rapids. We moved in there for the summer months, but it wasn't winterized, so we could only live there till the fall. Then we moved in with another of my sisters, but she had two kids and was crowded also. I had my first baby when we lived there. While we were staying there we found out about an old house on the reserve where the old man living in it had died. We moved into it and stayed for two or three years.

One winter when Frank was in the woods, working for relief, we had no bread, no flour, no food. This was still in depression times. My other sister was so poor she couldn't help us. She only had a few potatoes and salt pork for her kids. My kids were asking for food and Frank had to go to work with nothing for lunch. I took a sled on the ice down the river to McPhail's store, practising all the way what I was going to say to McPhail, the Indian agent.

I asked to speak to McPhail and was waiting, waiting. Finally he would speak to me, and I said, "I have no food. Nothing for lunches." I said, "I only want some flour so I can make bread, so my family can eat." Him sitting there in his nice, warm office like a little king; I've been freezing. He made me sit there for a long time, wouldn't answer me. Finally he said, "Why didn't you buy flour last week?" I told him last week I had to buy oatmeal, salt, beans ... no money left over to buy flour. I could only afford to buy flour every other week.

He said, "Don't make a habit of this. I will give you a little order this time only," as if he was giving it to me out of his own pocket. It was ten cents then to ride the train back from town, but I had no money, so dragged the flour all the way back along the ice on the sled. Made *legalit* (fried Indian bread). My husband was so surprised, so happy. He had *legalit* to go to work.

One November when we had four kids the house we were living in burned down. My husband was in the woods working for McPhail—no pay—when it happened. I was home alone with the kids, around four p.m. I had beans in the oven, was wearing slippers, ran out, took the kids out. People came and helped with the kids. It started from rotten stove pipes and we couldn't save it. By then Frank was back. Lost everything. My aunt had a big family, but she took us all for a while.

Nuns lived in the convent then. One called in to ask me about the fire, and after that she talked to McPhail for us. He gave us two beds and some blankets. That was all the help we got from him and here we were with four kids. Nothing left. Somebody gave us old stove, somebody gave us old table. People did what they could. That was before I started to make baskets.

That spring my husband started to make a log cabin. The man wanted his house back where we were staying. Frank could cut the logs himself, but he had no spikes. McPhail refused him spikes so my husband ended up getting them somewhere else. He was a barber, made twenty-five cents a hair cut and saved that money for spikes.

When Frank had logs half way up he asked McPhail for a little lumber for roof. The Indian agent refused him, so he got old lumber for a little money. Then my husband went to McPhail again, said, "We just need one door and two windows." McPhail refused him again, so he made a door with old lumber. Had no door knob; he used a piece of leather. All he got from the Indian agent for that house was two half windows, small.

But we moved in. Floor was rough—rough old lumber. It was a cold winter and we almost froze. We spent two years there with five kids by now. It was small, twelve feet by fourteen—had one bed and then another Frank made for the kids out of old lumber.

Frank taught me how to make baskets around that time, so we could earn a little bit more. We had to pay $5.00 duty to sell baskets in the United States. We did better selling them over across but sometimes we had to sell them in Canada—when we couldn't afford the duty. Then we had to sell them to the store-keeper down in Perth.

We managed to save a little money and bought an old house on the reserve for $300; paid so much a week until we finally owned it. We moved back, bought some used furniture. It had no electricity or running water. We had ten kids by then and my husband was still having a hard time trying to make enough for the family. When two of our oldest sons were teenagers, he said, "Those boys are old enough now to help me make a living." I said, "But they are still going to school."

We had a daughter married and living in Bridgeport, Connecticut. I guess they must have told us about jobs down there, because we ended up moving to Bridgeport. My son-in-law helped us find a place to live, and get jobs for the two boys in a factory. My husband got a job too, in a factory making shoes. But after a while the boys were laid off. Since Lilly was living in Brockton, Massachusetts, she suggested we move there where the boys could get jobs. By now it was the 1950s and I had eleven children.

I was working out every day in Brockton as a housekeeper. Actually I had worked out doing housework a good part of the time the kids were growing up. By now it was the 1960s and I remember getting $1.00 an hour, not much but enough to make a living. One of my sons was in the service down there and I received an allotment of $40.00 a month from him, so that made things a little better. Altogether I lived in the States twenty-four years before moving back here. My daughter Loretta had a real good job, and paid for the moving truck to bring my things back.

I lost three sons after moving back to the reserve. The first son I lost was Ronnie who died in a motorcycle accident. He was married with one child. His wife moved away after that happened. Then my oldest son, Lenny, drowned down here in the river. I was living here across the river from the reserve at the time. I had gone shopping and Lenny was drinking with a friend. They decided they wanted to go over to the reserve to visit some buddies. They had no way to get across except an old boat that was lying near the shore. It wasn't safe but they used it anyway, and they both drowned. My third son that I lost was Ernie, who died of a heart attack at the age of forty-four. He was married and had three children. So you see, mine is a sad story. A lot of very sad stories.

I had hard times, very hard times, but all those years I never got sick, until this winter was never in hospital except for having babies. I was sick December, January and February, in the hospital for ulcers and low blood. It was then I realized I always had my health and had never thanked God for it. Now I still thank God because I realize that your health is the most important thing. I had hard times, but I had my health.

EVA SAULIS

Gookum means "aunt" in Maliseet and that is what everybody calls Eva Saulis Gookum, perhaps because she was the only daughter with nine brothers, so she is actually the aunt of many children. In her sixties now and coping with diabetes, she has been, until recently, extremely active in fighting for better conditions for women and children, both in the occupations of the band office and in lobbying for "Indian rights for Indian women" outside the reserve.

The Tobique women trace their coming together as "the Tobique Women" back to the time in 1977 when Gookum and her niece, Glenna Perley, called upon women and whoever would support them to protest against the conditions women and their children were facing on the reserve.

Ida and Lilly are my first cousins and there were seven or eight girls and one boy in their family. Their mother died when they were quite young. Nobody ever sent children out to orphanages. Families took care of their own. Elderly people were looked after by their own children too. When my grandmother wasn't able to look after herself, she came to live with us. I remember Ida living with us for quite a while when she came back from Edmundston. Their father was my mother's brother, that made us first cousins.

My grandparents had two boys and one girl, my mother, Lilly

and Ida's father, William Laporte—people called him Billy—and one other boy, Andrew Laporte. Lilly's one brother was named Andrew after his uncle.

My mother was only twelve when she got married. She didn't even know she was going to get married. The parents arranged it. This man was from Edmundston. His name was Simon Simon. She didn't even know him. There was no cars then; they went over across to Fort Fairfield (Maine) by horse and wagon to buy her wedding clothes, but they never even told her then. They were in the store in Fort and this man, Simon, who was living over there with relatives at the time, walked over to my mother and tried to give her some money. My mother wouldn't take it; she said, "No, I don't want your money." That's when her sister-in-law, Lilly's mother, told her, "You're going to get married to him."

They had to get her to try on her dress. She said her waist was so small it was the same around as her head size. Well, she was only twelve and still playing with dolls. At that time they didn't know anything about—how should I say?—how they made babies. Now little kids even know what's going on, but at that time they didn't know nothing about that. She was so innocent. After she got married, they tried to explain to her in the Indian language what to do and what to expect now that she was married, which wasn't very clear I guess! (laughs) Anyway, she stayed married for ten years, even though she never loved him. They didn't have no children.

The old people had a lot of superstitions. People around here have seen them "little people"—they're like little elves—*golawodamoosseesik* in Indian. I've seen them around. As far as I know, I've heard tell of them in Eastport and Old Town (reserves in Maine) too. I think they must be related to the Indians, or something. I heard ladies talk about them in Old Town. One of them said once on a real moon-lit night they could see "little people" moving around outside.

There was a bridge here across the Tobique River at one time and people claimed they used to see a lot of them down under there. That bridge was burned, though. (My mother told me that one of them white squatters burned it; they didn't want us Indians travelling over there. He wanted the land for himself.) That bridge wasn't the only place those little people were seen though. They were seen all over the place. I told one of the children, "When I see them, I'll say, 'Hello, little man. Do you want a cup of coffee?'" (laughs)

My grandmother from Grand Falls was French. The men from here used to go on log drives up the river and work in the woods. That's how she met my grandfather. Her sister married a man here too. I don't know whether their parents disowned them for marrying Indian men, but my grandmother never saw her parents or her sisters and brothers after she married. Never. When she died we never even went to look for her relatives because they never came and saw her. She spoke perfect Indian.

Our parents were very strict. During Lent we had to stop eating candy, cake. Boy, we really looked forward to Easter. Really appreciated our food! (laughs) We didn't really mind, though I wouldn't do it now. We celebrated Easter, but in our family we celebrated New Year's more than Easter, even more than Christmas. It was a French tradition. They'd prepare days for that, have a banquet and a gathering. Mass would be at ten o'clock in the morning and after church relatives would all get together, greet each other with, "Happy New Year!" Then they'd have a big feast—well, it wasn't that fancy—but everything: corn soup, pot pie, meat pies, big roasts and potatoes, all kinds of pastry. No drinking. They'd just get together and really celebrate. Later on my parents bought a piano and people would sing, others would play cards. My uncle, William Laporte, played the fiddle.

The old times were good for my mother; good for us too, really. Sometimes when Louis, Raymond, Peter and I get together, we talk about times when we were growing up. Louis said, "After I got married and had children I realized that our parents had to do what they done—be strict. Teach us responsibility; how to take care of ourselves and our families." Because when the boys were old enough our father used to take them to the woods and teach them how to cut wood; also how to plant gardens; how to make baskets; even how to cook, wash clothes and knit. Everything. When they were told to do something, they did it.

There must have been Indian celebration days and stories, of course, but the priests were so against anything traditional, I think they tried to break all those traditions. When people say, "The missionaries christianized the Indians," that means they tried to take their language, their traditions, their legends, everything. I heard a lot of jokes about that too. For example, "When the missionaries came they told us to bow our heads and pray. When we looked up, our land was gone." They were stealing our land while our heads were bowed! (laughs)

Some *practical* things we kept, though. Like we had midwives until the hospital was built here. Before that, ladies had their babies at home. The hospital was built in 1924, about the same time as they built the church—after the old church had burned. The doctor use to come here by canoe—the people would go after him. Same thing with the priest. Until the early 1900s there was no priest here; he used to come in four times a year for baptisms, marriages. If somebody died, they'd have to go after the priest by wagon or canoe, then take him back again.

When we were real young we didn't have that much freedom like children do now. We were just kept right at home; we had a big yard all fenced in and that is where we stayed. The only time we were let out, they let us go to church, to school. We didn't go into other people's yards, especially evenings.

I had nine brothers in all; I was the only girl. We had one horse, one cow, chickens, pigs. Where I'm living now, my family cultivated all that in garden. So that provided food for us all winter. Each one of us had our chores; my parents put it down on a sheet near the door. I didn't have to go out and work in the garden or anything, I helped my mother wash clothes by a washboard, scrub the wooden floors twice a week, bring in water, heat the water.

By the time I was born everybody was Roman Catholic here, but quite some time ago I interviewed some elders about their religion before Christianity. One ninety-year-old lady told me that they had their own religion when she was young. She had a real good memory. She said, "We had people teaching Indian ways, and I think it wasn't right when the priests forced that Catholic religion on us." She said, "My parents would tell you, 'If you do this you'll burn in hell.'" Even her parents were so scared into it by the missionaries. She said that it was like forcing that religion on us; scaring us into being Catholic.

My father had a brother who had moved to the States and came here with his wife. They couldn't stay here because they were married by a justice of the peace and the priest told them to leave. That's the last time my father saw his brother; he never came up again. They couldn't afford to go travel in those days. There's a lot of stories like that. This same old lady I mentioned told me in the summer time people used to go play cards in the woods so the priest wouldn't see them. It was that strict.

So much has changed on the reserve now. In my time there was fishing and then hunting in the fall time. My mother used to tell me about her parents and I guess they had harder times then. The men used to go in the woods in the fall time and hunt all winter. They'd come home Christmas time. That was her father's generation. The women stayed home and took care of the family, made fancy baskets.

In the spring—they'd call it *sobekwatook* ("going to the coast")— they'd go by canoe down to Saint John. They'd take their furs and baskets and sell them because that was where the traders were, I guess. Some of them even settled in Saint Andrews (by-the-Sea). I was talking to this elderly lady in Eastport, Maine. She was from here originally. She was telling me this same story. She said, "I was seven years old when we left Tobique." She said, "I remember coming to St. Andrews, but I can't remember how we got to Pleasant Point (Eastport)." She remembered these old people from here, even my grandmother.

So our people used to grow their own food, go trapping, go hunting and fishing. My father used to salt that salmon in crocks. They didn't have no fridges or freezers then; they had like a closet outside where they'd hang the meat up in the fall time. Some of it they smoked, some of it they dried. By my time they no longer dried meat, but my grandmother used to dry berries—blueberries, *looweemeenals* (chokecherries), loganberries. That was from before people had canning. The women made all their own clothing too; knit the socks, mittens, made moccasins, snowshoes. My mother was very practical, very resourceful. She done all of that besides cooked for all of us, washed clothes, kept house and then made moccasins and snowshoes in the evenings.

The whole family would move over across (to Maine) in the fall time for potato picking. My father would take a job and then he'd hire some pickers and take the whole family over there for the season. We'd all pick and my mother cooked for the whole crew. We had good accommodation—a house. We used to pick for this farmer in Limestone for many years. When my mother had twins, that's the first time we had a cow. That farmer gave us a milk cow to bring back here.

We had a band agent here but people worked back then. The people who didn't or couldn't work got help—$1.50 a week for a single person and $3.00 for a family. That was in the '20s and '30s. Everybody worked except the people who were sick or old, widows. There was no separation then; marriage was "for better or worse." (laughs) Being separated or living with somebody else was unheard of then.

Families helped their own family, their elders. They didn't have no old age homes. My grandmother had her own place until she was too feeble to look after herself; then she moved in with us till she died. It wasn't very long. In those days the elderly were real active, strong, healthy. My grandmother died in her sleep, and she smoked all her life. She smoked a pipe; my mother did too.

My mother did Indian medicine, and we spoke only Indian until we went to school. That's when we lost our language because we weren't allowed to speak Indian on the school grounds. It was hard for us when we were little. My parents spoke Indian and French at home. We could hardly understand anything at school and that's why it took us a long time to learn. Once I spoke to the nuns who used to teach us here. I went to visit them at their "home base" in Saint John. We talked about the old days and the nun said it wasn't their idea; it was the rules laid down, the policy that we weren't supposed to talk Indian. She said, "We had nothing to do with it ourselves. We were just doing what we were told." I said, "I don't think it was right because that's how we lost our language." I guess they intended that for us.

We didn't have the same opportunities as they have now to go to college. The nuns taught us girls weaving, knitting, crocheting and cooking—those kinds of things. I was in grade six when I quit school. Well, that was as far as you could go. After that I went for a course in Andover (the nearby town); I took this course in Home Ec. They had a girl's club in the school basement and they taught us all these crafts. I tried to learn everything they taught us—dress-making, quilting, and so on. White girls went, too. We learned cooking too, though I learned cooking mostly from my mother. All those classes came in handy when I had my own children; I could sew and cook for them.

When I was about fourteen I started working off the reserve, doing house work. I used to work in Plaster Rock for a white family every summer. $4.00 a week. My brothers and cousin were working there too, peeling pulp for the man and I was working for the lady. Then I worked in Aroostook for a lady whose husband was an engineer. He travelled, would be away all night, weekends. I stayed with her and she paid me $4.00 a week. I was able to buy my clothes.

Then during war time I worked in the Presque Isle Laundry (in Maine) and started to get more pay. My cousins were working in Bangor, Maine at a shoe factory and they asked me to go down there with them. I went but I couldn't get a job in the shoe factory, so instead I got a job in the laundry, then later at a soda fountain in a drug store. That was during World War II.

My brothers were all overseas in the war; all but my oldest brother Nick. My parents had to have one son at home to help look after the family. The men volunteered in those days. One brother didn't come home, one of the twins. He was nineteen when he was killed in Italy. Oh, I could hear my mother crying at night when she heard that news, and for a long time after.

I got married at twenty-three when I came back from Bangor. I was married just six years when my husband died. I had four children. The youngest one was four days old when my husband died. He had an operation for his stomach or appendix in Woodstock, then he came home. He was supposed to stay in bed for ten days and he didn't. Apparently there was a blood clot in his lung and he only lasted six months after. He had to go back to hospital and he died at the sanitarium. They said he had TB but it was that blood clot that was lodged in his lung.

At that time I was very fortunate because I had my family—my parents, my brothers. After my husband died, I moved in with my parents. After I'd stayed with them about a year, Indian Affairs built me a new house.

The welfare we got for the five of us after my husband died was $59 a month. I was born in 1920 so that was about 1949. I received a clothing order, but they didn't give any for the children.

That dressmaking course I took came in handy. I made the children's clothes by hand, even their Easter outfits. I didn't have no sewing machine. I used to take a pattern from an old coat or little girl's coat and make my own patterns by hand. I should have kept them. I used to make little moccasins out of old felt hats; little booties. We never wasted anything. I'm still the same way, I save everything (laughs)

I married again, but not till eleven years after my first husband died. So I pretty much raised the kids on my own. When I got married the first time, I didn't know how to make potato baskets. I learned by myself, working with my parents when they made them. Growing up I learned to make fancy baskets from my grandmother. When she lived with us she used to make fancy baskets, and I'd sit behind her chair and copy her. She'd say, "What're you doing here?" and get mad at me, but that's how I learned to make them. But I didn't know how to make potato baskets until after my husband died. Then I had to.

At Christmas time I worked even harder so I could buy extra stuff for my children. I used to make cakes and sell them. I had orders; even made paper roses and dipped them in wax. I had my responsibilities so I didn't drink. Well, I never saw my mother or my grandmother drinking. There was a lot of women who didn't. It hurts me when I hear white people say, "They're all drunks. They're dirty." It hurt me when I started going out to meetings and to lobby, hearing this. I know for a fact that my mother and grandmother were real religious. The only time my father drank was Christmas time, one night and that was it. He couldn't, there was so many of us kids and he had to look after us. The only other times would be a wedding or some special occasion. Practically everybody worked. When white people say, "Indians are lazy and get everything free," that isn't true, right up to now. You have to work. Some people get a house, and we get a few extras, but we sure don't get everything free.

Gookum's story continues at the opening of Chapter Two with her recounting how as early as the 1950s she began to see how women were being treated unfairly on the reserve.

Shirley Bear

MAVIS GOERES

Mavis is one of those people it is hard to track down because she is so active. Besides taking courses to upgrade her work skills and working virtually full-time on the bingo committee, she manages still to find time for her large family which includes grown-up children, grandchildren, nieces and nephews *and* their children.

The first time I met Mavis was at a First Ministers Conference in

Ottawa where she was a representative for the New Brunswick Native Women's Council. Her hotel room had become the busy and crowded centre of the Tobique women's lobbying efforts. I remember the excitement in the air as history literally was being made, and I remember Mavis, full of energy, right in the thick of things.

Mavis—or "Mave" as her friends sometimes call her—has what my father calls "the gift of the gab"; hence she is a delightful person to interview. Her early story evokes a tangible *feeling* of what it was like to grow up on the reserve in the 1930s and '40s.

When we were growing up, you didn't see alcohol; you didn't see people out drinking. When we had parties, it was Indian games we played, like "Old Man Soup" or "the hat game." We didn't have electric lights; we used lamps. We all had our little jobs to do. Mine was washing the little glass chimneys and filling the oil lamps every day.

At a very early age my brother quit school and went out to work in the woods with my father. They'd be gone all winter long. My father was a very good provider, he would buy cases of milk, cases of tomatoes, vegetables. We had a garden too and my mother would put all the garden stuff away. The meat we had would either be dried or in the winter time, in two barrels in the shed. The meat would stay frozen and we had plenty of fresh meat. My mother even used to make her own salt pork when we'd buy a pig and they'd butcher it. My mother would take all that fat and salt it down in a crock.

I even still do that because I remember these things. We had a few chickens and my mother would put away eggs. She wouldn't use them for us to eat but she would use them for cooking, baking a cake or donuts. She was a good cook. I don't remember *our* family ever having a hard time.

We had Indian medicine, and, oh, my father swore by that medicine. Like that calamous root—in Indian it's *gilhiswas*. That is very good for a cold; we were always taking that. And *buggelous*, that's also a root. A fern root. You steam it for a high fever. Same with calamous root. You cut that up; put it on the stove and steep it; you don't boil it. Another plant—I don't know what you call it but it grows right on our lawns here—that's good for boils or any cut or anything that is got an abscess or any puss to it. That will draw it right out and dry it right up and heal it, and doesn't leave a scar either. Those are some of the medicines that we have.

My father, he always used to use tea bags for eye infection, any kind of eye infection. You'd look kind of funny with the tea bags on your eyes, huh? But after he'd make tea—in those days we didn't even have teabags, we had loose tea, so he'd make little sacks. Cool them off and put them on your eyes, and it draws the infection out of your eyes. They're even good for "pig sties." There's a lot of Indian medicine, really.

My father used to go and get hazel nut trees or bushes, peel the bark and steep that. He'd use the water from that for rubbing alcohol—for arthritis and sore joints. And it worked I've kept those traditions because I see that they really and truly work. Another thing, like I've had nine children, right? I don't remember what my mother and father did for me when I was a baby but when my babies were growing up my father came and stayed with me for a while. We lived forty miles away from a doctor. (This was after I married out.) One of my children had a really bad chest cold and where I had moved, I didn't have access to the calamous root or the *buggelous*. My father made me fry up an onion in lard, not till it was crisp but only transparent. Then I'd put that on a cloth and put it on the baby. That cleared that congestion right up, whereas the baby probably would have been admitted at the hospital for pneumonia or something. It stunk, but my God, I'm telling you, I was *amazed* at how good that was!

It's things like that, that I still remember, and still use. Lots of times now with my grandchildren, I teach my daughters these little things, and they find out that they work, sometimes better than when you're running back and forth to the doctor.

We had a lot of fun growing up here. We never planned things. We'd meet and then start playing. One favourite was Indian baseball—*eswabaswusik*. Four people could play it and there's just two bases. You have two people at one base—one to bat and one behind to catch—and two people at the other—one to pitch and one behind to catch. The batter runs and if you're out, then it's your turn to get in back and catch the ball. You keep score by seeing how many times you can go back and forth before that ball gets back to home base or you're tagged out. If they get the ball back while you're still running, you're out and it's the other side's turn.

Another was *moosoomee-kasawboom*—slang for "old man's" or "grandfather's soup." You would take an article of your own, like a ring or it could be a watch, a hat, and you'd put that in a container on top of somebody's head. Then we'd designate one person and she'd be the *moosoomee*, the one to tell people to do things. She don't know what this person is putting in the container, eh? She'll say, "Oh, I want the person to, say, act like a monkey." Then she would take one thing out of the hat, and if it was my thing, I would have to get up and act like a monkey. She doesn't know who it will be and neither do we. Then a whole bunch of us would play "kick the can"—it's something like "hide and seek." And we used to have scavenger hunts. We made our own fun and there wasn't any drinking or drugs involved.

When I was quite young our house burned. My father moved away, down to Old Town, Maine and he got trained to make hand-sewn moccasins. My grandfather before him was a leather craftsman —he used to tan his own hides and make all different sorts of leather work, so my father kind of liked leather work. After he got trained in Old Town, he came back and got me. By then my mother had died—she died when I was three—but I had a step-mother.

I started first grade in Old Town, Maine. I didn't know how to speak English so at first found it very hard at school. When my father got into the shoe factory, he moved the whole family there; and from Old Town we moved to Bangor, Maine where he worked in another shoe factory.

When I was eleven, my oldest sister got sick and asked for my help, so I came back the reserve. I still knew how to speak my Indian language; I didn't lose it. By jeez, every chance I got I spoke Indian. (Even to this day I'd rather talk Indian than English, really. To me you can explain things better.) I enjoyed being back and staying with my sister, though I missed my parents a lot. By then my step-mother was just like a mother to me. I really, really loved her as a mother because, well, I was only three when my mother died, and my step-mother more-or-less filled the gap. They didn't have any children until I was twelve and I always called them "my parents."

When I came to live with my sister she was married to an Indian man and she had quite a few children. It seems like she was pregnant every year. She really did need help. Her husband was a barber and he had a little barber shop on the reserve. She made baskets, used to boil her clothes and wash by scrub-board.

This place I'm living in now used to be the hospital. The nuns ran it. I was never sick so that I had to be in this hospital, but I remember coming here to visit my sisters when they had babies. I guess my mother died right in this hospital, but of course I don't remember her dying. My sister had three children die, two right here in this hospital, and one right at home. My sister had been in this hospital before she was transferred to the Fort Fairfield hospital where she died in 1949. That was my oldest sister.

When I was fifteen years old I went away to pick potatoes. I was in the eleventh grade and I met a man and got married. So I moved away again (laughs), and that time I was gone for twenty-some-odd years. That was 1949. I got married in June and was living in Oxbow, Maine when my sister was pregnant again. She started going into convulsions and they couldn't stop them. At the Fort Fairfield hospital they thought, if they took the baby—she was seven months pregnant—if they started labour perhaps it would relieve whatever was causing her convulsions, but then she started hemorrhaging. So with the two things wrong, she didn't make it. But as a result Stella was born. (My sister's name was Stella too.) So my husband and I took the little girl and she's been, well, you might as well say, my first-born. I've had her ever since her mother gave birth to her.

I lived in Oxbow, Maine for seventeen years and then in Brockton, Massachusetts. You know, the man I married was white and he wouldn't let me speak my Native language or teach my children the Native language, so when I got away from him didn't I ever talk Maliseet.(laughs) My youngest daughter, Susan, is the only one that can really speak Maliseet. The others know just little words, bits and pieces, but Susan can speak it when she wants to. It's a shame, though, she doesn't because the other kids don't speak it; we're losing our language.

All of my married life, I still worked. I even took the children out when I worked. I drove school bus. Oxbow, Maine is a very small community and I could bring my young children with me while I transported the school children. Then I would be home to do my work until it was time to pick them up again. After I brought the children home from school I cooked supper. In the fall I would pick potatoes and in the spring cut seed (potatoes) ... help keep our family that way. We had nine children but not once were we on welfare. We had a garden and the children were brought up to all pitch in, putting the garden in and also taking stuff out. They'd help me clean beans or whatever had to be done. We'd pick strawberries, raspberries, wild strawberries. By that time we had a freezer.

Things weren't working out in my marriage and finally I divorced my husband. As I said, my husband was white and wouldn't let me talk my Native language, wouldn't let me teach it to the kids. The divorce was hard—well, in a way it was hard and in a way it wasn't, because I had always worked out. I just kept working pretty much the same as I always had.

My sister had a very small apartment and she had a child of her own. I dropped in on her with seven kids and myself. The landlord wouldn't put up with it but I got a job right away. It didn't pay much, I think $130 a week. It was a day job. I found I couldn't get an apartment with that so I got a night job too. For seven years I worked two jobs, as well as raising the kids. It wasn't easy, but gee, my sister helped me a lot. We are a strong family; we help one another. For example, when she was going through her divorce I kept her daughter for about five years along with my own family.

I finally came back to live on the reserve in 1975. By then the kids were all grown and on their own except Susan, the youngest. I had a letter from Peter Nicholas and he asked me to come back. His wife had died and we had always been good friends. His youngest girl was the same age as my Susan, about seven at the time. I came up and stayed about a month; then went back and hired a truck and moved all my furniture into Peter Nicholas's because there was nowhere else to go. When I asked about housing there were no empty houses anywhere.

Peter's family didn't like the idea of me living in their home. I was brought up differently than they were. I like things in their place and I like a clean house. I even put some of my own money into Peter's place up there. His house wasn't finished; all he had was a bath tub and flush. I put in the lavatory, bought tile and put in a shower. He started drinking, and one thing would lead to another. There was just too much interference. Finally, one of his girls came in and literally took a bottle and hit me with it. I said, "This is it. I'm moving," though Peter and I still get along to this day.

I went to the band office and told them I had nowhere to live. By that time this place was vacant—the nuns had gone. Well, Alfred Bernard was living here with a white woman and her white child, but the place was way too big for them to occupy all of it. I saw the chief and he agreed that it could be fixed so that I could live here. I'll never forget the time we moved in. The guys moving us didn't even bother setting up anything. My daughter Susan and I finally got a bed set up upstairs and we went to sleep. We didn't have no food, no lightbulbs—somebody had taken all the lightbulbs; no curtains, no window shades. We hung up sheets in the window so we could sleep that night. We had no stove—our stove wasn't hooked up.

Edith Sappier came down with a hot plate. I had no money for food or anything—nothing. A whole bunch of women—Edith Sappier, Lilly Harris, Glenna, Eva—came with a bunch of stuff. Garbage bags, lightbulbs, toilet paper, eggs, bacon, a coffee pot. The women were supportive then. Oh yes, I guess they were some of them don't even belong to the Tobique Women's Group, but everybody helped out.

It was February 22nd and there was no heat. I went back to the band office and the band manager told me there was no money, they couldn't help non-status, but he said, "In this case I'll see that you get heat and I'll send somebody to fix the windows." See, these windows were still partially boarded up. And he put in two electric heaters.

Mavis' story continues in Chapter Two with her account of how she found out when she returned that she was "non-status"; that she had lost her Indian status when she married a white man.

Shirley Bear

JOYCE (YC) SAPPIER
(*WITH DAUGHTER BET-TE PAUL*)

Joyce Sappier, or YC as everyone calls her, is an energetic woman in her early 50s who speaks her mind and takes no "bullshit" from anyone. She lost her Indian status in her second marriage since her husband was American. After living in several of the United States that marriage ended and YC returned to the reserve in 1976.

Having lost her Indian status, she encountered numerous problems upon her return, and the next year got involved in the women's occupation of the band office. I interviewed YC with her daughter, Bet-te Paul, who also is one of "the Tobique Women." Although, as they freely admit, they have had their share of differences in the past, the two women have a good relationship now. Bet-te's own story follows.

YC: Women have had a hard time on the reserve for a long time. The reason I moved away was because my ex-husband kept going over home and busting the windows. He was scaring the kids—I couldn't even go to the dances here on the reserve after I split up with him. I was living in my grandmother's house after she died and he kept on bothering me and bothering my kids there. I finally had to leave the reserve.

BET-TE: I remember the time he scared the hell out of us.

YC: And there wasn't a goddamned thing I could do no matter how much I reported him, the cops always more or less favoured him. They never done nothing to him, so I was scared for the kids. I wasn't scared for myself; I could take care of myself.

BET-TE: That night that he really scared us, you were at the dance and I was home babysitting the kids and he busted the door right in. I didn't know who it was and I ran to the door and the little ones were all behind me. I was always scared of him because he was really cruel to me. I'm not his kid, see. He was not just cruel to me, he was cruel to you, too, Mom. I remember him, the other ones don't remember, they were too small, but he was a cruel man. I remember that night—he was like a giant to me.

YC: How did you get out of there, to run to the hall to let me know?

BET-TE: I went right under his legs and he tried to grab me. I think I was about nine. I was so scared and was looking up at him, you know, and he was going to grab me, so I went right through his legs. I was so scared I didn't even think of the kids. I was running up the street screaming.

YC: You came running up to the dance hall.

BET-TE: I found my cousin, Janice, and thinking back now, he could have done something to the kids, but I was so scared. Then people found you and they came running down to the house—your boyfriend, that was my step-father eventually—run after him. You and Suzy, too. He ran out of the house, nobody took him out of the house but he saw everybody coming down, so he ran outside.

YC: Vern got him behind the back.

BET-TE: Vern took a big piece of wood from behind the wood stove and hit him right in the back. He went running down the river bank and took off.

YC: He'd never do anything when I was there—well, I could hear him going around the house at nights but I wasn't scared of him because I always slept with a butcher knife underneath my pillow-case. If he'd come near me, boy, he'd a got it.

BET-TE: I remember women didn't have no recourse really.

YC: No. If you called the Mounties, they'd say, "We don't want to get involved in family." Same with the police constables right on the reserve. In fact, when the wife left they'd try to force her to go back into the house. Back to live with the husband.

BET-TE: We lived in an old shack, so then we lived with our grandmother.

YC: That last time I left Roy, my mother took care of you till she died. That's at the house that's down by the river. That's supposed to be mine, but my uncle who was a councillor then stole my grandmother's will. I went and put my grandmother's will over at the priest's house in a vault. Little did I know that my uncle would get ahold of that will. He lied to the Franciscan brother, told him that I wrote to him and told him to take it but I didn't.

I left Roy a good many times and moved in with my grand-mother. She had brought me and my brother Sandy up so I always considered her my mother.

BET-TE: You see, that has always been the case with women and housing. You always had to live with your relatives. You didn't have no place to go.

YC: I guess it went on about five or six years. I had Cookie when I left Roy. I had left him before but went back because they made me go back to him—the priest and the cop and everybody else was sticking their nose into it. But the last straw was one day when I went and cleaned my mother's house—she was crippled. When I came back he was burning the last stitch of clothes I had. All I had left was the old tee-shirt and an old pair of jeans I had on. He had burnt every stitch of my clothes. I could of died. That's when I went to my neighbour—it was just her and her two daughters that lived there—and I took what little clothing there was left of Bet-te's over there.

Then I got my Uncle William, I told him, "After it's dark, take me across to Uncle Sam's, but don't let Mom know where I'm at." I took off in the middle of the night but Mom found out and she made me come back. (laughs) Come back and put up with more abuse.

BET-TE: She was really religious, too. Catholic—man and wife should stick together.

YC: Till finally she seen the abuse herself. Then she told me to fight back. She said, "Grab anything you can get ahold of." So one time when he came home from work, I was cooking supper for the kids—spaghetti in tomato juice—I had a whole pot there. He hit me. I grabbed that pot and I hit him. You should have seen him, spaghetti was just rolling down on him. I grabbed the stove poker and I hit him. It landed him right in the hospital. He got blood poisoning or something out of it and I wouldn't go see him. (laughs) He was a cruel man.

I took care of my mother till she died. We were living in a small house and I met Peck who I later married. After my mother died there was actually no reason for me to keep putting up with that hassle. At the time my present husband Raymond's brother was chief and my uncle was a councillor. I told them to put Verna Nicholas in my house because she had nowhere to live—she was living in an old shack.

BET-TE: When did we leave the reserve? It was when *Meemee* (grandma) died. If I was nine or ten then it had to be 1959 or 1960. First we moved over across to Fort Fairfield; then when I was twelve we were in California.

YC: We were living in Fort Fairfield when I had Debbie. I lived with Peck about a year before we got married. I was the one that didn't want to get married, but then his mother wrote wanting us to, so we married in 1962.

I turned forty-one when I moved back here. I remember because the next day was my birthday and me and Gladys partied— just the two of us together. It must have been 1976.

> YC's story continues in Chapter Two with recollections of how
> she resisted the pressure to "sell her rights" after she married Peck,
> and of how she got involved with the women's protests when she
> moved back to Tobique.

JUANITA PERLEY

Petite in size with long braided hair, Juanita Perley has a strong, direct presence. During our first interview, she spoke while cutting out the pattern for a traditional Indian dress. Another time we talked while she worked on a children's beaded vest, with the coffee perking and grandchildren playing throughout the house.

Born in 1939 and married in 1955, twenty-one years after her wedding her husband forcibly evicted Juanita and her ten children from their home. However, instead of quietly accepting her plight, she challenged the band administration by becoming the first woman to take over a public building on the reserve.

I was born here but when I was an infant my parents moved because it was during the Depression and they were very poor. Although the Depression has never really left the reserve, it was worse then. So they moved into the States—all over Maine— wherever they could do seasonal work, the potato harvest, and make baskets the other times. We lived there about eight years, then they brought me back to the reserve.

Times weren't much better then for making a living. I was born in 1939 so it would have been 1947. What really struck me when I first came here was the hospitality; there was a warmth here that was lacking in the white communities where I grew up. Nobody locked doors.

When we got here it was in the middle of winter and Henry Bear's family took us right in; gave us their bed—my mother and me; and we stayed with them until we found a place on the reserve to live. I thought that was awfully nice of them. I never did forget that.

The reserve was a really beautiful place to live, for children growing up especially. It was so different from the way I had been raised among the white community. How they lived here was like a fairy tale. You could go and swim by the river all day long and nobody ever drowned, amazingly enough! Grapes and berries grew along the river. There is no way you could imagine how beautiful it was. That was before the dams (were built).

Then gradually what they call progress started coming in— first with the Tobique dam in the early fifties. Then when they flooded the valley, there went the fiddleheads, the blueberries, the salmon. What you once got for nothing you couldn't even buy any more—you couldn't afford to buy salmon. The Indian men would earn money as guides, and that went with the dam. It was really a drastic change. I've often tried to tell my children what it was like but there is no way you could imagine the beauty and the unity that was here among the families. You could walk into anybody's house and they fed you, they fed the kids. You never felt like an outsider anywhere. You didn't have to knock first.

Here now it has changed. You would not dare leave your home open now, or even leave it for a weekend.

All the older people were kind, it seemed. Strict when they taught you. Everybody corrected you when you were a child, but in a gentle way; they would jokingly correct the things you did wrong. I couldn't speak too much Indian. I understood Indian well because that's all my parents spoke, but I would answer back in English. The older people here would always make me answer back in Indian or they wouldn't listen to me. I don't think too many of them understood English back then, anyway. Just enough to get by on in the stores and outside.

When people went shopping, they never got money to buy the groceries; the Indian agent would write up a purchase order at his own store—McPhail's store. I can remember how they ridiculed the Indian people who came in there and even as a little kid I resented it. But you had to go in there with this little piece of paper that said you could have, say, $10 worth of food, or whatever struck his fancy at the time. They'd be making fun of the Indian people that came in—they called us "gimmes"—like "gimme this," "gimme that."

The way we talk, you never say, "Please," in our language because nobody was ever made to beg. So when Indian people said something in English they translated it literally from the way we speak and it sounded like a demand. I always resented the way the white people treated us and even today I resent it—I don't like them one bit, and I don't care if that is printed in the book, either!

Mind you, some of the white people along the riverbanks, the squatters that are directly across from here, got along well with the Indians. But the Indian people back then weren't as aggressive as this generation is. One of the farmers commented to me one day, "It's really strange. We used to get along with your fathers so well. Nowadays we can't get along with the younger generation at all."

I think this generation just began to wise up to the white man. They were "all done giving." The more they educated the Indians, the more aggressive we got. I don't think they really counted on that when they started teaching the school system to us. I don't think they thought we would use it against them. Most of the educated Indians turned around and started using their education for the benefit of their people. That's when things started getting sticky. Whites liked the Indians when they were being passive.

We had a convent here and schools, but gradually as years went by, everything was pulled away. I used to think, every time we lost something here it was added onto Perth (the nearby town) and Perth really grew. Then the welfare system that came in updated the old way. There weren't purchase orders any more. It was cash and Perth grew even faster, the cash just flowed into town. When we lost our post office, Perth got a new one.

They started integrating our kids—supposedly to make them get along more in white society, but it was a big mistake when they did that, pulling children out of reserves. You don't get any more graduates now than you did back then; even less, I think. We used to have a good priest here. His concern was always for the Indians. That was Father Sam. He was here when I moved back in 1947 but then they moved him. He was probably too good! I can remember in a Sunday sermon he said to the people, "Whatever you do, you stay away from those (federal) elections. You don't need that. It's just another step in the direction of taking away what little the Indian has." I can remember that so well and it is about the only thing I ever listened to as far as church was concerned.

As time went by and we gradually began pulling away from the church, we began looking for our own way. I discovered that most of where the Indian is today, the missionaries had a great deal to do with it. The Roman Catholic church had a lot of influence on the reserve, but they are losing it. There are a lot of other denominations here now—the Wesleyan, the Pentacostal, the traditional people. The priest doesn't have too many of us down there any more.

As I said, the Depression was really hard for people on the reserve. Before the war, people only got fifty cents a cord for wood—that was for a day's work if you did get hired. My brother lives in Fredericton now and he says he will never move back here.

Welfare back then was unknown on the reserve. I know myself how hard it is to be poor, but the way my brother describes it, things were worse then. One of my sisters even starved to death after an operation. A doctor did surgery on her at home for infected glands. They cut her open on her neck and her throat swelled up. She couldn't have anything but soup and all our family had was potatoes, so they gave her juice from the potatoes. Finally she just died. You must as well say she starved.

When we moved back in 1947, my father was crippled and he was old. I remember a time when we had nothing to eat other than what we planted in the gardens in the summertime. My brother would go hunting. We didn't own a gun so he snared rabbits, and that's what we had. Around '48 or '49 one day the chief came around and my mother asked if we could get help like the rest of the people. He said, "Not if there's an able-bodied man in your home," meaning my brother. He said, "He has to provide for you."

My brother had stayed here that winter—snared rabbits trying to keep us going; piled wood for us. But then, after he heard the chief say that, he said, "You know, you guys might be better off if I left. At least you'd get more food and you'd even get wood." So that spring he left and that fall he burned to death. He had no place to live over across (in Maine) and there were hardly any jobs.

It was harvest time when word came to us that he was burned to death in a fire. That was the youngest boy of the family and my father was heart-broken. I have often thought, I wish my parents could be living with me now. They would consider this a luxury, considering how they lived then.

They brought my brother home and the priest said they could not bury him in the blessed part of the ground and he couldn't be taken into the church because he hadn't done Easter duty according to Christianity. My father was devastated. As young as I was then, I went and asked that priest, "How do you know that where he is isn't with God? In what you've taught us in catechism and the Catholic religion we're not supposed to judge people and yet you judged him."

The priest said, "Well that is the law of the church. If you don't practise your religion you don't come into the church." It was a big deal to my parents—terribly hard on them. In any event, he was buried outside the blessed ground with no ceremony.

I still love the reserve, though. The warmth and friendliness of people here you couldn't find anywhere else. I really had fun growing up on the reserve. Back then it didn't have as much materially as it does now. Also, there weren't too many outsiders that came in. We were isolated mostly. The kind of fun you had was clean fun because still in our generation there was not much alcohol. By then, all the veterans from the war had settled down, become AA members. But then I married early which probably was why I didn't know what was going on! (laughs)

I was sixteen when I married. We moved away the first year until I came home to have my first baby. Then I never wanted to go back out there. I never liked the cities. It always felt like you were in a small box and people were so unfriendly. If you talked to somebody or said, "Hi," they'd look at you kind of weird as you walked by. So we moved back and I was married for twenty-one years.

Juanita's story continues in Chapter Two, with her account of the episode in 1976 in which her husband threw her and their children out of the family home.

Pamela Harris

SHIRLEY BEAR

Shirley was one of the first Tobique Women I met. She was in Toronto with Carolyn Ennis and Karen Perley, doing some campaigning for reinstatement in 1983, and since I was committed to the cause and wanted to meet them, I joined in their campaign.

Towards the end of a hectic week, we went out to a restaurant recommended to Shirley, and it turned out to be one of *the* most exclusive establishments in Toronto. Everyone laughed that here we were, all virtually penniless, dining out in such style.

A couple of days later, when taking her to the airport, I offered my services as writer and researcher to the Tobique Women. Shirley informally accepted, and, by a circuitous route, that work has led to this book.

Shirley is an amazing woman. She has a highly developed analysis of racism and sexism; is a gifted artist, a shrewd "politician," and above all, a woman who knows both her own mind and her own worth.

One of the first things I remember about the town of Perth is that we used to go to the movies on Saturday afternoons—we had to wade across the river to catch the train, and if you took younger ones you forded them over on your back. Usually it was no deeper than up to your knees.

After the movies there was usually a truck that brought groceries to the reserve from McPhail's General Store and we used to hike a ride on his truck. I used to like to think he was kind and waited for the kids, to give us a ride when there were a lot of us. (laughs)

The thing I remember the most, though, was walking along down in Perth, being called dirty Indian kids, and not understanding it. They would say "dirty brown" or "dirty black"—"there go the dirty Indian kids." I don't remember feeling bad or even mad about it. I remember feeling really embarrassed. I guess I didn't intellectualize those things. I was embarrassed, and I think it is easy for a person of colour to be embarrassed about themselves, to wish they were any colour but. I also remember going home and trying to wash it off in the summer time.

If you look at Ramona, my daughter who is seven, her hands are dark brown in summer. One time someone said to her, "Did you wash?" That's racism. I remember instances of racism from my childhood, but I don't remember doing much about it at the time because I didn't have a name for it.

I was one of the darkest ones at school, too, not that I've changed much over the years! Georgina and I were the little dark ones in the school and Doreen was the little white one. There was definite favouritism shown for the lighter ones. For example, it was a "privilege" to erase the chalk board and to hang around a little longer with the nuns after school, and it was always the lighter kids who got such preferential treatment.

The racism wasn't visible always, or else we didn't know what it was. Even the Indian people would, and still do, make jokes about those who are darker. I don't know why they do it. Maybe they've had good training from the nuns and the white people from close by communities or television.

When I went to convent school in Edmundston it was a girls' boarding school run by nuns. At the time it was geared for either very wealthy kids or very troublesome ones. There was no discrimination in those categories as long as people were around who could afford to send their kids there. For example, there were some very young white girls from Woodstock who started sleeping with guys and were sent to the school "to put a leash on" those desires.

Five or six of us Indian girls who were there were considered English-speaking even though we didn't know how to speak English. When we left grade school here hardly any of us were very good at English. I wasn't. Our first language was Maliseet. But the nuns encouraged us to speak English to the French-speaking girls and they in turn had to speak English to us. That was quite an exchange for someone who didn't know how to speak English in the first place, so we took English courses by correspondence.

One of the reasons I went to the school was that my good friend Doreen was there and we used to spend a lot of time together. She liked reading, and I didn't because I couldn't read English very well yet and could understand even less. She would read to me and because I knew how to draw and paint, the nuns assigned me an art teacher and studio. I didn't realize then how privileged I was in that respect. We would go up to the studio or to the back porch; Doreen would bring a book and read to me while I worked.

At the end of the year they read out our grades and invited the whole village to come and listen. Even if they were bad you got them called out. The first year I went I was the third lowest of those who passed. I said to another girl from here, "Do you really want to stay for this?" She said, "Not really, but I don't know what we can do." I said, "We already have our tickets and half of our luggage is already sent down, so let's take the rest and go home." She said, "You know, that is a damn good idea, but what about next year?" I said, "We can always say, 'School's all done.' They'll never know." So we hopped a train while everyone else was on the way to the ceremonies. I had been embarrassed the year before and I didn't want to be a second time.

After that I went working in the States and eventually got married; I never did go back to that school. The priest had a lot to do with where we went for our education; it was on his recommendation and he did all the writing for us as to where we went to college. I said, "I want to get ready to go to university and I want art." He said, "Oh Shirley, you don't want to waste your life like that." He had been the one who encouraged me to paint and draw, listen to "good music." I thought, "The hell with you, then." I had so little knowledge of university I didn't think to take whatever I needed to work my way into the arts; but one thing I did know was I sure as hell wasn't going back to the convent school.

I was eighteen when I went to the States. My aunt and uncle were there, otherwise my mother wouldn't have let me go. My friend Eunice and I rented a place, and she went to work at Walgren's Drug Store while I got myself a job waiting on tables— which I had never done before! It was fun and it was good experience. When I quit there I worked myself into a job at a department store; I started at Christmas doing gift wrapping and was pretty good at it, so they kept me on and put me in ladies wear. I stayed a few months until I got tired of it; I was getting a lot of noise from here that I should be coming home as well.

I guess my parents thought city life was degenerating and that we were doing all these awful things down there in Hartford, Connecticut. I remember that we couldn't bring food into our room, but because I had a job as a waitress I could eat right there and feed Eunice too! No matter what they said, I'd say, "she's got no money. She has to eat." They'd say, "Then use your tips." My tips were ten cents here and there! (laughs)

I came back and there was nothing to do—no life. I didn't want to go back to high school where I still had two more years to go, so I met someone, figured it would be easy—"easy living"—to be married! Basically I thought I was in love. We all do. (laughs) It was that whole idea of getting away, since there was nothing here. But it never works—you never get away—you take it with you.

I started working for a research lab—Sylvania—in the States at a time when integrated circuits were brand new so they were doing a lot of research in that area. I moved from one position all the way up and I remember one time two women were trying to get a union in, but the research plant would make raises similar to the union to keep it out. We didn't know that much about unions in those days, but these two women kept wanting one in—they said besides raises we would get more benefits. We already had a lot of sick leave and basically all the benefits that went with the union, though, so people kept voting it down.

When there was promotion I bid on every job going, and asked a lot of questions—but I was also very slim and pretty and dressed well. When I'd get a promotion, one of the union women would say, "If I knew how to swing my ass like you do I'd get a promotion too." She said something to me then that I've thought about a lot, especially with the women's rights movement. She said, "One day when you're older"—of course she expected to see me at that plant till I died—"your ass isn't going to do you any good, then, because there will be someone who will swing their ass better than you."

I used to think about her a lot, that she must be so bitter about something. Is it true? Did my ass get me this job? What got me out of the plant—and I was never in the production area where they made items to test—was talking to women on the production line. I thought some were pretty old but they were in their forties!

(laughs) I loved talking even then and would stop to chat with these women and they'd sit and talk. Then the boss would come around. The women would get all shook up, put their heads down, start working hard, say to me, "Don't talk to me now. Here comes the boss."

I'd look at them and say, "Christ, he's only a man." They'd say, "Oh, he's my boss. He can fire me." I'd say, "But there are so many jobs." It was in the '60s and there were a lot of jobs everywhere. You could go from one plant to another on (highway) 128 in Massachusetts and get a job. Good pay was about $3.05, $3.50 an hour, and if you were making that in one plant you were sure to get that and more in another.

I was standing there watching the women one day and thought, hell, this is what I've got to look forward to? I couldn't believe that there were women who worked there twenty-five years doing just about the same job. None of them moving up. I don't know if they ever bid on better jobs, but they were doing the same thing and I thought, I don't want this; so I left that plant for another to find another job.

I applied for engineering assistant thinking I would go to university—the plants were paying for your degree by incentive programs if you wanted to take evening courses. I took my general education test and passed it so now I have a high school diploma, but I still couldn't see spending my whole life working for somebody else.

I figured, I can paint, so why not try it on my own in that area? I've been poor ever since! (laughs) I thought it was such a big, fantastic decision. I'm independent. I'm free. That's what started this whole thing, painting, making baskets for a living. Because it wasn't long after that when I left my husband and came back—we all come back somewhere, sometime.

When I came back to the reserve I was no longer married; I'd gone through the whole change already. I came back with two grown up kids in 1972, and my daughter Stephanie stayed here. By then I'd known Peter—now my husband—and he and I moved around. I was here one year and then we moved to Peter's reserve, Big Cove, on the other side of the province.

Shirley's story continues in Chapter Two with her realization that she had lost her Indian status when she married a white man.

Shirley Bear

GLENNA PERLEY

On my first visit to the reserve in 1983, Caroline Ennis who has been one of the most active and high-profile Tobique Women, told me, "When you meet Glenna you may not realize it, but you are meeting the 'quiet strength' behind the Tobique Women." Having come to know Glenna as a friend, I know that she would resist being singled out in this way, but I do believe that Caroline is right.

Not only was it Glenna and her aunt, Eva (Gookum) Saulis, who initially gathered women together to mount a protest against their unfair treatment on the reserve, but also as the Tobique Women's collective story will demonstrate, Glenna has been at the heart of the struggle ever since. One example among many is the fact that, taking the case of Sandra Lovelace to the United Nations Human Rights Committee was originally Glenna and Dan's idea.

Although she would never seek credit for them, many of the ideas, strategies, and analyses of the Tobique Women have been initiated by Glenna. Her solid common sense and keen grasp of issues has never ceased to amaze me, and beyond that, her "quiet strength," compassion and courage have been a source of inspiration to everyone who has worked beside her.

Although I was boarding with Glenna over the year or so that I was taping interviews, it took a long time for us to finally sit down with the tape recorder.

The earliest memories I have are of my great-grandmother on my father's side. A lot of people say she was mean, but she was kind to me. The other day I was telling Ida (Paul), "I remember my great-grandmother," and Ida said, "She would talk nasty to me." There is a picture of her and I and a bunch of other women, relatives mostly. I was only about four and was standing next to her and she had her hands on my shoulders.

I remember my great-grandmother as being a nice, old lady. She always gave me apples and oranges, and used to tell me not to tell my cousin Pat or my uncle Tony. She'd take me into her bedroom and she had this wood stove and this big trunk where she kept all her goodies. (laughs) She wouldn't let anybody else have them, just me! Chocolates and dulse. I remember her milking cows. She used to take me up to the barn; it was quite a long way she had to walk up the hill. I used to go with her and Pat. Pat would do all the work but she would be there to supervise.

She would pick sweetgrass. I remember my grandmother going to the same places picking sweetgrass and Indian medicine. They'd go down by the river for medicine plants. I don't remember when my great-grandmother died. They must have kept it away from me; maybe they took me to my other grandmother's. I would have remembered if I saw her in the coffin.

My father's family (the Nicholas's) always had a big garden and chicken—they farmed. What is now Gookum's big back yard was all garden and I remember helping my grandmother there. She put up jams and vegetables. She didn't have to buy much food, but what she bought was all in bulk. And she was always feeding other people. She made baskets too.

My other grandmother and her family didn't have it so good. They had a garden, but not a big one, and I think they used to make baskets. I don't remember that grandmother so well because I spent more time with my father's mother than my mother's. My brother Lloyd must have been a baby then since he is four years younger than I am. I had older brothers and sisters, but they died when just infants. After my older brother and sister died, my mother didn't have another child for five years, and then she had me. Pat is my cousin, but my grandmother brought him up because his mother, Molly, had such a hard time raising her kids. A lot of times they didn't have a place to stay.

My father's mother always told us to help each other. She'd say, "When I'm not around I want you to help one another." She helped a lot of people with Indian medicine. A lot of times when the kids were sick—not even her relatives—they'd come to her and want advice from her on what to do. Some of the people that didn't like her called her a witch, but she just laughed, said, "I wish I was a witch. I'd put them in their place!" (laughs) She didn't care what they called her. She said, "I'm not doing it for them. I like to help people."

My own mother must have been close to my father's mother because I remember when my mother died, my grandmother was mad at my father—because he was drinking, I guess. She said to him, "I don't even want to see you." I don't really know what they were fighting about. Then I heard her say that she wasn't going to let my father bring me and my brother up. I think it was because my father drank quite a bit at the time. He was good at making money, he always had good ideas and they always worked for him, but I guess the alcohol got the best of him. No matter what he tried he always made money.

After my mother died, my father drank a lot more and then he married my step-mother, Connie, and they moved away to Maine to make baskets and work in the woods. They had my brother and I down there for about a year and a half. I was about eleven. The only difference from here I remember was the language. I had a hard time with the English language, but I didn't have any trouble getting along with the white students—Lloyd and I were the only

Indians. People were so friendly, it was like almost the reserve. There weren't many families, altogether about twenty-five houses along the road, one store, a post office and a church. Mostly people worked in the woods, had gardens, but they had a hard time, just like the reserve. It would have been about 1949.

Before that we went to school on the reserve. I liked school till my mother died, but I hated it after. I don't know why; I think I changed after my mother died. I just hated school and didn't want to learn; I didn't care if I made grades. It stayed with me, too—I guess that's why I never got a good education. The nuns always made us speak English. I think I took my mother's death out on everybody, everything.

I hadn't stayed over across in the United States with my father and step-mother very long when I wrote my grandmother to come after me—I wanted to call her but I didn't know how to use the telephone. I didn't like it because they were drinking too much and my brother and I were left alone quite a bit. I had to babysit my cousins, Vaughn and Wayne and Iris, and I was only ten. My grandmother came after me in a taxi. (laughs) It must have cost her money! Lloyd stayed there longer, until our father and Connie finally broke up, then he came to stay with my grandmother, too.

Back when I had returned from the States to live with my grandmother, the nuns put me back a grade which made everybody my age all higher than I was in school, and that was discouraging. I quit school four years later and went out to work as a baby-sitter for a short while; but then ended up in a sanitarium at St. Basile. Actually I didn't realize I was sick; I just had a shadow on my lung. It was not TB yet, but if they let me go I probably would have got TB. You had to get a lot of bed rest to get that shadow from your lungs.

Gee, there were a lot of kids from Tobique there. I felt so sorry for two of my cousins when my uncle took us away in the van— Wanda and Gloria were only about six years old and had their dolls with them; they didn't know what was happening. Altogether there were three little girls and two little boys, then about six teenagers, plus adults all mixed together—about twenty of us going all at one time. Some people from the reserve were already there, too. Seems to me there was always at least one person from the reserve in the TB hospital when I was growing up. I went at the time they started bringing in those mobile clinics.

Mostly I remember being very lonesome—well, being a teenager and all of a sudden locked up in there. But you could go to classes two or three times a week, depending on how bad off you were. We had movies once a week or so in the auditorium. Sisters ran it and they weren't too strict. You had to be in at certain times and when you were getting better you could get overnight or weekend passes to go home. A couple of times my uncle came to see me. He wanted to take me out to dinner and all I wanted was a hotdog. (laughs) He said for me to order anything I want and I ordered a hotdog! The boys were on one floor and the girls on another, but once a week you could visit other floors. We would talk to the boys at the canteen or outside, too!

Most of the people there were French. I learned some French and made quite a few friends. I didn't see much difference in the French; if it had been all white—that is English—people, it would have been different, but for some reason I always felt closer to the French.

I remember my grandmother was very religious. She always had her rosary and was always praying. I remember that the older people and everybody used to listen to the priest; whatever he said, it had to go on the reserve. Before they made a decision, a lot of people would go and talk to him. They wouldn't go against him!

When I was living with my grandmother, she would talk to me a lot about her religion—but, even though she was a good Catholic, it was her Indian religion she would talk about. She would teach me what the Indians believed in. She said they never used to have confession; would just go in the woods and pray. That is why I like going in the woods so much, and when I do go in, I usually end up praying! My grandmother said there was no such thing as confession; the older people used to talk to the trees. She used to laugh at that; said, "I wish some of those trees could only talk!" But she did go to church too.

That's why when I heard these medicine men at a spiritual gathering, I felt I'd heard it already. I told one guy, "I've been sitting here about two hours listening to you, but everything you've said, I've already heard it all." He asked me where I'd heard it, and I told him, "From my grandmother." She told me prayer is just being alive and helping people: "Your life is a prayer, the way you help one another—just as long as you don't deliberately hurt a person or steal from a person." You have to forgive somebody when they do something against you; you don't go out and try to hurt the person just because they hurt you. Like the medicine man said, you have to let God take care of it. He said, "Just you watch and see, whoever hurts you, they end up hurting more than you do."

I've seen it a lot of times. Like a lot of people who are greedy, or take things away from other people, they never live long enough to enjoy what they got for nothing. That's why, when sometimes I hear a person saying, "This one has more than I have," I try to teach my kids that it doesn't matter who has more. I know having that in mind helped me a lot to *survive*. I don't care what the other person has, and if they win anything I'm glad for them.

Without the ways my grandmother taught me, maybe I would have turned to drinking, but I know I'm strong and that's why, I guess. I don't think I would be if I wasn't brought up by her.

She saw the humour in things and she told a lot of stories, but I've forgot most of them. My grandfather was alive then too. He was kind but he had a bad temper. When he got mad everybody was scared of him. He wasn't too good with his Indian language, spoke mostly French. When he'd get mad he'd start talking French. I do the same with my kids—when I get mad I start talking Indian and they really jump. (laughs) Tiffany said, "Mom! You sound so scary!" Same with my grandfather. He was partly French and brought up in Quebec. I don't know how he ended up here; when he married my grandmother, I guess.

My grandmother was married before. Her first marriage was arranged by her parents—she was very young when she got married. She said, "I was still playing with dolls. I even went back to school after I got married." Arranged marriages used to be quite common. She said she cried and begged her mother and father that she didn't want to get married. She didn't even like the man, he was so ugly. (laughs) It didn't help—they said he was a good provider, a good worker, and she wouldn't need for anything. He was almost forty.

She had no children by that man, but eleven children, I think, by my grandfather—there was a few that died. The first one died, I know. My father had just one sister, Gookum, and all brothers. I was twenty when my grandmother died, but she wasn't that old, around fifty-eight or sixty. She said, "I'm lonely. All my friends are gone, all my family's gone."

My grandfather had been killed in a car accident—a car hit him. He was working on the construction of that big airforce base in Limestone, Maine. My uncles and quite a few men were working there. He must have been a good worker, like my Uncle Raymond, from what I heard—he was always working. After he got paid on Friday or Saturday he started hitch-hiking, walking home and he got hit by a car on one of them crossroads. I was about eighteen at the time.

I worked there at the base when I was going with my husband, till we got married, that is. Also, when I started going with Kenny I was taking a hairdressing course. Actually he was working in Connecticut so we didn't go with each other that much—just summer vacation, spring vacation, then the following year we got married! Actually it was my grandmother that pushed it. She was dying but they didn't tell me how bad she was.

She died that fall and I got married at Christmas because she had asked me, "Will you get married?" and I'd said, "Yeah, I will," as if it eased her mind when I said I would marry Kenny. Looking back I feel as if it wasn't my choice, it was like a promise to her. Maybe that is why it didn't work out. Maybe she thought I would be looked after, because before she would never insist on me doing anything. She had asked to talk to Kenny before she died, but he would never tell me what she said.

I got close to my father after I got married and he was living a short ways from me. I starting looking after him right away—

that's when we noticed he had arthritis. I wasn't that close to him when I was growing up.

Kenny and I moved down to Connecticut for two years till I had Kim and Tina. I also worked down there—in a plastics factory, but it was hard to get a babysitter and we couldn't get a good apartment with the kids. They were able to say, "No children" or "No pets," or they'd take pets and no children. I thought, gee, I don't want to bring my children up here. Kenny was starting to drink heavy then, but I thought if we moved up here there was no liquor stores. He got worse instead of better! (laughs) He probably thought, I'll fix you.

Kenny's uncle was chief then, Charlie Paul. We were sort of lucky that we got a house when we were only here a year. But the same thing is happening now—they move from a different place, come here and get a house right away. I don't think that's fair. The people who have been here and waiting on the housing list should get it first. I think there should be a waiting period.

I noticed when we came back that the chief had a little bit more say than before—before that everything was what the Indian agent said. At that time—about 1964—they still had only two councillors, Paul Perley and Pauline Nicholas, because there weren't many people on the reserve then. I think the Indian agent—by now called superintendent—was located in Woodstock. McPhail must have retired. Then from Woodstock they moved Indian Affairs to Fredericton. It kept getting further away! I guess you had to write to them if you wanted something, but there wasn't anybody asking for things. I guess they just accepted what was given to them. Everything was just accepted.

> Glenna's story continues in Chapter Two with her recalling how, even before her own marriage ended, she began to notice the problems women were having on the reserve.

Harvey's Studio, Fredericton

CAROLINE ENNIS

Ever since Glenna Perley asked her to arrange for media coverage of the first protests in 1977, the Native women's cause has claimed a central place in Caroline's life. Her personal motivation can be traced back to the difficult times her mother faced raising a family single-handedly, and to the childhood experiences of living in a series of other people's already-overcrowded homes.

When the Tobique Women decided to stage a Women's Walk to Ottawa in 1979, Caroline took on the responsibility for all the outside arrangements—an enormous task which she often says she only accepted "in her naiveté." Nevertheless, the walk was an event that received widespread media coverage, alerting the national consciousness to the plight of Native women throughout Canada.

Not one "to suffer fools gladly," I have seen Caroline verbally pin a prominent cabinet minister to the nearest wall. She is fearless and unrelenting in her pursuit of the Native women's cause which she sees as one of basic human rights. Shirley Bear, herself hardly a shy and retiring person, smiles with recollection of how Caroline—

"this tiny, little person"—can command such attention and respect.

I interviewed Caroline while we were relaxing at her aunt Lilly Harris' home after clearing brush for a house site one day. Although Caroline was one of the first Tobique Women I met, it was in working together in the out-of-doors that I felt I became friends with this strong woman.

I don't remember much about my father but I know my mother left him because he used to drink and he'd beat her up. I didn't know that at the time, I was too young. I must have been quite young because I don't remember much. Anyway, she finally left him for good. My father did come home for a short time after my mother finally got a house. I was about twelve and by that time I was used to being on my own—literally bringing myself up. I was pretty independent by the age of twelve since I got very little supervision. It wasn't my mother's fault—she had to go away to work in order to support us. Nobody really cared what we said or did because we were just somebody else's kids.

I remember running away from school when I was older, but when I started school I liked it. I think because I liked reading; I really picked it up. When I started school the nuns were talking English and I couldn't understand one word they said, but I guess it doesn't take kids very long to learn another language. The teacher would read us stories at the same time every day and the kids around me would fall sound asleep. Except for me—I couldn't wait for that time of day. I just loved it.

Our school didn't have a library. Each grade would have a reading text, and as soon as I could, I read all the readers—because there were stories in them. Do you remember those old-fashioned texts? There'd be stories, and in between a poem and something else. I'd read right through the whole thing and then borrow somebody else's who was either a grade behind me or a grade above. When new texts came out, I'd just love it. Now and then you'd come across some comic books or those "True Romances." Some people must have read because I remember going to houses that had those True Romance type of magazines, and I read them all too! This was when I was about ten years old, I read anything I could get my hands on. People would hide books if they saw me coming because they couldn't stand to see me reading one book after another. I must have been in the way but I didn't realize it. (laughs)

As poor as we were, Tobique was a nice place for kids to grow up in. You made your own fun. I think people were closer, they communicated. Like on Christmas Eve, for example, you'd go and visit every relative all night long, and there'd always be lots of people laughing, laughing, laughing. Especially at my aunt's— she must have liked a lot of people being around her because there was always a huge crowd there. They'd play cards and always be laughing. I guess times were bad, but you didn't know it as a kid.

The Roman Catholic church was part of everything you did on the reserve. For example, they used to have a church service every night—benediction. We'd all go and giggle and laugh and look at the boys. (laughs) I didn't mind going to benediction, it was kind of fun. It was a social, where you'd see everybody. I didn't like going to church at Lent, though. We had to get up and go to church every morning before we went to school. I think the church dominated our whole life but parts of it were really kind of fun.

I loved it when we dressed up in white every 26th of July for Saint Anne's Day. The men would go out and cut young poplar trees from the woods and line every street on the reserve with these poplars, about every ten feet. Wherever the poplars led, that's where the church service would be. You would leave the service at church and everybody would walk in a procession to the person's house where the service was that year. They would have made up an altar on their porch. The *whole* community would be there, plus Indians from other reserves. It was a great big happening, like a festival. Your mother would give you extra money and there would be all these events as well as the service where you got to dress up.

That was the only way you got to meet your relatives and other people—that is, people from other reserves. I never visited any other reserve until I was grown up. I knew they were there, but was only aware of the ones people talk about—Woodstock (down river) and Sebiak in Maine. But they used all Indian names so I never knew where they were. They only mentioned three or four other reserves so I thought that's all there was.

All summer we swam in the river and nothing ever happened to us. I remember only one kid drowning but he wasn't from here. There was a log run every spring, so a long boom thing was built so that the logs wouldn't go up on shore. We'd jump off that thing and swim in the river. I remember seeing great big eels in there where we swam. This was before they built those dams. There'd be a huge rock sticking out of the river and you could swim out and lie in the sun on that rock.

Everybody played baseball all spring. You couldn't wait to get out at recess. Right after school, as soon as you dropped your books off at home, you'd go and play baseball, play till supper time and in the evening go out and get another game in. So we had really good ball players; they used to beat all the towns around here. Until very recently when Tobique went to Indian Summer Games, they won every baseball game. I remember hearing one Micmac say, "Oh, those damn Maliseets, they're born with base-balls and bats in their hands!"

I remember when we finally got a little house—actually we got it because this other family didn't want it. We were all so happy, all my brothers and sisters came in with their little possessions before the place was even finished. It was ice cold in there—a brand new house but it was built so badly that it was really cold. No bath, no insulation and wood heat. The water we used to wash with would be frozen every morning. But it didn't seem to bother us—we didn't see it as a hardship.

I didn't *feel* poor because everybody else around here was poor too. It didn't bother us at all—kids are pretty adaptable—but it must have been hard for my mother. She never talked about it; she was very strong but very gentle and very religious. She must have had an awfully hard life, but she was happy. She'd be cooking in the kitchen and singing away, singing all these old songs.

Our only source of income was from the potato harvest in Maine. In order to supplement our food supply, we would pick potatoes in the fall. We had to pick all the small potatoes that were left over in the field. We'd have two or three barrels of them; and would bring them home from Maine when we moved back at the end of harvest. They'd last us all winter; my mother was a very good manager.

That's the only way people on this reserve survived in the '40s and '50s when times were still really bad. If it weren't for the potato harvest in Maine, I think a lot of people would have died of malnutrition. That was the only thing you had to keep you going. As recently as 1955, people were still only getting $2.50 a week to buy groceries with. I think they called it relief because it was relief from death by starvation. You were certainly not meant to eat well on it. Now, that's not very long ago. There were four children plus my mother and $2.50 a week doesn't come to a hell of a lot. I tried to check that out with the Department of Indian Affairs and I could never get the information, but some of the people here, like Raymond Tremblay who was either councillor or chief at the time, remember.

I was sent to a boarding school in Newcastle for high school. It was run by nuns and real strict. That's why I left it, because here I was so free, going to dances and having a lot of fun for a fifteen year old. Then I went to a boarding school where you went to bed about nine o'clock at night; got up at the crack of dawn to go to church. Your whole life went by the bell—they rang a bell and you jumped up and ran down to eat... and I guess I just couldn't take it. I stayed till tenth grade, then I left.

I came home and talked to one of the guys who worked in Connecticut then. I asked him if I could go with him to Connecticut. I must have been damn brave. Not a cent to my name! Here I went off to Connecticut and found a job baby-sitting—I lived in with a white family. The man was an executive of an advertising company in New York City, and they lived in Westport—really exclusive. I worked for them one winter, before coming home for a year or so. Then I went to where my aunt was living in Brockton, Massachusetts.

From Brockton I went to Bridgeport, Connecticut where my brother was living. He was still married at the time, so I lived with them and started working in country clubs because that was where my sister-in-law was working. It was really good money for that time; we were making $5.00 an hour, plus what we made at extra parties. I wasn't married then, so all I did was work. I bought a car and lots of clothes.

That's where I met my husband. Actually I met him before that in Brockton when he was still in the service. His family is originally from here but he grew up over across in Caribou, Maine. When he got out of the service, he was living in Westchester, New York which is not far from Bridgeport, Connecticut, only about an hour's drive. Anyway, that was where I met my husband, and we got married. I continued to work in those country clubs, before and after I had the two boys. My husband knew he couldn't get promoted unless he had a civil engineering degree, so he decided to come up to Canada to go to university full time. This was around 1971.

When I could not find work, I also decided to return to school. I graduated from St. Thomas University in 1981. It was while I was attending university that I was contacted by Glenna. She was in the middle of the first protest by the women of the Tobique Reserve. She asked me to contact the media, women's groups and whoever I thought could help.

Caroline's story continues in Chapter Two with her looking back at the hardships women suffered on the reserve which led her to recognize the problem of discrimination.

Shirley Bear

SANDRA LOVELACE SAPPIER

Sandra is nationally the most well-known of the Tobique Women because of the publicity generated by "the Sandra Lovelace case." In 1977 Sandra agreed, as a woman who had lost her Indian status through marriage, to take her case to the United Nations. The U.N. Human Rights Committee ruled against the Canadian government, causing Canada international embarrassment and putting pressure on the federal government to remove sexual discrimination from the Indian Act.

Since Sandra's case was taken to the United Nations, she has been interviewed so often over the years that her name has become identified with the issue of 12(1)(b). In 1985 a one hour CBC television dramatization of her story was shown on the *For the Record* series.

Slim and attractive with a strong personality and a no-nonsense approach to life, Sandra grew up in the all-female household of her mother, Cora, and three sisters. Two of her sisters, Karen Perley and Barbara Nicholas, also were involved in the band office occupations; and Karen and Sandra often went out lobbying for reinstatement together. Since their father is a brother to Eva (Gookum) Saulis, Gookum is their aunt and Glenna Perley their first cousin.

We were really poor because my mom brought us four girls up by herself. At that time the Indian agent would hardly help anyone. Sometimes she would have to go down town and tell him, "We have no food"; he would give us food orders but that would be the only help. Before school started in the fall we would get clothing orders and that was the only clothing we'd get.

At first we went to school on the reserve. The nuns taught us and we couldn't talk Indian—every time we talked Indian we'd get spanked. They used to tell us we were dirty—they made us ashamed we were Indians. After grade six we went to school down town and there was a lot of, "Go back where you come from." The white kids would make fun of us, put us down because we were Indians, so I quit school about grade eight. I couldn't take it anymore; I figured if this is what the world is like, I don't want to be around white people.

I left home at about seventeen; went with a bunch of girls to work at a potato factory in Maine. I worked there for a couple of years, hardly ever came back here and that's when I met my husband—he was stationed at the airforce base. By that time my mum had remarried and moved to Philadelphia. I moved to Pennsylvania where my mum was and worked there, then when my husband got out of the service he moved there too. That was where we got married, worked for a while, then moved to California for about six years.

We split up in California; I got a divorce and everything over with by the time I moved back here. I decided I wanted to come home and be with my people. By then I had a son, Christian. First I stayed with my sister for a while, but you know how it is with two families; the kids didn't get along, so I pitched a tent and my son and I lived in it. That's when I heard that the occupation at the band office was happening.

Sandra's story continues in Chapter Three with her finding out upon her return to the reserve that she permanently had lost all her Indian rights when she had married a man who did not have Indian status.

Shirley Bear

KAREN PERLEY

Although not as well known as her sister, Sandra Lovelace Sappier, Karen has been extremely involved, both on the reserve and out lobbying, in the Tobique Women's cause.

As I have gotten to know Karen over the past few years, I have come to realize that, like Glenna Perley, she is one of the "quiet strengths" amongst the Tobique Women. She is kind, intelligent, committed, and has a marvellous sense of humour. She is a beautiful person in every sense of the word, though her humility would cause her to resist such praise.

Growing up on the reserve was all right; we didn't have much—we were poor just like everybody else. It was happy though. It wasn't like it is now where kids are so bored and restless. Back then we always had lots to do, made up our own games.

My memories of school on the reserve were all right. I know I was afraid of the nuns, perhaps because they spoke a different language. I don't know why for sure, but I know I don't have very happy memories from later on when I started to go to school downtown. We were always being looked down on because we were Indians. I was self-conscious because I didn't speak English as good as I thought I should. We always spoke Indian at home—didn't speak any English till school here when we had to communicate with the nuns. I remember thinking what a strange language English was! But the teachers pounded English into us so much that now it is all the kids speak even at home. Some parents will try to talk Indian to their kids and they'll say, "What does that mean?"

I grew up without my father being around. My mother and father were separated as long as I could remember. That part was unhappy, not having a father around; he was always away in the States working. I remember a couple of times Gookum saying, "Your father is here. Why don't you go see him?" We would go see him but it was so strange. He would give us money and buy us stuff if he was around and then he'd leave again. I started to get to know my father when he moved up here and I was about thirteen. My mother used to tell us not to go over there but we'd go anyway.

We did have a house—it was a veteran's house that my father had started to build—but it wasn't finished. It was a big house, cold in the winter, hot in the summer. I remember sometimes being hungry. We'd have oatmeal, put it in a glass with a little bit of brown sugar and milk and mix it up like that without cooking it. It would get all mushy and we loved it, but that would be all we had. Other times we would have stale bread—I didn't really know the difference from fresh bread when I was a kid. We preferred bread you bought at a store to home-made. (laughs) Isn't that something? Now I'd rather have home-made any time!

In this little school on the reserve the nuns used to show preference to the light skinned kids, and kids with light hair. Fair kids would get all kinds of attention, be allowed to run errands for the nuns. I think that is when I started wishing I had blue eyes and light skin and blond hair. I was really religious and I used to pray every morning, every night and sometimes in the afternoon because the nuns would say if you pray hard enough you'll get what you want. So I would pray that I would wake up the next morning and have blue eyes. Isn't that sick? When I got a little older I still did a lot of praying. None of my prayers were ever answered; I was too dark! Now if I had believed there was a black God.... When I started hearing about diseases and how people die I used to pray, "O God, please don't let me die of TB, cancer, heart disease ... " I used to pray for everything. The reason I did that was the nuns used to say that God did love all children, no matter what colour. Yet they would turn around and favour the light kids!

My mother gave us as much attention as she could but back then there was hardly any welfare so she had to go out to work, plus raise four kids and we were all small. She tried and my grandparents tried to help her out as much as they could, but back then everybody was in the same situation.

My grandfather was chief for a long time. Around election time they'd say (in Indian, of course), "Somebody is going to run against your grandfather." I had pictured the two running a race. (laughs) My mother would let us go down to the band hall once in a while to see a whole bunch of people, a celebration.

There was Indian medicine then but hardly any Indian traditional practices or ceremonies—because of the nuns and priests. I know my mother was religious because her mother and father used to make her go to church, so she made us go to church. We went because we had to, not because we wanted to. The nuns would make a game of it. You would get a star every time you went to church and the one with the most stars would get a prize at the end of Lent. So you tried!

There used to be Indian dancing, especially for the little kids. I'm not even certain it was the way Maliseets used to dance or whether we adopted them from other tribes. We were once matrilineal and women had more decision-making power then than later on. I think that was kept alive though, because it was always the woman at home making all the decisions for the family. The man was out working somewhere. Even now, such as yesterday at a housing meeting, I noticed it was the women speaking out! I suppose the husbands had something to say too, but the women did most of the talking and it is just accepted.

I think the women are getting stronger again now. There was a period when the male was the person who "wore the pants in the family." Maybe they used to think of him that way because he went out and made money. He'd work and get paid for it while the woman stayed home and didn't get paid. Now it would really be something if it went back to the way it was with the matrilineal type of system. But there would have to be a lot of changing done. First of all we've got to lobby our own people; try to vote some women into the council.

I remember one funny thing from when I was growing up without a father. When we started school we would ask my mother, "Who's our father?" She'd say, "The Indian agent is your father. He's the one supporting you, so he's your father!" Honest, one time the Indian agent came to the store—Mildred had a store then. He was sitting there and I thought, gee, this guy is my father and why isn't he showing me any affection or paying any attention to me? My mother shouldn't have said that, because I started to believe that this guy really was my father! (laughs) I used to hear a lot of negative things about that Indian agent. I don't think the adults talked much about reserve politics when kids were around, though, because you know how kids are—they go and spread things they hear and most of the time they don't get it right.

I started going to school in Perth in grade seven—all the grade seven kids used to go on the school bus. That is when we started pressuring our mother to buy us nicer looking clothes. She tried. My sister Sandra and I started at the same time and Mom bought a whole bunch of material to make us dresses and skirts. They were all right but we ended up wearing them most of the time and you would see the little white kids down town coming in with something different, new things on every day, it seemed. We were "trying to fit in."

Some of the white kids weren't really that bad. Even the lower class whites, the poor whites, were discriminated against and looked down on. Not as much as us, but they too were treated badly. The French too. I thought the closer we could dress and look like the white kids, the more they would accept us. They too favoured the lighter skinned ones amongst us. The darker ones would get called the names—"dirty Indian," "squaw"—be given a harder time. At school in town we were always told to speak English, too.

Whenever anything got stolen in that school the principal would call through the PA system for all the kids from Maliseet to come to the auditorium. He was the biggest bigot. He would call us all to the auditorium and say there was some money missing from a particular place. He'd point out to us that we were outsiders; that if we kept stealing we weren't going to be welcomed. But he just assumed it was one of us.

I went as far as grade ten. My mother made us keep going; I always thought it was important to get a good education, too. Even when I quit I had made up my mind I was going to go back, but not to school in Perth. I couldn't stand it there. I was fifteen and that's the time young people start thinking they know more than their parents. That's when I went to live with my father and started getting into trouble, drinking. It would have been 1964.

The year before I quit, the school board had decided they didn't want Indian kids going to their school any more, and they told the chief and council they didn't want us. This biogoted behaviour was coming from supposedly respectable people from downtown. The chief at the time was Raymond Tremblay and he went to the media about what was happening. The school finally took us back in the fall but you can imagine how we felt—knowing we weren't wanted, yet we had to go. Our parents made us stick to going to school. One headline said, "Little Rock, Arkansas in Perth-Andover," because the Blacks in Little Rock had gone through the same thing, I guess.

The reason I quit school was because of that incident and that I had failed grade ten. I had to repeat it and started to, but by that time I had met Carl. You know the rest! I met him that fall and picked potatoes in Maine, then started back to school but only went a week. It was 1966 when Carl and I left for California. I was fifteen.

Carl was going to leave for California and by then I had left my father's then. Carl and I were picking potatoes and living with a friend in Limestone, Maine. I had gotten into some trouble with my father who didn't want me to see Carl because he was older than me—twenty-six—and still married. When I kept seeing him anyhow, my father didn't like that very much and I left.

I had Beverly in California. We lived there a few years and travelled. Moved to Michigan, stayed there a year, then back here for a while. After that we moved to Worcester, Massachusetts for about a year, and from there to Bridgeport, Connecticut where we lived the longest, five or six years. From there Carl got a job offer to be a special constable on the reserve. His mother was sick at that time and he wanted to be close so we moved back. That was in 1975.

When I came back the reserve had grown—there were a lot more houses. People were treated a lot better, with welfare and a few jobs. Even my mother had drapes on the windows and a real washer. She even had a telephone. That was something.

When I came back to the reserve a lot of the kids I had gone to school with were still on the reserve; most of them hadn't left. A lot of the women involved in the various protests spent time away, though. It wasn't long after we came back that the protests over housing started and I joined in.

Karen's story continues in Chapter Two with a conversation with Glenna, recalling the reasons behind the demonstrations for better living conditions for women and children at Tobique.

Shirley Bear

BET- TE PAUL

For my most recent, extended stay at Tobique I boarded with Bet-te. Even before then we had become friends, and in asking ourselves why we seemed so often to be on the same wave length, decided that it stemmed from both being "children of the '60s."

Living with Bet-te, Ne'Pauset, her son aged seven, and Sebosis, her eighteen month old daughter, I learned first-hand the pressures and demands of holding down a full-time job *and* raising a family as a single parent. The work never seems to end, even though the children are delightful.

Bet-te agreed to become "president" of the Tobique Women's Group a couple of years ago when the women got tired of being asked who their president was. Until then they had resisted having a slate of officers—a foreign concept in conflict with their values of shared leadership and responsibility. However, in order to function in white society, the women informally chose "officers," with Bet-te as president.

During our interview we talked not only about the external events of Bet-te's past, but also about Native spirituality and the tensions involved in trying to be faithful to traditional ways and values in today's world.

Bet-te is a strong, determined woman with an independent mind and a deep commitment to her people.

I left the reserve when I was eight or nine and we moved to Maine, then to California. I didn't start living on the reserve again until I was sixteen. As a small child I remember speaking our language; we never spoke any English until I started school and the nuns literally forced us to learn English. I got cracked on the knuckles all the time in the convent school, and my braids got yanked.

After my grandmother died and my mother re-married we moved away and I went to different schools. We lived in California till I was sixteen, then my mother moved back to Limestone, Maine, but I wanted to be here on the reserve, so I came back and went to school here. I lived from relative to relative, trying to go back to school, but I was always treated like the "poor relation" or "shirt-tale cousin" (laughs). Instead of the other kids being told to clean this, clean that, do this and do that, it was me.

Still, this was always home. Outside I always knew I was different, I guess. I always knew I was an Indian but it never made any difference until I lived off the reserve. White people would say, "Oh, you look Italian. I didn't know you were Indian."

I lived here for a couple of years and then, when I was seventeen, just went off on my own and started travelling around. It was the 1960s and a lot of young people were on the roads. I lived in Montreal for a long time; went up to Toronto and lived there for a while; came back down this way and went to see my mom in Limestone. She had re-married to this jerk. I lived there with her a while and then moved up to Edmundston, stayed there and worked on odd jobs; lived in Madawaska—right across from Edmundston in the States.

Usually I travelled around with friends, people I would meet on the road, but lots of times I hitch-hiked alone. By now it was the late '60s and early '70s. Most of my friends and the people I met were white. I stayed up in Edmundston until I was twenty or twenty-one, and that's when I got into "the druggie stuff," but I don't want to talk about it ... I was into the hippie thing—just took people for what they were, regardless of whether they were white or Indian. Well, I was just doped up; I probably didn't give a shit, you know. I was high all the time at that stage.

I didn't really become politically aware until I got involved in a Native youth group down in Fredericton. We went out to St. Regis and we took over the Indian Affairs building. It was a national story. The people there asked for help. There was going to be a big youth rally on the island in St. Regis, across from Cornwall, so I went. I was going to university at the time.

Up around St. Regis and Cornwall there are a lot of industries and I got mercury poisoning. The night before we were going to take over Indian Affairs I got sick and was really in a lot of pain. I was in the hospital for quite some time, and while there found out it was due to the mercury poisoning. Everybody else went up to Ottawa that next day, while I was in the hospital. After they'd finished up there, Art Manuel—he was a "big wig" in youth rallies at that time—came back to get me and transport me home.

You got the poisoning from drinking the water and taking baths in it. I didn't know the water was bad—I wasn't paying a lot of attention to it. Could have been that the people living there built up a resistance and that I was particularly susceptible, but the people did have skin diseases. The cows drank the water too; people grew food. The water stunk, though. Probably health officials didn't care because just Indians lived there, but that was those people's home, their land base, so they wanted to stay.

That's when I started getting politically aware of the federal government and their attitude toward the Indian people—the early to mid '70s. Then I went back to Fredericton and started to go to craft school. I lived with some people on a farm in communal-type living. While there I decided to go the Manitou College up in La Ma Casa, Quebec. I got more politically aware with the situation of our people because it was a Native school—totally Native—the traditional ways, regular arts training for your painting, jewellery, pottery, political courses.

The government wanted to close the school down and we said, "No way!" The students took over the school—we blocked off the entrances and said, "You're not closing it down. We're keeping it open." But as it turned out, they closed it down anyway. I guess that is the first time I started raising guns; getting really "radical" as they say, but to me it's not; it's just a label people put on you because you stand up for something you believe in.

From there I went back to Fredericton and tried to go back to university. It must have been 1976. Along the way I learned about Native spirituality and traditional ways, but when you're living in this day and age you have to think about a combination some how. Like, you can't just say, "This is the way it was with our people," when we ourselves don't know, it's been lost so long. What I think is important is keeping the spirit inside of you; having a communion with nature and with other people. I don't think you can just rely how the old ways were—in a spiritual sense, yes—but in a practical sense, I don't think you could possibly live that way. Not when you're used to being brought up the way we actually have been; we didn't evolve to this day and age for no reason. I don't know what the reasons are, but God didn't give us minds for nothing—they are not supposed to lie there and vegetate—I think we have to question things. I don't belong to any religion. I can't even claim to be a traditionalist, because I'm not, totally.

We've always been taught that how we are supposed to relate to other human beings is already in us when we're born. It's in a baby, like her (pointing to Sebosis, her baby). I'm just a guardian, it's built in us how to relate to other people and beings of the earth. You know what right and wrong is; that's even there in animals if you really look at it. They're not going to attack you for any reason at all, unless you are hurting them in some way. When animals go out and kill, it's nature, whereas with us people, I think it is social surroundings that cause people to go out and harm others. Especially in today's society with the gross things that are happening. Like people who have been brutalized—who have had bad things done to them in the past—go out and harm others. For an animal it's instinct—their territory or need to eat or survive. You don't see animals doing the crazy things to each other that people do! (laughs)

During the time I was living with my white boyfriend on that commune, I had what you would call a really strong spiritual experience. I was in a really sad, sad state of mind. I was in tears and just needed to escape from the bullshit that was happening in the relationship and the commune. Him and I had a fight but really it started from all of us, so I just went out and got lost; I thought I was going to lose my way. I found this rock and there was like a natural bed in it. I went up there and was crying my eyes out, feeling real bad. I was sitting there and all of a sudden this rain came down on me, but I looked out and all around me the ground was dry. The rain was just on me, in one spot and I couldn't believe it! Hey, what's going on here? Am I hallucinating again? But I didn't take anything.

I thought, gee something's going on; that's when I started feeling something coming. I was way in the woods and I looked out—there was no rain clouds, it wasn't a sun shower, the sky was blue. It was strange. Before this all started happening I was sitting there thinking, is it worth it all? Is it worth living to go through all this bullshit you have to go through with people? Suddenly I felt a jolt! When I looked around me I saw all the fallen trees—somebody had been working in there cutting all these trees down—and I started thinking about all that was happening to the earth. All of a sudden there was a connection to the earth like I'd never had before. It was overwhelming.

It's so hard to explain that experience, but that was the first time I thought along the lines of me being a part of nature—not anything special. I'm a human being, yes, but I'm just like the other animals, like the earth, a thing that grows. That's sort of when I started thinking about the religion part of my culture. I stopped being a Christian a long time ago, but thinking along the lines that we don't have to go pray to God. We are a part of him—it's in us. We have a mind to think for ourselves and a soul and a heart to care. I think in that way we are gods, ourselves. Maybe that's the wrong word to use, but there's a little part of the Creator in all of us.

I got off talking philosophy! (laughs) A lot of things that still are strong in me were beginning in those mid-'70s. When I came back from Quebec and was going to university in Fredericton was when I started getting involved with the women's housing issue. After the school year I got a summer job at the Métis non-status association as an assistant co-ordinator on a research project. Barbara Nicholas called me and made me aware of what was going on.

Bet-te's story is continued in Chapter Three with her account of her participation in the 1977 demonstration in front of the Indian Affairs building in Fredericton, and her involvement in the picketting of the band office on the Tobique reserve.

Shirley Bear

CHERYL BEAR

Married at fifteen, with a child to raise on her own by the age of seventeen, Cheryl Bear actively became involved with the Tobique Women while still in her teens.

As we sat in the kitchen of her small house, Cheryl's youngest children played in the background, occasionally coming up to talk and sing into the microphone of the tape recorder. As well as looking after her four children, she was busy at the time taking upgrading courses to improve her education.

The grandparents of whom Cheryl speaks so warmly are Louis and Madeline Sappier. Madeline, who was the older sister of Ida Paul and Lilly Harris, died a few years ago, while Louis, who was born in 1890, is the oldest living member of the Tobique band.

I enjoyed growing up on the reserve—I had a good childhood, no problems and school was no problem except for the nuns. They used to be pretty bad. (laughs) They were cruel, as a matter of fact. I was raised by my grandparents; I was spoiled, I guess, to put it bluntly. We didn't have too much to play with as far as toys went but we made the best of it—used to play kick the can, hide and seek, different games.

I have three brothers and two sisters. My mother went to the States with her husband and I stayed here with my grandmother. My grandparents raised my uncle's first son, too, so there were two of us. I knew some other kids that were raised by their grandparents, also, but I don't think it was a big deal or a tradition—that's just what happened.

My grandfather is the oldest living person on the reserve now. My grandmother died just a few years ago. I remember there was so many kids on the reserve that used to get jealous; they'd say, "You're rich," or "You've got money." But my grandmother would get a catalogue and she'd ask you which clothes you would like and then make whatever it was. She never measured you. She'd sew and sew and then bring it back to you.

There was times at rummage sales she'd pick up something, fix it all up and you'd have a really nice dress or coat. She was good. Same thing with her cooking—she never measured. I would say, "How do you do it?" and she'd say, "I don't know, you just do it." (laughs)

My grandfather had a hard life as a young boy. His whole family died of TB—I forget how many, but it was a large family. His mother died when he was fifteen and his younger brothers and sisters half starved, he said. I guess the mother and the baby went at the same time. I only heard him mention his father once. I asked him, "What was your father like?" and he said, "He was a drunk." That's all he said. You didn't have to say no more. And you could tell he thought a lot of his mum.

He married my grandmother when she was fifteen and he was twenty-seven. She lost her mother, too, and she didn't have nobody to take care of her. When he married her he took care of Lilly, too. They took care of three of my grandmother's younger sisters at different times. The Indian agent would never help them out, either. My grandfather told me once he was so mad at McPhail. The reserve had gotten potatoes that were supposed to be for every family, but McPhail gave out something like a couple of bags to certain families and was going to sell the rest. My grandfather got mad and went over to his place. I don't know whether they went at it physically or just verbally, but anyway, he ended up getting a bag of potatoes.

Every time my grandfather would see that band agent down town, boys, he'd splutter under his breath—"that #*!#*!" That man was not loved on this reserve—he was hated. I remember when McPhail died, though. My grandfather said, "You're not going to see tears from my face." I thought he was going to say, "Good riddance," but he said something else like, "Hell's gates must be open."

He was always supportive of women—maybe it had something to do with his own mother. I know a lot of times he went to help different women, like when they moved away with white men and were fighting, I guess. He'd go after them if they asked; would get the family and move them back to the reserve. He did that for a woman down the road, always used to help her out.

I remember he sat me down once when I was just a little girl and said, "Whatever you do, don't marry a white man. Once they take you off the reserve they treat you any way they want and then you and your kids will have to pay." He said, "You're better off here; at least your family is here." I promised him, said, "No, I'll never marry a white man."

Those things happened to a lot of women and he seen it. I remember Shirley (Bear) telling me about what she went through. I could hardly believe it, and I know what my mother went through when she married a white guy and moved away—of being beaten. Sometimes I think I had a pretty good childhood. I didn't have to put up with what a lot of kids had to—seeing their father beat up their mother, or their father an alcoholic—things like that. I just feel lucky a lot of times I didn't have any of that.

I went to grade five on the reserve with the nuns, then we were shipped downtown. We were the bad ones down there. (laughs) It wasn't so much the white kids as it was us! We used to take advantage of their fear for us; we would make them bring us candies and stuff like that. Thinking back at it now, it was bad, but it was all in innocence back then. There's a lot of white people down in Perth now that are really bad as far as discrimination goes, but you can almost understand it! (laughs)

I think the generation before us had a hard time in school down town, but our generation fought back—because that's about the same time the "red power" trip started coming up. It was the early '70s. Of course, after a while you got to know the white kids and you become friends with some of them. There were times, too, when you were scared to admit you had a white person for a friend.

Sometimes the teachers would phone my grandfather and he'd have to come downtown looking for me. I used to skip out of class quite a bit. We'd just take off for the hell of it. I quit school in grade eight.

I regret quitting school almost every day now. (laughs) I should have stayed. But when you're young you don't really think ahead about your future; you don't feel like going to school, so you don't go. After I quit school I just hung around the reserve, then got married when I was fifteen.

I got married to Shirley Bear's youngest brother, Jeffrey. He was eighteen, three years older than me. We lasted about a year; had one daughter. First we lived at his mother's for a little while. His brother's marriage was breaking up, so Jeffrey rented his house, but then we started breaking up.

Cheryl's story is continued in Chapter Two with an account of her taking over a house at the encouragement of her grandfather.

II
ORGANIZING

The Telegraph – Journal   Saint John

WE'RE NOT TAKING IT ANYMORE

ON MY FIRST VISIT TO TOBIQUE I asked Eva (Gookum) Saulis exactly when it was in the mid-1970s that she first noticed women were being given a hard time. Gookum told me, "Oh, we always knew what was happening to women was wrong. We just got to the point where we weren't going to take it anymore." I was surprised by her answer because I naively had assumed that the women's protests began when they first realized something was wrong.

Even as children, several of the women interviewed saw the hardships that women faced, in particular with abusive husbands and in raising children alone. For instance, Caroline Ennis recounts her own mother's continual struggle to eke out an existence for her family. Caroline notes how she was aware of the problem as a girl growing up on the reserve. Then, when she saw the pattern of discrimination repeating itself from generation to generation, she felt compelled to get involved with the Tobique Women's campaigns.

Returning to the reserve only to find themselves labelled "non-status" and, hence, "outsiders," women such as Lilly Harris became painfully aware of sexual discrimination. Lilly and other women interviewed who lost their Indian status tell of the problems they encountered. Stripped of their rights, these women automatically were excluded from most housing and jobs, and became actively involved in the protests. They all received threats and ridicule because of their involvement, and many other non-status women chose to support the Tobique Women more indirectly.

In early September 1977 the women began the occupation of the band office which lasted four months. In what follows the women speak of both their rising consciousness and of the incidents that led up to that dramatic 1977 uprising. Already two women, Juanita Perley and Cheryl Bear, each had taken independent action by taking over houses not allotted to them. Increasing numbers of women and children were being forced out of their homes by husbands, and, as Eva Saulis explained, "We just got to the point where we weren't going to take it anymore."

CAROLINE ENNIS

For a long time before I returned to Canada I was aware of what was happening with non-status women. In the back of my mind I always said to myself, that's really terrible. I was aware of it but I didn't try to do anything. Actually it wasn't the non-status issue at all. It was status women that were having problems with housing. Like my mother; throughout her whole life she never got a house— not until about two years before she died, so she never really got to enjoy it. She was seventy-three when she died and this was the first home she could call her own. Even when she was trying to get it the chief at the time said, "Oh, she's going to die pretty soon. She doesn't need a house."

It was the following fall, after a terrible winter, that my mother decided to move away. We must have been freezing again and the chief didn't give a shit—he was warm. The nuns were warm and the priest was warm. I'm sure my mother must have gone to those people for help. We kids were too young to do anything at the time, but it must have shaped my character because when I got older I decided that I wouldn't let *anybody* push me around.

When I got involved in the demonstrations and lobbying, it wasn't for the non-status thing; it was purely a women's thing— because of the kinds of things they were doing to women like my mother—to women like Yvonne who used to get beat up by her husband all the time. The same thing happened to Glenna and I could see these things happening generation to generation down. So I guess that was kind of my motivation—I wanted to change that. I didn't think it was right that those things should be happening to women.

The desperate situation experienced by Caroline's mother was seen by other people on the reserve. Women such as Glenna Perley and her cousin Karen Perley remember how Molly Laporte and her children had to "steal" wood from the nuns in order to survive the harsh New Brunswick winters. Karen's own mother, Cora, also encountered many obstacles as a single parent raising four daughters. In the course of my interview with Karen and Glenna, they recalled those times.

KAREN AND GLENNA

KAREN: My very first recollection of women being treated badly was when my mother had tried to get some help with the house; her coming back and being angry, saying in Indian, "The men are getting helped more than the women are." Like asking for wood— she eventually would get it, but only after a lot of problems. That was when I was a little girl.

GLENNA: I never noticed anything when my grandmother was alive.

KAREN: In the families with men, the men would go out and cut wood, but the women by themselves weren't able to. When my mother did get the allotted wood, she had to hire somebody to chop it up to fit into the stove. Us kids had to bring it in, throw it down into the basement, go down and pile it. I hated that job. There were no boys in our family so Mom would ask Irvine. He'd be down there splitting it while all four of us girls would be sitting on the steps watching him—amazed or something, I don't know. Mom would say to him, "Irvine, chop up a quarter's worth of wood," so he would chop as much as he would think for a quarter. But he was generous—he did more than a quarter's worth. (laughs)

Sandra Lovelace Sappier, Karen's sister, also recalled how their mother would run out of food and have to go down to Perth to ask McPhail, the Indian agent, for food vouchers. McPhail, a white man who was a store-owner as well as Indian agent, issued food vouchers for the purchase of food in his store. Nevertheless, he is remembered mainly for his mean-spiritedness; his usual practice was to humiliate the women before granting them their meagre rations.

MOVING HOME AFTER ''MARRYING OUT''

With greater numbers of marriage breakups in the 1960s and '70s, and women returning to the reserve who had lost their Indian status through marriage, the injustices became even more evident; upon moving back to the reserve, women who had "married out" were shocked to find that they were considered to be no longer Indian by the band administration. Though many had lived "away" for a considerable number of years, all had kept close ties with the reserve, having returned for visits as often as they could. Lilly Harris tells of the ordeals she went through after moving back home as a widow, and Mavis Goeres, "YC" Sappier and Shirley Bear tell of their experiences as women now divorced from their white husbands.

When we were growing up nobody talked about status and non-status. Even fifteen years ago we had a chief who didn't know too much; he wasn't educated, was siding in with the Indian agent, like a puppet. He just helped his family. When I married I lost my status but I didn't know it at the time. I didn't find out until I moved back in the mid-1970s.

I came back and was living with Milly's mother. I was paying her board; it wasn't very much. She didn't want much board—maybe $20. I didn't think that was enough, so she said, "Why don't you go to the band office for help?" I said, "I'd hate to do that. I'll pay you myself." But she said, "No, it's coming to you too." Because at that time I'd have been running out of money if I didn't get some help.

So I did, but how I hated to go up there. I asked the man if I could get welfare. He said, "Yes, what's your name?" I said, "You know my name, Lilly Laporte" (because my sister had said, "Use your maiden name"). He looked up at me and said, "I thought you were married." I said, "Yes, I am widowed." He said, "What's your married name?" and I had to tell him. I got it; it was only about $50 every two weeks but it helped.

But if it weren't for my sister telling me, "Go ahead," I didn't feel I could just go—it was to me like begging—but she said, "It's all Indian money. You don't have to feel bad. You go up there, tell them." But I didn't stay on it very long because Mildred hired me to work for her. She needed someone. Also my other sister, Marie, was sick so I helped her. I had two jobs and later on three jobs since I was working for Frank, Mildred's husband, as well as doing housework.

When I had sold the houses in the States I got $15,000, so when I came back I thought I could build a little house if I had land. I went to the chief and he said, "I can't give you land. You're not an Indian anymore." I said, "What do you mean? You know I'm an Indian, you know I was born and brought up here." Well, he had been a little boy, but he remembered because I'd come home every summer.

He said, "No, when you married that guy, it made you white." I said, "I just need a little piece of land so I can build a house." With all the land here! He said, "I can't do that. You can't own anything here, any land." So that's why I bought the trailer which was $12,000. But it cost me a lot of money to move up here. What I should have done is leave my furniture down there, but I didn't want to because that was all I had.

I was so surprised when he told me I was non-status. I said, "How come these white women living here are Indians and I'm white? You can tell the difference when you look at the white women and when you look at me." Then he said, "I know, but that's the way it is."

I couldn't get even a little piece of land. I wasn't asking for a house. I was going to build my own little house. He said, "None of the non-status people can own anything." It was so unfair. I felt so bad. If it wasn't for Louis, Mildred's father, I don't know what I would have done. I said, "I could buy a trailer, but I don't know where I could put it." Louis said, "Bring it in here and if they say anything I'll kick them out."

So that is what we did. I told them it was his trailer, because I thought that if I said it was mine maybe they wouldn't have let me bring it in. I put it in his name but I paid for it. It is hard coming back where you were born and somebody tells you, "You don't belong here anymore."

I was paying my own mortgage too on the trailer I had bought. I didn't know you could get your mortgage paid until my sister died. They didn't help you with oil either at that time; not me anyway. I was having a hard time with three jobs. Five dollars from Mildred, eight from Frank and five from Marie; I used to have to get up early to get all three jobs done.

But when Marie died I wasn't making enough to live on, so I went up to the band office and asked, "Haze, can you help me with oil or something? When I had three jobs it was okay, but now I have only two." He started asking me questions. I hadn't managed to pay off the trailer—I was lacking $2,000, so I was having to pay off a mortgage. He said, "Mortgage? Can't you see that?" They used to have a sign on the wall saying that if you're paying a mortgage, they'd pay for it. Was I glad! So they paid the rest of it. Then I could pay the rest of my way by working.

Lilly's story is continued in Chapter Four with her memories of the Women's Walk to Ottawa in 1979.

MAVIS GOERES

Mavis Goeres also was shocked to find out that she was "not an Indian any longer" when she moved back to Tobique in 1975. To make matters even more difficult, she encountered seemingly endless "red tape" with immigrations officials over bringing her youngest daughter, Susan, back from the United States. Many other women in Mavis's situation still are experiencing what they view as harassment from the Canadian department of immigration.

I'd married out, you see, so when I came back I was considered "non-status." But I didn't know anything about it until 1975. Well, I was gone away so long, huh? I leave in 1949, come back in 1975 and all of a sudden somebody tells me, "You know, you're not an Indian any longer." I say, "I'm not?" I find out that *white* women are Indians now, but *I'm* not. Honest to God, I was shocked. I couldn't believe it. I got to talking to some other women and find out it's true.

At the same time I had a long struggle to bring my daughter, Susan, back home. Immigration wasn't going to let her stay; I had to get a permit for her to live on this reserve because it is in Canada and she was born in the United States. The permits were only for thirty days—a paper with a red seal on it stating she could only stay thirty days or she would be deported out of the country. Finally I had to get a passport for her.

It took me about three years before I finally got it all settled so that the immigration officials didn't come around and bother me. Really. And she's *my* daughter. She's got as much Indian blood as a lot of these people around here. Maybe even more so. There's even people living here who don't have any Indian blood in them who can vote in band elections. Also white children that have been adopted into this reserve. I think it was done politically under certain band administrations, to ensure a bigger number of safe votes for the chief at election time. Things like this come out in the end, though ... everything comes out in the end.

Here when I came back men could kick their wife and children out because the Indian Act made the man sole owner of the house; the men were domineering over the women. So you see, what we women were after was equality. How come a man could marry a white woman and she became Indian? But if the Indian woman married a white man she was no longer an Indian? This we couldn't understand. We had our culture; we had our language. The white women who came in, they didn't have the culture, they didn't have the language—with the exceptions of very few.

Before the '70s I don't think people were aware of status at all, because when I got married nobody approached me to sign anything, and I never, ever did. But I understand that later on the government was going around having women sign a paper that signed their rights away. Some of the women from the reserve did sign them and the government would give them a certain amount of dollars. I don't know how much. Thank goodness I was never approached. Probably being so young at the time I would have signed it. Figured the dollars was a good thing, you know.

When all this was happening—women losing their rights and men kicking them and their children out—that's when we first started becoming aware of these things. Of course there's very few instances where the man would keep the children; the children all went with the Indian woman. Where were these women going to go? They had to go and move in with relatives, with friends. I remember when Glenna got thrown out of her house—had no place to go. She lived in Peter Nicholas's cellar. Finally I think she even moved into Eva's old house that was condemned.

This is what women had to do, move into condemned houses or over-crowded situations, so that's when the women finally decided, my goodness, what the hell's going on here? Let's get together; let's do something about this. It all started with getting housing—to get housing put in both names so that the children would be covered, would have a place to stay.

Joyce (YC) Sappier was one of those women who was pressured to "sell her rights," but who steadfastly resisted. Like Mavis, she returned from the United States to live on the reserve in the mid-1970s. Her conversation with her daughter, Bet-te, illustrates how easily women's loss of status could be manipulated by a band administration to its own political and financial advantage; exactly who did and did not lose their status could depend upon the individual's relationship with the local powers.

BET-TE: Did you know at that time that you'd lose your status when you married a white guy, Mom?

YC: No, I never knew I'd lost it because I didn't sell my rights. The other women were selling their rights, but I wouldn't sell mine. They kept on writing to me to get me to sell when I was in California. I wouldn't even open the letters; I threw them in the garbage after I seen the first two. One of the councillors and the chief told me, "You'll get some money for selling your rights." I said, "No way. Why should I sell my rights?" And all the years we were away from here them son-of-a-guns kept collecting money for me and the children.

That's how I got to vote one year. I found out I was still on the band list, even though when we came back I told the chief and his wife that I was Lane now. They said, "No way. You're a Bear." They issued me a status card—my Indian card—even though they knew I'd married out. Until I defied them at the election. That's when they went and turned around and claimed I was non-status.

I know that for a fact because just before that particular election Rena was with me and she said, "I'll go call Ottawa." I said, "Yeah, you make goddamn sure you hear everything that's going on. Find out about Lillian too." She came back smiling, "I knew we could vote. You're still on the band list. Go get Lillian." We went and got Lillian and we voted. The chief knew we voted against him, so the following election he went and got our marriage certificates. They went to Fort Fairfield and Limestone, posed as Indian Affairs, too. If we would have voted for the chief he would have kept us on—it was all political.

I was for the women from the beginning because I'd been going through all that bullshit before I left here. I believed in what they were fighting for because—especially when I came back—I could see what was going on, on this reserve. All the favouritism, all that was wrong. A person that's been away from here for quite a while can see that when you come back home. I noticed how selfish people were; how they weren't together; they didn't help each other out like we used to.

I saw all that and it hurt—to see my people just caring about that god-almighty dollar. And before, you would give the last thing you got, like when we got pregnant—me and Marjorie, Rena and Juanita— the baby clothes and the maternity clothes kept going around and around. If somebody needed food, we were always gathering food for the family that needed it. They wouldn't do nothing like that anymore.

BET-TE: Some of us do.

YC: Some of us, yeah, but damn few. I saw changes even with my own family. We were so far apart. I fought and helped myself. Just like when I lived with my brother, I didn't live there for nothing. Holy Christ. A week alone there I spent $300 on food. Just one week, mind you. Gave them things they needed that they didn't have. I didn't get thanks for that; I got kicked out because they believed some nonsense their daughter said.

Times have changed on this reserve, and not for the better.

YC's conversation with her daughter continues in Chapter Three with their vivid memories of the 1977 band office occupation.

Shirley Bear moved back to New Brunswick from the United States in 1972. Her marriage had ended, but like many women, marrying a white man meant that she had lost her Indian status. After spending about a year at Tobique, Shirley moved with Peter Clair, to whom she now is married, to his reserve on the north shore of New Brunswick.

Here she recalls her disillusionment with the provincial non-status organization; although many of its members were women who had lost their status as had Shirley, they had virtually no voice.

SHIRLEY BEAR

For me coming back wasn't difficult, though I realized then that I was non-status. The non-status and Metis association had already started and I went to a few meetings, but what I saw in there was Indian women married to white men—in this area many of them poor whites. The women who were in the organization weren't doing much leading. The men were making a lot of the rules and talking for their women and I didn't like it, felt I didn't need it. But I knew there was something wrong.

I didn't have the political sophistication at the time to know I could do something to change it. Then I joined the Native Women's Association of Canada—it had a small provincial branch. I became a secretary-treasurer in that organization and never saw the books. The woman that was running it enjoyed doing the whole thing, never shared anything with anyone. That was around 1974. I was painting and did a couple of exhibits the following year, 1975, the Year of the Women.

In 1974 I started a painting I first called "Women's Statement," then changed to "Rape." At the same time Peter and I were building a log cabin in Big Cove, so we were busy, but I knew the injustice. I'd learned about the women's movement in the States.

I knew some women who went through horrendous experiences with back room abortions; women dying with cancer in the womb—due I think to the kind of birth control things they were taking. I knew a lot of women having hysterectomies to avoid having more kids.

Actually I knew about that even before, right here on the reserve; women used to be able to talk doctors into giving them hysterectomies because they didn't want more children. In the Roman Catholic Church they were very strong against any birth control other than rhythm—abstinence—but who abstains? I knew all those things and felt an injustice against *me* in a lot of those instances, but at that point I was never vocal about it.

Shirley's story continues in Chapter Five with her telling how, in 1980, she took part with Tobique women in planning the first aboriginal women's conference in New Brunswick.

TAKING ACTION

The 1970s was a decade of rising consciousness for many women on Tobique Reserve. Women who were being forced by husbands out of their homes found themselves in desperate circumstances. These women had to get some sort of accommodation for themselves and their children, which usually meant depending on the help of family and friends. While a number of women saw the unfairness behind so many women becoming victims of dire circumstances, it is one thing to see injustice, and another to risk doing something about it.

When people give the credit to Glenna Perley and Eva Saulis for initiating the Tobique women's protest movement, they correct that impression. Instead, they give the credit to Juanita Perley because it was she who first occupied a public building on the reserve. Here Juanita, herself, tells of what happened.

JUANITA PERLEY

This business about women being kicked out of their homes, it goes way back. It is just that nobody ever really made an issue of it until I got kicked out. Then all hell broke loose. There used to be women out on the streets even when I was a little girl. What has stood out mostly in my mind is women being beaten by their husbands. I guess they probably thought, where would they go? Where could they go back then? Nowadays there is a bit more for us than there would have been for them back then. They just took it, I guess; had no place to go. The children would see it all.

I hear it was even worse after the Second World War. There was no way for the men to get work and that is probably what frustrated them most. Politics had a big hand in it, too; the political powers even back then didn't treat the people *equally*. I remember my brother and father talking about not being able to get jobs. Only certain people got jobs back then and our family wasn't one of them; we weren't good supporters of the chief.

I remember my daughter's twentieth birthday. That was the first time the kids and I got thrown out of our home. My husband had became an alcoholic and things just went from bad to worse. I had ten children and a grandson by then and I thought, where in the world would I take my children? Where's a place big enough? Then I thought, there is the band office. Nobody lives in the band office—they only work there. So we moved in. It was Labour Day weekend of 1976 that we first got thrown out.

When I moved all the kids up to the band office the RCMP showed up. It was the first time here that *anybody* had occupied a public building. The police said I was going to be arrested for breaking and entering. He said, "I'm going to charge you with B and E." I said, "What's that? Bacon and eggs?" (laughs) He said, "You'll find out. I'm going after some more RCMP." I said, "Go ahead. Get your whole regiment. You're not getting me out of here. I have to have shelter for me and my children and this is just standing here doing nothing. I may as well use it."

The Mounties contacted the chief and the chief said, "Leave them alone. We'll just move our offices to our homes until we get that family a place to stay." In the meantime my husband must have been really embarrassed by all the public attraction we were getting over there. He said he would move out and let us move back in. I thought, well that's a pretty good deal, so we went back.

My husband did pretty good until December 7th when he kicked us out again. I remember that day so well. It was storming to beat hell outside and I thought, oh my God, where and the hell are we going to go now? So I called the band office and told them I was coming back up to the band office.

The chief said, "No, no. You don't have to do that. You could move into the arts and crafts building—this building I'm still living in now. I said, "All right." They even sent the band truck down to move us up. When we got in here we didn't have a damned thing. All my husband let us take was our clothing and he wasn't drunk when he kicked us out, either. He was sober.

We moved up here two weeks before Christmas. I thought, how in the world are we ever going to get by? Finally that same day I went over to the band office and said, "At least we need a stove and a fridge, a place to keep our food." So they got us a stove and a fridge and one of the stores from downtown brought and hooked them up for us. Then we didn't have any food. We laid out all the mattresses in the living room that we could get a hold of for beds, and a few blankets. This place was like a basket. The wind was coming from everywhere, it was so cold. Finally we got a food order, and got some food. By the time everybody was settled it was about 10 o'clock at night. After that I thought, well now at least we have a place of our own.

I got a lot of support from the people on the reserve, though there were the odd few that didn't support me. One man came over when we were living in the band office and tried to come in through the door. I said, "What do you want?" He said, "This is still the band office." I said, "Not any more," gave him a shove and pushed him out the door. I said, "This is my house. Until they replace everything—whatever I lost down there—this is mine. If they can treat a man so high and mighty, then by jeez, they had better start treating women equally too." As soon as we moved in here we started working on the band council to give us a table—all that was here were the craft tables, no chairs. Finally after six months of fighting with the chief and council I got the barest necessities—dishes, pots and pans. But we managed to get by.

The band office tried to get my husband out of the family

house. He held a certificate of possession which the chief and council tried to cancel through Indian Affairs in Ottawa but they couldn't cancel it. Indian Affairs wouldn't budge; said it was "an internal dispute" and they couldn't "interfere." I said, "Okay, fine and dandy. You molly-coddle the drunken men on this reserve. I guarantee you, I'll get everything I lost and then some!"

In the meantime my husband began coming over here, still trying to beat us. Finally one day I thought, well, I can get a peace bond, so I went down to the court house and the prosecutor had a big laugh. He really thought the whole thing was hilarious. I didn't say anything; I just turned around and walked out of that court house. I thought, who's been helping me all my life? It's at the end of my own arms; I'll help myself. So on the way back I stopped at the hardware store and bought a box of buckshot. I thought, if that man comes back, they'll have to scrape him off the porch. At least he will leave us alone then.

When I got home a friend of mine from down the road stopped by; asked, "How did you make out?" I said, "They laughed at us. They laughed us out of court." So he called Ottawa. It couldn't have been more than an hour—I was cleaning up the house, mopping—when there was a knock at the door. There stood this sergeant. He said, "Are you going to be coming down to lay charges?"

I said, "No. You already had your laugh. If I need any protection I'll protect myself. I've got a shotgun in here. If he comes up here you can come scrape him off the porch after. Anybody who tries to arrest me will be scraped off the porch too." The sergeant left, and wouldn't you know it? I didn't even have to go down and lay charges—the RCMP laid them. After all that. (laughs)

Then my husband seemed to realize I meant business and he cooled off. I bought my divorce; figured I may as well cut the tie and go from there. I got custody of all my children; never asked for anything else. I thought, I don't really need anything more than my children. My baby was ten at the time. Then that follow-ing year, 1977, one of my sons got sick.

We didn't know what was wrong with him; at first I thought it was emotional because of the divorce and everything. He had just turned thirteen. In the spring he got worse and worse, and no matter what doctor I took him to, they said it was nothing; that he just wanted attention. He was shaking his head and always losing his balance. It got to the point where he couldn't control his bowel movements. I thought, somebody has got to listen to me somewhere.

That winter we had taken him to the hospital and they thought it was meningitis, but the tests and spinal tap all came out clear. I thought maybe if I took my son down to emergency in the Fredericton hospital, knowing a lot of specialists were there, maybe somebody will believe me that he is sick. So I took him down, plus a change of clothes because I knew he was going to wet his pants. He'd be walking along and you'd see it just pouring down his legs.

When we got him down there, the minute that intern saw him he took us aside and said, "How long has your son been like that?" I said, "He's been like that since February. I've been taking him to doctors all over our district and nobody believes me that he is sick." Immediately they admitted him, ran tests, and found a brain tumour. I remember that day so well.

That same day one of the specialists told me that they were transferring him to neurology at Saint John General, so the next day we packed up and took him on to Saint John. We had just got in there, and I looked up at the hospital from the motel room I'd rented. I could see the light on in his room and it was the middle of the night, so I called the hospital. They said, "No, Hal is fine." The next morning when I got there, there were tubes in his head. They said he had gone into seizures during the night because of all the pressure inside his head.

They knew he had a tumour somewhere but they couldn't locate it; said they would have to do an exploratory operation. They took him into surgery that morning and he was there all day into the evening. They found the tumour right at the base of his brain—it covered three-quarters of his nervous system there—and they couldn't touch it. After they ran tests they found it wasn't cancer; it was some kind of growth he'd probably had since he was born, but didn't start growing at a rapid rate until he hit his teens.

The doctors put a shunt in him and he ran into complications. He died for a while and then he started coming back, but was paralyzed on one side; he couldn't talk, couldn't breath on his own. Finally they got him past that stage; had him in a rehabilitation centre in Fredericton for a couple of months. Then I brought him home and began giving him physiotherapy myself. He had been in the hospital ten months.

Finally he started talking, I think because he was at home. At first he couldn't swallow, so I would mash all his food and feed it to him. They said he needed to gain weight because he only weighed sixty-five pounds. Gradually he started gaining weight, talking, and even starting to walk. He just died this past June. The growth started growing again inside him, but he had an awful life, all the years he did live with that growth in his head.

Sure, he was walking, talking, but he was always in pain. He just never said anything. When he took sick at the end, he was only sick two weeks. When they got him to St. John he was dead in two days. He would have been twenty-one in July. He was a nice looking boy—smart too.

My children have always helped a lot. A couple of years after we moved in here we got a grant to make bedrooms in the basement. Then when the children worked on their summer projects they'd chip in and buy something. Finally we got the house liveable. They knew it was a place of their own where they wouldn't be afraid to come home. But it has been a long ten years.

When I first had my problems individual people supported me but there were no meetings—nobody rallied around to support me. I think people were a little bit afraid of me because I was so aggressive. They were used to having women take the lumps, but I figured no man is worth that.

In Chapter Three Juanita recalls how she became disillusioned with the new chief in 1977 after an incident once again related to housing.

Although Juanita Perley's direct action of taking over the band office is best remembered, Cheryl Bear also took action around the same time by moving into a house not originally allotted her. Here she recalls that period in her life.

CHERYL BEAR

When Jeffrey and I started breaking up there was this older lady who was getting a new house and she knew I was stuck. She said to me, "When I move out of this place, you move in." She told me that I should because the chief and council were going to give it to a man who was by himself with no responsibility or nothing. But meanwhile, some of her relatives must have talked her out of it— not to get involved—so she backed down.

But I had a friend who lived right next door to her, and as soon as my friend seen her moving out she came after me and told me. When that lady moved out, she left the doors unlocked, so I just moved right in. Holy, the chief was mad because it was his own brother that was to get the house. (laughs)

The chief came in and everybody was arguing. My grandfather and my grandmother and the baby were just sitting there, and I said to the chief and his friends, "Look, I need a place to live. If you want to kick us out, you'll have to pick us up and move us out." The chief and them took off and called the RCMP who then came after me. I told them exactly the same thing. The cops said, "No, we're not going to do that," and that was it; I never heard any more.

That was in the spring, the first time I split up with Jeffrey. Later we got back together for a while and he even tried to kick me out of there once. I told him where to go. (laughs) He wanted to stay in the house and no way was I going to let him—boy he had a lot of nerve. I told him, "Don't even think about it!"

That kind of thing used to happen a lot. See, the woman was supposed to move out with the kids, and it was the man's house. That's how they used to sign the houses; the certificate of possession was issued to the man, until the women started getting up and getting mad. Then the administration began issuing joint certificates of possession in both names.

The funny thing about it was that my grandfather encouraged

me. He told me, "The way it used to be here is nobody owned any houses." He was telling me about how the reserve used to be. The houses were there; they were built and if a family moved out and another family was in need, they didn't ask anybody, they just moved right in.

After that, things just started changing on the reserve. Women were coming back and finding out that they'd lost their status, too. They weren't even aware of the Indian Act or anything like that. They just figured, "I was born an Indian and we're Indians, and that's all there is to it. When my aunt Lilly first married, she didn't realize it, and I don't think my mother did when she lost hers. It just became a topic when women started coming back. This is when people started bringing it up, saying, "She's a non-status; she has no rights."

A lot of the women coming back were divorced or widowed and just brought their kids back to take care of them. It was harder for them, though, especially because of the attitude some people had towards them for being non-status. It wasn't the non-status women that stood up for themselves, though. It was the status women that stood up for them because of the attitude the non-status had about themselves; they sort of looked down on themselves, like, "I have no right to do this, no right to do that, because I am non-status."

Everybody was telling them that "you're not an Indian," but it was the wrong attitude. So when we did occupy the band office, it was the status women that were in force—we were the ones with more guts. The non-status were more afraid. In fact, the same thing is still happening—like my brother is non-status and I've told him, "If I was you, I wouldn't let nobody call me non-status. If you want to call somebody a non-status, call all these white people living on this reserve non-status. You were born an Indian and you'll always be an Indian. That's all there is to it!"

Men and women should have the same rights anyway. Why are just men given the freedom of choice to marry white or Indian. Why can't we have that same choice? Why do we have to give up something just because we wanted to marry a white man? It's unfair, that's what it is. Even when my girls grow up, I'd like them to have that choice, to marry whoever they want.

Some people say that traditionally Maliseets were matriarchal; that women had more of a say. I don't know too much about that, but in the household I was raised in, it was true. It was my grandmother; she always had the say—what was right or what was wrong—and my grandfather seemed to almost automatically honour or respect it. There was times he spoke up and when he did speak up we listened. (laughs) But the times were really rare; he didn't interfere all that much. He let her run the household and finances an everything pretty well all the time. I think that he strongly felt he had to.

I know right now my grandfather has more faith in the women on this reserve than he does in the men. He said to me, "I don't think there are any more men left." If something happens on the reserve, he always says the women should do something about it. He's got a lot of faith in us and it feels good to me. A lot of encouragement. He said once us women should get together and give that old chief a good beating. And all the fights the women had, he was always there supporting us. He always seemed to support and encourage us, tell us we were not to give up.

In Chapter Three Cheryl tells of her part in the 1977 band office occupation and her continuing struggle over housing.

FROM AWARENESS TO MOBILIZATION

In the mid-1970s agitation was building over the housing conditions of women and children on the reserve, and now we hear from the women who went on to become centrally involved in the ensuing struggles for change. Eva (Gookum) Saulis and Glenna Perley talk with Caroline Ennis and Karen Perley about some of the incidents which led up to their own strong commitment to the women's cause. Then they recall together how in 1977 Gookum and Glenna mobilized Tobique women to protest against injustices they refused to tolerate any longer.

GOOKUM: When titles to houses and land were first issued, I noticed that's when things really started getting bad for women, because the title was always made out in the man's name. It was that time in the 1950s when the Indian Act was changed and really enforced on the reserve. This wasn't just the non-status women, status women had no right to property or anything on the reserve. Therefore they could be kicked out, kicked around. See, before the 1950s there was no such thing as title. There was no deed or paperwork, it was just your land; you cleared it, and everybody respected that land as your property.

When I first noticed women being evicted out of their homes and having a hard time was in the 1950s. I seen a lot of that; a lot of women had to leave the reserve. I think I started noticing when I had my own family. People would make fun of those women, "So-and-so is moving out again!" People laughing at them. Especially before we started making our protests. That's when I really started thinking seriously, there's something wrong. Something has to be done. Then it happened to my own daughters.

CAROLINE: It was just the workers and the chief's relatives that were getting help. Others on fixed incomes—like war veterans, women and the elderly—were told there was no money to help them. The chief or band administrator would send the men who were working over to repair their own houses and not to anybody else. That went on for years and years; they kept fixing their own houses over and over, while in the meantime everybody else's housing was falling down around them.

GLENNA: Everybody was complaining, but nobody was doing anything.... I know on our street I dreaded to see the weekend. Every Saturday night one of our neighbours would be beat up, or Kenny and I would be fighting and we'd keep moving the kids back and forth. Alice would come over to my house, or Barbara Perley's kids, Edward and Nora—they'd come and sleep over at my house. There was a lot of drinking and people splitting up.

Every Monday morning we would see a truck going by—some woman got kicked out or couples had separated. All the men would be standing outside the band office laughing. That's what made me mad one time. A woman was moving and they were making fun of her, but they did it to not only white women, to everybody. They'd say, "Where is she moving to now? Who got kicked out now?" It was a big joke for them to see a woman moving. That's when I got mad and I started thinking.

When we'd first moved from Connecticut I didn't really know what the women were going through. Kenny was a councillor soon after we moved back and a lot of times women would come in and sass him. At first I thought they were asking for too much, or just being nasty. After a while I didn't even listen to the ones who did come in and complain.

I was still living with Kenny when I told him, "Gee, I feel sorry for these girls that don't get housing." He said, "We can't help them." I said, "Why?" and he said, "Because they are non-status; because they were married white." That is the first time I ever heard of "non-status."

KAREN: I remember Mom talking about women selling rights—enfranchisement—but non-status, I don't know where that word came from.

GLENNA: I kept telling Kennie, "But it is not right. Those women were born here; they are from here." He kept bringing up the Indian Act—"That's the way it is." One time I said to him, "Well, why can't they change it?" He replied, "You can't change the Indian Act!" Right away I thought, "You wait!" We would argue whenever we started talking about it.

KAREN: I shudder every time I think what the men would do to us if it was written in that Indian Act.

GLENNA: When Kenny'd say, "You can't change the law," I'd say, "Why not? It was made by men; it could be changed by men." And in my mind I thought it could be changed by women, if enough women worked together. I began wondering if other reserves were going through this trouble, but I didn't know.

Later, when we started going out and meeting women from other reserves, we found their complaints were the same as ours. Sometimes even worse. It's still the same for some reserves now.

It was around that time I was unable to cope with Kenny's drinking. He kept telling me, "You've got no place to go; with five kids nobody else will take you." He'd keep bringing it up. I stood it until he started getting cruel, picking on the kids. He'd come home around six o'clock in the evening drunk, and send the kids to bed, saying, "Go to your room. Go to bed." Before when he was drunk he didn't bother us; didn't start getting cruel till around that time. Kept calling names. Finally I moved out into my uncle's house.

KAREN: Into the basement, right? I remember that.

GLENNA: Yes, I stayed there with the kids a few months. Then a friend let me use his house for two summer months while he was in the hospital. But the day before he came out he wrote me a note that I had to move the next day because he was coming home. I only had twenty-four hours and didn't know where I was going to go.

All summer, though, I had a car and had time to look for a house trailer. I kept going to the band office to see if they'd find rent for me or some place to stay. Hazen is the one who helped me. He said, "You know if you could find a trailer anywhere, we have to pay rent for you."

GOOKUM: Gee, I used to feel sorry for those women, like Juanita and that ex-chief's wife. If I hadn't owned the property I lived on for so long, I would have been kicked out too. My second husband tried to throw me out one time. I hung onto the door and he couldn't do it. If he had a deed, though, he could have. But I felt so bad, seeing this kind of thing happening to the women and children. It got worse as time went on. The men kicked their families out and then they'd move their girlfriends in.

My daughter Marlene moved out on her husband after they'd gotten a house. It was in his name and when they moved into that place Marlene says he changed completely. He started always bringing up, "This is my house, this is my house," and Marlene had worked so hard to furnish it. She used to work out (off the reserve), buying stuff for the house with the money she earned— fixed it all up. I guess her husband was real mean to her. Maybe it takes two, but she couldn't stand it any longer. They came over to the house fighting a couple of times.

Finally she packed her suitcase and walked out. She left everything she'd worked for and everything I'd loaned her too—clothes, everything. She stayed with us for a while, then went away to work. She never went back to him.

KAREN: Juanita was the first woman really to do something; the women's protests really began with Juanita and her sister, Marjorie.

GLENNA: Yes, the year before the occupation, Juanita's husband kicked her out just before Christmas. She had a few supporters and they had to keep going to the band office before they got any help. All that year and into the next summer, whenever a woman would go in and ask for help, she'd be refused.

When you'd go from one house to another you'd hear that it was always the women that didn't get help. We'd start to ask each other if building material came or if someone got help and it was never the women. We'd see a truck coming in with lumber to somebody's house and it was always a man building a porch or something. Women started talking about it, that it was unfair. There seemed to be a lot of drinking and fighting at the time, too.

KAREN: Remember in 1976 was really our first protest, when we set up a camp at the entrance of the reserve and blocked that house trailer from coming in? The chief and council were going to get a trailer for a white woman who was separated from her Indian husband, and we said, "No way!" We stopped it right at the entrance and she didn't get it.

GLENNA: Yes, she got a new house instead. (laughter) The band council retaliated by granting her a brand new home.

It must have been around that same time I was threatened with jail over my own trailer. (laughs) I started from April asking for a skirt around the trailer but they kept telling me there was no money. Two hundred dollars would have done it. I kept waiting and they'd say, "next month." Finally it was October, late fall and the water was frozen in the trailer; it was cold in there; the furnace kept breaking down. My trailer was falling apart.

I had heard the money was there since September, so finally

early one morning I kept the kids home from school and I called the chief, told him the kids couldn't wash to go to school because the water was frozen. He said, "I'm not helping you any more." I told the kids, "Get ready, we're going down to the band office." The chief had left for Amherst or somewhere, but I still stayed there. Then I got reporters to come up and I told them everything, named off names.

That was the year they built the new school on the reserve, but they didn't have enough money to help me or Marjorie winterize our homes. A day or so later, they had just boarded up the windows of the old school, so I went to borrow a hammer and ladder and crowbar. I went down to McPhail's Hardware and bought a skillsaw—must have had good credit. (laughter) I said to my uncle, "I want that plywood off the windows at the school." He said, "Wait a minute, we just put that up this morning." I said, "Well, my kids need that more than the school does." My son, Sterling, and I took it off by ourselves. Everybody driving by looked at us.

I would take about eight sheets off at a time and bring them back up here. Irvine was a constable then and he drove in about an hour later. He told me I stole that material and I said, "I didn't steal it; it belongs to the band and I'm just borrowing it for the winter." I was cutting away with my skillsaw as Irvine was talking, so he just started laughing and got in his car and drove away. Before he left he said, "I'm going to have to come back here this afternoon with the RCMP." I said, "That's fine. I'll be here."

I was kind of scared and when the RCMP didn't come around till the kids were home from school I was glad. When I asked him who sent him, he said the band council. He asked me if I was going to take the materials back and I told him, "No." He said, "Then I'll have to charge you." I told the RCMP, "That's all right, but make sure you first find a babysitter for me." (laughter) He looked down at the kids and didn't know what to do. The kids said, "Mom, are you going to jail?" I said, "No, he won't come back."

I was waiting for him the next morning, but he never came back. Maybe he couldn't find a babysitter.

But you know, you were forced to do crazy things like that, just to get help. Men didn't have to go through anything like it. Only after that did I get any help.

KAREN: Remember that time in 1977 when Elaine and her husband were fighting, you, Glenna and Gookum, went to help Elaine? That—plus what was happening to other women—led to the band office occupation, didn't it?

GOOKUM: It did. Elaine got kicked out so many times—I don't know how many times I had to put her up with me and she had to sleep in the basement since we just had a small house. Once I remember her husband told her, "You have to be out of here by six o'clock," so we had to move her out. Another time was when we began that big protest. Glenna and I went up there because he had told her to move out. Him and Elaine were fighting, so Glenna and I just stood outside—we didn't want to interfere. When Elaine came out with her little girl, Jennifer was hugging her knees, crying, "I don't want to leave my home." Oh, I had a great big lump in my throat; I felt like crying, too. I said to Glenna, "We'd better do something about this problem. It's about time!"

GLENNA: I remember that, too—Jennifer hanging onto Elaine, saying, "Mummy, I don't want to go anywheres else." Gookum said to me, "Elaine wants us to go in and help her." I wanted to tell her, "No, I'm not going to help her move out. Tell her to stay there." But something hit me right here inside of me and I couldn't. So I stayed in the car and Gookum went in for a while. But that is when we went to Marjorie and Juanita's. We told them, "Elaine's husband just kicked her out. Why don't we get together and do something?" Juanita said, "Sure," so we started planning at her place that same day. Then we met again the next day and kept going from one house to another, gathering women. Everybody we talked to was ready to go do something right away, they were all so fed up. Well, there were some that were afraid.

KAREN: Yes. Even after that, right? Some just didn't want to get involved.

GLENNA: Some would say, "I support you, but my husband doesn't want me over there." We didn't force it if somebody was reluctant; we didn't want to give anybody else trouble. We already had enough trouble. (laughter) But there were other women who told their husbands to go to hell and they did join us!

CAROLINE: Actually, we didn't organize, though. It just sort of happened. Something would make you mad enough that you called a few people and pretty soon everybody was involved. It was Glenna and Gookum at the beginning and they gathered supporters, but nobody said, "Let's organize into a group." Nobody said that, somebody'd just phone around and say, "We need some help."

GLENNA: And explain to them what we were doing. At first I'd ask them if they had any problems of going to the band office and being turned away or refused help. Most of the time the answer was, "Yes," and then they'd tell me what happened. What we didn't realize was that so many people were being treated the same way, and they were just glad that somebody was finally listening to them. They said they supported us and they were glad somebody was finally going to do something about it.

CHAPTER THREE

ALL FOR A DECENT HOUSE

ON AUGUST 31, 1977 THE HEADLINE, "Women Occupy Band Office —Want Indian Act Changes," appeared above a story in the Saint John *Telegraph-Journal*. This was only the beginning of virtually daily media coverage Tobique women received over the next several months, as the demonstration against the housing practices of the local band administration developed into a lengthy siege. What follows is the account of that year by several of the women who were centrally involved.

Here we witness outbreaks of violence. The violence seems to be "horizontal," in other words, of women who identify with the band administration fight the women who have risen up against it. Soon the entire reserve becomes polarized into those who side with the women occupying the band office and those who side with the chief and his administration. As new crises arise virtually on a daily basis, the protesters collectively develop strategies to deal with them. For example, Glenna Perley recalls that they made the decision never to respond to taunts and name-calling. However provoked, "We never answered back. That was our policy." They always discussed situations at length before taking particular actions.

The women occupying the band office were dealing both with the immediate pressures and problems on the reserve and at the same time seeking assistance outside Tobique. They sought help at the district Indian Affairs office in Fredericton, the Union of New Brunswick Indians, the regional Indian Affairs office in Amherst, Nova Scotia, the National Indian Brotherhood (the national status Indian organization, now renamed the Assembly of First Nations), the national Department of Indian Affairs in Ottawa, the Human Rights Commissions in New Brunswick and Ottawa.

While seeking help further and further afield, and usually "getting the run around," a picture was coming into focus. The women were gaining an understanding of the bureaucracies and organizations which make up the Native Indian political reality in Canada. They were coming to see the enormous government bureaucracy of Indian Affairs which lay behind the local chief and council. They began to see more clearly the Indian Act, that piece of legislation which regulates almost every aspect of reserve life. In struggling to get some assistance for women's housing, they broadened their horizon to see the world which lies beyond the reserve, yet has an immense impact upon it. Here the women share their unique perspective on that world.

After Eva (Gookum) Saulis introduces the discussion, she leaves most of the story to "the younger women" to tell. During the occupation, however, she was a prominent spokeswoman. Sandra Lovelace Sappier became involved early in the occupation, but since much of her own story is of lobbying for change outside the reserve, more of her personal account is in Chapters Four and Five, where she also explains how she was persuaded to be the test case for the Tobique women's challenge of section 12(1)(b) of the Indian Act.

GOOKUM: After my daughter Elaine got kicked out of her home that spring of 1977, me and Glenna went around talking to other women who had been evicted by their husbands. We'd get statements from them telling what happened. Then we'd get a lawyer from Grand Falls to write those up in a document and send it to Indian Affairs in Ottawa. One woman really cried when she was writing up hers. We didn't get to all of them, but we got five to sign statements.

Also, we had petitions circulating around the reserve calling for property rights for women. The issue didn't include non-status yet—we were against the Indian Act giving sole property rights to men. By May most of the voting members on the reserve had signed the petition and we sent it to Warren Allmand (then minister of Indian Affairs) early in June, but he never acknowledged that petition.

CAROLINE: When I was going through the House of Commons a couple of years ago I met Warren Allmand in the hallway, I asked him about those petitions and he said he never received any. So either the bureaucrats kept them away from him or the guy was lying. After that, whenever we wanted to get something to a minister, we sent somebody to deliver it personally; we found out it stops at a certain level if you don't.

GOOKUM: In July we went down to the Indian Affairs building in Fredericton. Glenna said we should go and protest right there and we did.

JUANITA: We demonstrated over housing conditions all that one day. Even the women who had housing weren't getting repairs, and if you were a single mother, you weren't getting anything. The administration would stuff you in a house only because you moved in there anyway. Then they'd never repair it. That demonstration was just before my son got so sick.

GOOKUM: The Indian Affairs superintendent told us it was "an internal matter" and the best thing to do was for us to apply pressure on the chief and council up here. But we kept demonstrating outside with our placards and signs until finally he promised to meet with us and the chief and council in two weeks. He never did.

BET-TE: That's when they said, "We don't want to get involved."

GOOKUM: We never got a reply from the minister of Indian Affairs until November when they got a lot of pressure from white women's groups, and we'd sent those petitions in the spring.

GLENNA: That Indian Affairs official in Fredericton wasn't any help, he just did what the chief wanted. It was a waste of time when we went down there. *Empty promises.* Same with the human rights commissioner. We went to him, but he said he was provincial and we would have to go to the federal.

CAROLINE: When I went to Gordon Fairweather, the federal human rights office was so new they were still opening boxes. They said they couldn't help us, either, because the Indian Act didn't come under their charter. By the end of August we were so frustrated— band officials wouldn't even make a *pretence* of listening to our grievances—we decided to demonstrate in front of the band office.

GLENNA: That very first day it was me, Juanita, Marjorie, Linda Bear and one other woman. Eva (Gookum) didn't show up, but she said, "You're doing right and I hope you get something done." A lot of women said they weren't able to be there, walking back and forth all day, but they encouraged us to keep it up, said things like, "We went this far; we might as well keep on!"

We had all kinds of placards and signs up, "Fed. Govt. Supports Mismanagement of Band Money," "Did We Hear Someone Say, 'The Chief Represents the People?'" "We Need Help Now, Not Next Year." The very first day of protesting up here the staff would open the doors or windows and call us names, but we just laughed. I'd just look at them and think, you don't know how you look; you should be on this side and look at yourselves!

Then we had enough supporters that we split into two groups, with some people going down to protest—Gordon Fairweather was in Fredericton—while others stayed right here in front of the band office.

CAROLINE: Actually I didn't know anything about the protest until the demonstration in Fredericton. We were living in Fredericton— Dan and I were both in university. We weren't too in touch with what was happening up on the reserve; were mostly involved at the university. The only reason I got involved was Glenna phoned me up to call the newspapers. I certainly wasn't going to say to Glenna, "That's your business!" (laughter) Glenna needed some-body to go to the media and talk about what going on so that they would contact the women.

GLENNA: You also got the students together. We got you working!

KAREN: In Fredericton we had signs, too, and walked around the old Indian Affairs building. That's when we got the students sup-porting us—the Indian students in university there. My sister,

Barbara, was in Old Town or Seybyick, Maine, but she heard about it and came right up.

BET-TE: Barbara called me and made me aware of what was going on. I was working for the non-status organization but I told her I would take the afternoon off work and go picket with them. That was the day of the protest in Fredericton. Then that weekend the women called and said they needed help here, so I came up. We were all outside the band office and the people inside were acting like it was a big joke. Here we were protesting for better conditions to live in and they were ridiculing us, making snide remarks.

GLENNA: For the first few days we were just outside, picketing back and forth. We'd go up there from morning to night, then go home. One of the guys from the Union (New Brunswick Union of Indians) was up, and actually it was his idea to go in. He said, "Girls, you aren't going to accomplish anything out here. Why don't you move right in? But don't tell anyone who suggested it!" We said, "That is a good idea," and went right in.

BET-TE: By then we had a lot of supporters—even white people on the reserve backing us—but it didn't seem to be doing any good; the chief and his administration wouldn't talk to us. Some of us were pretty radical at that time and we all got together and went in. We didn't really move in; we were just going to sit there until we got a meeting with the chief and council. That's actually how the occupation started. Never once did we tell them we were going to throw them out. The kids were *always* with us—well, where are you going to put your kids? You're not going to have a babysitter for all that time, so they were all there!

We all sat in the reception area and said, "No, we're not leaving." So they just left us there; like they'd come in the morning to work and we'd still be there. After a while they moved out—couldn't take it, I guess—but all we were trying to do was get a meeting with the chief. He still wouldn't meet or fix up houses for the women. He'd say, "We'll listen if you move out of here," and we'd say, "No way. We know you're not going to listen." He was just trying to fool us into giving up.

GLENNA: Really we went in mainly to try and talk to the chief. While we'd been on the outside, we would take turns going in to try and get a meeting with him. Either he wouldn't even reply or he'd say, "I don't have to talk to you." When we went in with all the kids, the people inside didn't say anything and we didn't say anything. We just sat down and they ignored us.

KAREN: The chief treated us like we were invisible. Like he couldn't see us.

GLENNA: But it was kind of hard to ignore us with all the kids. The chief's wife, who was also the secretary, was trying to type and the kids were running around. We kept them quiet but just our *being* there was a disruption. It's true we didn't kick them out. We didn't try to disturb them but there were a lot of us sitting around and the kids would want to use the bathroom, were going back and forth all the time. I knew it was bugging them.

The first day when the chief said, "We're closing up now," we didn't move; we just sat there. Then the band manager said, "We're going to lock the doors." We said, "We're not going to leave unless you have a meeting with us." The chief went out mad and that's when they got the constables.

So then the cops came in and told us, "The chief sent us over. You have to leave." We said, "We're not leaving. He won't talk to us, he won't help us, so we're not leaving." The cop said, "Okay, good enough," and went downtown to Perth-Andover and got the other cops, the RCMP.

The Mounties came to talk to us and we told them the same thing; that it was our building too and we weren't touching anything. So we moved our blankets and sleeping bags in. The kids were having fun—it was still a picnic to them. In the evenings after work a lot of people would come over to encourage us. The elders would tell us not to leave, say things like, "Don't leave ... don't let them chase you out. This is our building, too, now."

CAROLINE: The longer we were at it, we couldn't get out of it even if we wanted to.

GLENNA: No, we were getting too much support, and other things we hadn't even known about started coming out. Like the way the administration had treated veterans or certain individuals—telling them there was no money when we found out there was.

KAREN: A lot of reserve residents cooked meals and sent them over. Some stayed nights while others went back and forth to their homes. I remember coming home and talking to my husband, Carl. I was kind of reluctant to get involved at first because he was a band constable and I thought I wasn't supposed to get involved in reserve politics, but I did anyway. I was excited; I thought, wow, something is finally happening!

GLENNA: When you think of it, how did we dare do this? (laughter)

KAREN: It was great. It was brave!

GLENNA: It was a really good feeling when all of a sudden we *knew* they were afraid of us because what we were saying was true. We didn't have to be afraid of anything. At first the chief said we were lying.

KAREN: But do you think women with the responsibility of kids would do something like that for nothing? We had a good reason.

GLENNA: Then they wanted to put us in jail. We didn't care. We said, "If some of us go to jail, other supporters will come and take our place." Early in September we were served with an injunction from the chief ordering us off the premises. It went to court because the sheriff in Woodstock wouldn't or couldn't enforce it until the court ordered him to. I think it was Dannie who got us a lawyer from Fredericton through the Human Rights Commission. We got a lot of threats, a lot of harassment. First it was mainly name-calling—they called us "the troublemakers." Gookum wanted to answer them back—she would have, too. (laughter) But I said, "Let's just ignore them. It's not important what they say; what's important is what we're doing. We don't need to waste our time on name-calling or answering back." After that, no matter what we were called, we never answered back. That was our policy.

CAROLINE: But they tried to intimidate people; they threatened people. The situation got more volatile as the occupation continued.

GLENNA: Yes, our kids took a lot. When they'd get on the school bus, the opposition's kids would call them names, and they had to take all that; "Your mother's a troublemaker, a protester," things like that. One time someone almost ran my daughter, Kim, down with a car. It was deliberate.

CAROLINE: We called the RCMP and they couldn't do anything. There were one or two witnesses and they still couldn't do anything —at least that's what they claimed.

BET-TE: We were "the shit-disturbers, radicals, white-washed, women's lib ... You don't know what you want ... You don't have no rights anyway ... 'The Liberated Woman.'" They thought that was a big put-down to us, but we never considered ourselves "liberated women"; we were just women who needed decent homes.

GLENNA: At first we went in there for the women mostly, but when our story came out in the papers, the war veterans came and brought their problems, too. There are a lot of veterans here and most of them supported us. They told us they were on fixed incomes, the ones who were pensioned off. The administration wouldn't repair the houses they got after the war—said they weren't band-owned.

KAREN: The same things were happening to the elderly. Some got their heating paid for and others didn't. Some got help and others who really needed it didn't get any. It was really nice to see the elderly come and visit us.

GLENNA: We had them write out their complaints and we would put them aside. We collected a whole bunch of them and a long time after, when the welfare officer came back, he said, "You have a better system than we have!" We had all the elderly, the widows, women with kids who were living alone—separated and single mothers—non-status, all filed separately. Those people started to come in and support us.

GOOKUM: It was the band administration we were going after— what they were not doing. In one paper I saw the statement,

"These women don't know what they want"—they want Indian rights for Indian women and they want this and that. I told my husband, "The veterans should get together and speak up for themselves." It happened so many times that when people needed something, they would come to the Tobique women. The women had more guts, I guess. (laughter)

KAREN: We got a lot of press. We never thought too much about going to the media at the very beginning, but when our story came out in the papers it had such a big impact—we got a lot of phone calls and reaction—we thought it was good.

GLENNA: After that first day of the occupation, the telephone never stopped ringing and we knew we were getting a lot of support, even from as far away as Nova Scotia. Before that, the press didn't even know where Tobique Reserve was. There were so many calls coming in. I took some and Gookum took some.

You learn things as you go along. When I first started, I trusted the press, I trusted everyone. (laughs) But the press were pretty good to us all the way.

Of course, the reporters talked to the chief too. One time he told them, "Maybe you'd like to hear the other side," and he sent them to interview his sister-in-law and he thought she'd support him, but she said exactly the same things we were saying. It was funny. (laughter) Then another time the objectors were throwing rocks at a reporter because he had a camera. They threw the reporters out of a meeting, but it was good for us; the opposition really showed their true colours.

BET-TE: I couldn't believe that night not long after the occupation started when you got kicked out of your house, Mom.

YC: I got evicted because I believed so strongly in what the women were fighting for. Somebody even came and busted the big picture window at that place. My landlord blamed it on the women and threw me out. Why would the women come and throw a rock when I'm supporting them?

BET-TE: That's around the time the violence really started. Some of us couldn't go outside without being attacked after dark. The opposition kept coming around to the band office at night, so finally we got a spotlight in the back so we could see if someone was breaking in. We all took turns standing watch, because there were times they'd throw rocks, and some were threatening us with guns. They'd say they were going to come in with guns to get us out of there.

People were getting beaten up on the street; and even little kids threatened, like Glenna's and Juanita's. But then Juanita stopped protesting and she wouldn't have anything to do with us for a while. I don't know what happened; I don't know why her family made the switch, but all the time people were trying to turn our supporters against us. Rumours and accusations were flying around constantly.

GLENNA: I'd get calls—somebody telling me that they were going to burn my place down. Rocks were thrown at the window of the band office and at our cars.

One good thing on our side was that none of us drank in there, and most of our supporters never drank. See, that was a major difference between us and the opposition. We had a ruling about no drinking or drugs in there right from the beginning.

KAREN: Some of the people outside were drunk. We took the threats seriously—you wouldn't know what they would do when they were drunk. When they were sober they wouldn't say anything.

BET-TE: What I remember most vividly from those times was the violent things people tried to do to us because they wanted us out of there. It was mostly the chiefs' supporters. Rocks being thrown at the windows, flying glass just missing the kids and frightening them. But we never retaliated. We just stayed; we wouldn't leave. Actually most of the community was helping us out, bringing us food, and a lot of the guys were protecting us—they'd keep watch at night.

The occupation wasn't only hard on us; it was hard on the other reserve residents, too. Everybody was tense. You would go to bed at night and you wouldn't know what was going to happen by morning because the opposition kept coming and throwing rocks at the windows. People would be beat up.

When it got really bad we had guns in the band office. We weren't going to let the objectors beat us up; we were going to protect our kids. We told the RCMP that we had guns and they told us we shouldn't have them. But it wasn't their kids; it was our kids. One of the reserve constables told us, "You can keep the guns as long as you don't leave them out in sight."

BET-TE: We never showed those guns around, but the opposition knew we had them. They saw us taking them in.

YC: Some of them other women were *big*, coming after little old things like me. We had to protect our kids. I'd have used them if I had to, and they knew that. Big women.

BET-TE: Didn't scare me, though, because Mom always said, "The bigger they are, the harder they fall." We were getting threats— "We're going to kill your kids." The kids couldn't go to school because they were being harassed constantly.

YC: We took turns staying up all night—one of us downstairs looking out and one upstairs looking out. Gee, we had some hard times, especially weekends. During the week it was kind of quiet, but weekends was when they drank.

CAROLINE: It was like a "banana republic"—that's what Suzette Couture called it in that film [a CBC television dramatization based on the Tobique women's story].

BET-TE: Remember that time an ex-supporter and her whole family turned on us? It got even rougher then. We didn't participate with them too much when they went on the chief's side. Remember those opposition women lurking around in the bushes one night, trying not to be noticed? All the time we saw their cigarette butts sticking up. (laughter) Too bad we didn't have buckshot.

At Wounded Knee they had a chief who used some of the same tactics as the chief used against us here. Except with us nobody got killed—luckily. The chief had his goon squads here, but we had too much media behind us and they didn't dare do anything to the media.

But AIM (American Indian Movement) was ready to come in. Me and Barbara (Perley) kept after Glenna, "Tell AIM to come in so they can scare the shit out of these people; show them we've got protection and people believe in what we're doing." But we got talked out of it because people would have been really threatened by it. I can see Glenna's reasoning now, but at the time some of the situations got really violent and we weren't initiating *any* of them. Threats flying around and you knew they could be carried out. We were always walking on eggshells.

GLENNA: We never wanted to hurt anyone. We just wanted people to know what was happening; that we were being hurt. I talked to one of the AIM leaders and I think I kind of insulted him when I said we didn't want guns up here. It was bad then, but we didn't want our people to get hurt. It would always be the innocent that would get hurt.

KAREN: A lot of people were afraid because AIM is associated with being violent and guns, shooting.

GLENNA: We didn't want to scare our supporters away. We had to keep thinking about how what we were doing would affect them, because if it wasn't for them we wouldn't be anywheres.

KAREN: A lot of people didn't understand AIM. There always were such negative reports on them in the media. The only time anybody heard about them was when they were occupying some place; we never heard the good things they accomplished. We were no different from other people; we thought the same things, and we don't want anybody shot or killed here.

BET-TE: We found out a lot, like what they were doing with people and where the money was coming in. I think that's what they were afraid of. We didn't break into any files; they were just lying around open on desks and it was stuff about *us*. We should have had access to all that information anyway. Freedom of information.

YC: There were papers saying that this person and that person got special needs from welfare, and those people never did receive them.

CHERYL: That happened to me. The administration used to say things like, "We don't have any money"; "We'll *try* to help you;" "There's no way, girl." I remember one time walking in there—I forget what I was asking for, but I was sitting down and just happened to look over at this paper and saw it had my name on it. So I picked it up and it had all these repairs listed, supposedly on my house. I said, "What's this? My house never had any of those repairs!" Someone in the office said, "Oh, I must have made a mistake."

I know I was so glad when the women got up and moving. I think they had been in the band office about a day when I found out. I went up and when I found out why they were in there, I stayed to support the cause because I thought it was a good cause. Sometimes I would stay overnight, but I had my own little house to watch, too.

GLENNA: I suppose people used to believe the chief's administration when they were told the money was gone.

CAROLINE: But then we started calling Indian Affairs or CMHC (Canadian Mortgage and Housing Corporation), and would find out it wasn't gone.

GLENNA: We had some individuals at Indian Affairs helping us. If they thought it was information we should know, they'd make sure we found out about it.

CAROLINE: Well, they wouldn't *volunteer* information; we had to dig it out of them. Some would give us what was *safe* to give. Often it actually was public information everybody could have access to, but the history of this reserve was that everything was kept such a secret from the people, we didn't know any of it. Then we started finding ways to get it.

KAREN: Wasn't it when we didn't get any satisfactory results from Indian Affairs that we tried other women's groups and other people to apply some pressure?

GLENNA: Yes, because the press kept asking us if we were getting any results. We tried the Union (New Brunswick Union of Indians), other chiefs. They didn't want to get involved, said it was an internal matter.

KAREN: We tried to get help so many places. First locally with the band council. The councillors said they couldn't do anything, that everything was up to the chief. Then the other chiefs said, "We don't want to stick our nose into another chief's business." We got the same thing from the Union, and from Indian Affairs in Fredericton and in Amherst (the regional office for the Maritimes, situated in Nova Scotia).

GLENNA: The National Indian Brotherhood said, "We can't get involved." Amherst Indian Affairs officials came up and had a meeting with us. They kept sending telegrams to Ottawa and federal Indian Affairs would say, "It is an internal matter. We already gave Tobique money and the chief and council can do whatever they want with that money."

KAREN: After a while those Indian Affairs people just stopped talking to us, too.

CAROLINE: I came to the conclusion a long time ago that a whole lot of problems could be solved to everybody's satisfaction if government leaders would listen to women like us, but it seems they never do—most are men and chauvinistic themselves.

KAREN: We called an Indian woman's group and I got the impression that they didn't really want to get involved. I remember being disappointed. We seemed to be getting the run-around every place we turned.

GLENNA: The white women helped us a lot more. Right at the beginning Caroline got in touch with some women at the Advisory Council (of the Status of Women) and NAC (National Action Committee on the Status of Women).

KAREN: It seemed like every time somebody came up with a new idea I would think, "What a great idea. We're sure to get help there!" Then we'd get turned away. First I thought the district office of Indian Affairs would help us. Then I thought, well, they won't, but for sure the regional office will. No luck there, either. Nothing did work and look how long it took for women to get their status back!

GLENNA: The very first time we talked about non-status was when I was being interviewed by Barbara Frum on "As It Happens" (a CBC national radio program). I hated talking to her because one of the chief's office workers was sitting right beside me.

Barbara Frum asked me what the complaints were and how it all started. I said, "Some people feel that the white women are getting more than the Indian women. They label our girls who are married to white men, 'non-status,' and won't give them any help."

In interviews, that's when I realized non-status was the main problem I was talking about. Well, the problem we started with was housing and the administration not wanting to help the women. But as I went along I started explaining that it was the women who weren't band members who had the worst time. They were always being told, "We can't help you; you're not a band member." So non-status became one the bigger problems, though it didn't start out like that.

The media sort of woke me up to the issue, even though I was aware of it ever since Kenny was a councillor and we used to argue about it. The chief and council used non-status as an excuse, and I'd ask Kenny, "Why can't they help the non-status women? You guys don't seem to follow the rules anywheres else."

When the reporters would call and talk to us, the non-status issue just kept coming up. First came the housing issue, and then they would want to know more about the 12(1)(b). The media were so surprised that this kind of discrimination was still happening in Canada.

At first we couldn't get any of the non-status women to talk to reporters. Joyce (YC) did for a while but I wanted someone with small kids because that's what the reporters were asking about. So we asked Sandra and she didn't want to be bothered with it at first. We kept reminding her of how bad off she was and that she had to do it for her kids. It took her a long time; she was so shy. She isn't shy now. (laughter) We sort of had to coax her at the beginning.

SANDRA: I had gone to the band office before and asked for a house for myself and my child. I'd had to pitch a tent, because I couldn't find any place to stay. They'd told me I had no rights; that I was non-status. At the time I'd never heard of "non-status"—the Indian agent had always hid it from the women. Then the women occupying the band office approached me, "We heard you couldn't get help because you are non-status." I said, "Yes." I was living in that tent with my son, and it was getting really cold at nights.

So when they asked me if I would move into the band office and protest with them, I thought about it and said, "Yes." I remember the chief saying, "Squaws are trying to get us out of the band office." When the cops came to try and get us out, we block-aded ourselves right in. That was when Dan and Caroline Ennis approached me about taking my case to the United Nations.

KAREN: Caroline and Dan asked Sandra to sign that complaint, and they got the lawyer Donald Fleming to take the case, but actually it was Glenna that came up with the idea.

GLENNA: I was at the trailer one time and a number of us were talking about the non-status issue. That's when I mentioned the idea of going to the United Nations; said, "Why do we always just go to the Human Rights? What about the U.N.?" After that, Danny went to find out. Noel Kinsella (chairperson of the New Brunswick Human Rights Commission) helped us too, because he already had come up to see us a lot of times, over various complaints.

We had to have just one person to sign that petition for the U.N., and actually we had one woman before Sandra, but she ended up not wanting to do it. Then we convinced Sandra, so after that, it was always Sandra we'd have talk to the reporters about non-status.

SANDRA: I decided to do it, said to Dan and Caroline, "Yes, if it will help the non-status women." Most of us were so angry because the white women were getting all the jobs on the reserve. Meanwhile the Indian women were being treated like dirt. I told the administration I'd take any job; I was tired of being on welfare. I had my name in there, but ... nothing. We had a lot to protest about.

KAREN: It seemed that no Indian groups cared or gave a damn about non-status women until our protest started.

YC: I know why the chief was so much against the non-status women. The reason was because he'd been benefitting all them years by using our names and collecting from them.

BET-TE: Maybe that's what frightened him, because we were asking for an investigation of the records. He didn't want the records to go out. He was scared of us there, for a while, when he knew he couldn't buck us. But he wasn't about to give, either. That was the attitude of a lot of the men.

YC: The chief just wanted us the hell out of there. He liked to be in control, and he didn't like what was going on. He didn't want *women* telling him what to do. When we wouldn't get out, finally they started taking all the office stuff out.

GLENNA: The chief and his staff moved out of the band office around the middle of September. They said they couldn't work in there; that we were "disrupting the workers." So they took most of their files and moved them into somebody's house.

KAREN: Right after that, a lot of others moved in, started staying overnight.

GLENNA: Oh, yes. We gained a lot of support after the chief moved out because instead of dealing with the problem, he was turning his back on us.

YC: Even my uncle, Medec (Louis Sappier) who is ninety-five now, and his wife would come and visit. That time they heard the opposition was going to come and gas us out, he and Madeline stood right up with us. They both said they weren't leaving; they'd stay and get gassed along with us. He said he couldn't believe the opposition would go that far.

KAREN: When we asked for donations of blankets, clothing and food, people responded, even from different reserves. Some came and stayed right with us. Really from all over the Maritimes and from reservations in Maine. I remember a picture of one guy, Jimmie. He had a hard-hat on, and a gun or club with him, and somebody snapped a picture. It really made us look like "the radicals." (laughter)

GLENNA: A lot of women would phone just to encourage us. When we were downtown, people would come up and congratulate us.

KAREN: Women from other reserves came to us, too, and said, "Do you know the same thing is happening on our reserve?" I was shocked. I thought it was only our reserve. At the annual assemblies of the Union (of New Brunswick Indians) they'd come up to the Tobique women.

GLENNA: And the men were mad. I remember this one old lady from a Micmac reserve who had a house the administration there wouldn't complete. It needed steps and the way it was, she couldn't live in it.

KAREN: This cute little old woman, and they wouldn't help her. She had arthritis and high blood pressure. Somebody at the assembly kept telling her to get up and speak at the microphone. Finally I think she did and she did get interviewed by the media. After that she got some repairs done on her house, but it wasn't very good work.

GLENNA: She was telling me the same thing happened there as here—even worse, I guess. Every night before a band election, there would be big parties at different houses, and the band would pay for the drinks and everything. She told me, "Everybody sees it, but nobody will do anything. I am the only one here." And she must have been in her eighties.

We had a lot of outsiders, including younger men and teenage boys, Indian students, who were supporting us. I didn't even know them, but they'd come up weekends.

There was an election coming up here at the beginning of October, so we wanted to get a chief in who was for the women. Vaughn Nicholas was a councillor who we thought would make a good chief, and we talked him into running. At the time he was the only one who had a chance to win. We campaigned really hard for him. Most of the councillors always tried to help us, but it was the chief and the band manager that put blocks in their way. I remember one time I went into the band manager's office and said to him, "You weren't brought us like this. I know your mother didn't raise you to go around hurting people." He kept on saying, "I have to do my job or I'll get fired." I finally said, "But you're working along with them." He didn't say anything, just put his head down. But I don't think there was a time we went in there and called them names. I know I didn't.

CAROLINE: Some of those people, I could feel the hate coming off them. I never felt that from him when he was on the other side, though. His wife, yes, but not him.

YC: Then the chief ordered the Power Commission to cut off our power—no electricity, so no heat, no hot water. Bet-te brought her little wood stove in and that's what we cooked on. Raymond Nicholas and his boys hooked it up for us. We had light for a while when he started an emergency battery, but it ran out. After that we used kerosene lamps.

BET-TE: The men who supported us openly, like Raymond and Ramo, my brothers and a lot of the other younger guys, took a lot of ridicule and teasing from the other guys—"the women's libbers." But they stood by us.

GLENNA: The men, like my uncles and their sons, would bring us wood every day, and the women would bring pots of food. By then the Voice of Women from Fredericton was sending us donations of money, blankets, clothing. To the kids it was like camping out. They had fun till we were attacked.

BET-TE: It was pretty damn cold, but we were all moved in there and we stayed. For one thing, many of us had no place else to live. We stayed all through potato picking season, and some of us worked out in the fields—we had to earn some money. The band office became home.

YC: We never done anything right away, not until we gathered together and talked it all out amongst ourselves first.

BET-TE: We always made our decisions together, even if it took time. The chief was getting his staff to come and take out files, then put the blame on *us* for their going missing. So every time they came in to take out stuff, we'd make them sign a piece of paper and record what they took and the date. For a time, we wouldn't let them take anything out.

One good thing, though, was that they couldn't cut our phones off, because they were connected to the fire hall next door.

GLENNA: We ran up a big bill, called Ottawa, everywheres. We got so desperate towards the end, we were going to call the Russians. (laughter) The women are saying now, we should have tried it— scared old Canada. You see, we don't consider ourselves Canadians or Americans.

We had the phones, so people could call us, too. Also, the fire siren worked. The men supporting us said to let them know if the opposition ever came and touched the women or kids. We decided that, if we ever really needed help, we would turn the siren on. We used it a few times. The first time we had to sound the siren, initially there were some women outside throwing rocks; then we saw some guys coming, too, and there were quite a few. It was at night and they were all partying and drunk.

CAROLINE: There was that great big crowd standing around, throwing rocks and threatening to burn the band office down....

GLENNA: It wasn't *that* big ... the people were big though. (laughter)

CAROLINE: Was that first time when we called up the RCMP because the objectors were threatening to burn the building down? They didn't ever show up and we had to call Ottawa the next day to complain about the detachment. So the next time we called them they *really* showed up—in about four police cars.

That might have been one of the times we got served with an

injunction ordering us out. There were rumours of an RCMP riot squad coming in, and we were given an hour to leave, or we'd be "forcibly ejected." We barricaded the doors and windows and contacted the media—whoever we could reach—politicians, Indian Affairs; called the minister in Ottawa and told him any violence would be on their hands; they could have done something before it reached a crisis point. We gathered a whole lot of our supporters inside, plus some reporters, and the riot squad backed off. We never found out what stopped them, likely a combination of outside pressure, publicity, and uncertainty about legalities around the Indian Act.

GLENNA: Finally that injunction got thrown out of court because the chief had applied for it without going to the whole council—it wasn't signed by enough of the councillors.

Over the next few years we went to court several times—we always seemed to be getting served papers. The first time, one of our supporters advised us we couldn't get thrown out because the band owned the building, so we just threw the papers up in the air and wouldn't listen!

CAROLINE: We also knew that the injunction couldn't be issued without permission from the minister of Indian Affairs. That was in the Indian Act; and also the Act states that band property belongs to all band members. Actually our lawyer did advise us to leave, but we decided to take our chances and stay on.

As I remember, first a judge issued the injunction which we defied, then later in September we got served with another one. But we were determined to stay because that was one of the issues; office space had been expanded with funds that were supposed to be for repairing older homes on the reserve. So one reason women were living in the band office was because that's where money for their homes had been spent.

Before the occupation, usually the reserve didn't get involved in anything they thought was the business of chief and council, but all that changed with the occupation—then people had to get involved. Everybody split into two opposite factions, and things just got more and more volatile.

GLENNA: Even the priest got involved! He wrote a letter to the minister of Indian Affairs supporting us, then he got a lot of criticism over it. The objectors kept telling him all kinds of bad things were going on with us in the band office, that we were drinking. It turned into a big controversy on the reserve because some people wanted the priest to continue his support and some wanted him to mind his business. He was kind of caught in the middle, and I remember him being really upset over it.

After he got into trouble like that, he wouldn't support us openly any more, but by then he had written his letter to the minister, so I didn't care. (laughs) One Sunday there, he'd really praised the women in church; said, "This is the first time it ever happened on any reserve that women got up and helped themselves." It's a wonder he's still here! (laughter)

I remember one Saturday night when things really got out of hand. The opposition was drinking and they decided to get us out of the band office. That's what they told us, that they wanted us out. My son Sterling got sick that night when they started throwing rocks. He started throwing up so I had to call my uncle Ramo (Ray Sappier) to come after him, and they started throwing rocks at Ramo's car. That was one of the times we had to use the siren.

YC: I remember that night. Ray and I came racing up to get someone from the band office. I was out there then, because by that time I was living with Ray. They were rocking the car side to side and I was going to jump out and beat them up. Ray grabbed me back and Glenna yelled, "Get the hell out of here! There's too many!" That's when they started throwing stones and bottles at us.

CHERYL: Another time the opposition came over throwing rocks at us. We had most of the windows pretty well boarded up, so we were barricaded in pretty good, but we were kind of scared they were going to set fire to the building. We all went upstairs with the kids and everybody was posted at different angles to make sure we could see what they were up to. The kids were scared—they didn't know what to expect.

We were trying to get buckets of water, so that as soon as they got close enough, we could pour water on their heads from one of the upstairs windows to try to sober them up or something. (laughter) A couple of us ran into the fire hall next door, trying to figure out the hoses. We were going to spray them. (laughter) It was scary at the time, but funny when you think back.

BET-TE: Then another time later on, Debbie (Bet-te's younger sister) was attacked by two women. She was only school-age and they bashed her nose right in. All she'd been doing is walking down the street. Then election night, itself—I'll never forget that night—October 3rd. We'd campaigned really hard for Vaughn, and he won! He beat the chief by thirteen votes.

KAREN: The election was really a win for the women. We were so glad we had tears in our eyes. Oh, God. I was up there counting votes—a scrutineer—and as soon as I knew Vaughn was going to win, both Sandra and I had tears coming down our eyes.

GLENNA: I'm too nervous; I can't go up there. Even that election I had to come up here and wait alone in my house. Then as soon as I found out, I came right down and, as I was coming in, I met the chief going out. He had his head down, and I heard he didn't want to shake hands with Vaughn ... the falling of an empire.

That night everyone was down celebrating at the party at Gookum's old house. We were going to take turns watching the band office, but Cheryl (Bear) had said, "I'll stay with the kids, but come and check up on us once in a while. I had my car and Gookum said, "We should go and check up on Cheryl."

There was a car right behind us and I didn't know who it was, but it followed us right up to the band office, so I thought it was Karen or Caroline. When we got out, the door was locked and I was knocking on the door. I had parked right near the door, so I got there first and Gookum had come around the back of the car.

Then somebody grabbed my jacket. I turned around and said, "Get your.... " They'd been drinking and were trying to fight us, swearing at us. I grabbed hold of the railings and kicked back. By that time the person had given up on Gookum and come back at me, so I had to fight two of them. I hung onto the porch and was kicking to keep them off me till Cheryl opened the door. I don't know what she was doing in there, but it seemed like it took her ages to open that damn door.

When Cheryl did open the door, they started to come in. There were four women by then but I only remember the two who were beating *me* up. The wood stove was right there and it was hot. I had a chance to push one of them right onto that stove, but I remembered I couldn't stand smoke. I thought, I'll hurt myself if I knock that stove pipe off. And the kids were in there. I just hung onto the woman fighting me.

While somebody was pounding me on the back I was thinking, they're not going to get me on the floor, and they didn't.

CHERYL: There were two of the women fighting me while the other two were fighting Glenna, but we managed to turn the tables. One of the women attacking me let go and I ended up on top of the other one. Glenna was doing pretty good too. (laughter)

KAREN: Somebody came running to Carl's mother's house which is where I was. She was out of breath and said, "There's trouble at the band office." I remember Caroline and I started running. God, Caroline could really run, but I couldn't.

BET-TE: That election night I was partying up at Gookum's old house with everybody. Not all of us were drinking, but we were all having a good time, celebrating the win. I didn't want to stay much longer, so I started heading up the street. Edward, Barbara Perley's son, was in his teens then and he was walking up with me. I told him I was going to check in on the band office. As we were walking past the school, one of the objectors, who was night watchman there, started shouting obscenities at us over the outside loudspeakers. Then he came outside and, God, he had one of those blackjacks you hit people with. He tried to go after young Edward, and we hadn't said or done a thing to him.

When I got to the band office, they were still fighting and I grabbed one of the women and pinned her up against a corner. That's when the reserve cops arrived and started to get them out of there.

CAROLINE: By then a big crowd had gathered outside the band office. The whole damn reserve was there and it almost turned into a riot. That was scary when the chief lost. All his supporters knew they'd lost and they blamed the women.

KAREN: Election night, almost everybody was drinking, including the young punks. Different groups were hassling each other in the crowd. Some fights broke out, and there were bottles flying.

GLENNA: You didn't dare turn your back unless you knew who was behind you. I was scared for my trailer, thought they would burn it down.

Kathy (one of the women's supporters) doesn't drink, but that night she had a few. She was braiding her hair and saying, "You wait. They'd better not touch me because I'm ready. Has anybody got an elastic?" (laughter) Her hair was really long and somebody had said, "Kathy, they'll pull your hair out if you don't do something with it."

CHERYL: I know those girls good who attacked us, and what I think is that the old chief, his wife and that gang pumped them with booze and then provoked them into it. They didn't have the guts themselves, so they got young girls about my age to do it. That's how I see it, anyway.

BET-TE: They were scared, too. With the new administration coming in, they'd figure they had no jobs now. They were so used to easy money. That's what their fear was, I think.

KAREN: The next morning it was like nothing had happened. It was quiet again ... until that night. That was the time Debbie (YC's youngest daughter) had to go down to the hospital for smoke inhalation. She could hardly breathe.

BET-TE: It didn't start out as anything real violent that night. Two girls from around here came in as friends to visit. There already were a lot of other people there, too. The two women acted so innocent, and then snuck upstairs. No one saw them go up because there were people all around. All of a sudden we smelled smoke and we didn't see those two women who had come in. We rushed upstairs and it was ablaze.

My mother had all her furniture in one room and it was on fire. My sister, Debbie, tried to put it out, and that's how she got smoke inhalation.

YC: Some of us were at Karen and Carl's place partying when someone came running down and happened to spot Caroline outside; yelled to her, "Band office on fire." Caroline turned around and saw the flames. She came running into Carl's and we all made a bee-line over. I was running like hell in these little white shoes with heels. It was kind of muddy, had rained or snowed and the road was wet. My feet were soaked when I got to the band office. One shoe on and one shoe off.

KAREN: I remember me and Sandra rushing over there, too. Sandra ran upstairs because all her stuff was up there. Geez, I was scared because I thought that her son, Christian, was sleeping up there.

SANDRA: No, he just happened to be staying somewheres else that night, thank God. It was scary at the time, though. But remember, we laughed about it afterwards? I got my plants out. (laughter)

KAREN: You had your stereo, all your clothes, I don't know what all, in that room. I remember you went up and didn't really gather anything up—just grabbed some clothes and those plants. Thank God we managed to get the fire out, but it sure made a mess; ruined a lot of people's furniture and things.

YC: People had already rushed Debbie down to the hospital in Perth, and then they had to rush me down there, too. The way we were treated when we got to that hospital. I was so worried about Debbie and all they would tell me was that she was "all right." I told the doctors not to dope her up, but I guess that's the first thing they did because they wouldn't let me see her or tell me what room she was in.

They gave me a shot to calm me down and put me in a bed. I had to pee, and wasn't to get up by myself so rang the buzzer. I had my hand on that buzzer for the longest time and the nurse wouldn't come. Finally I crawled to the bathroom. I got mad and I got dressed. The nurse came in then and asked me, "Where are you going?" I said, "I'm going home. I could pee my pants or die and you guys wouldn't give a shit."

She said, "You can't leave; you have to sign this paper." No way would I sign that paper, and goddamn if they didn't call my brother and he signed it. I could have killed him. Assholes down there, but typical of the treatment we'd get. I'll never forget that night. I still have a singe on my couch where it was burned, and all my plants were gone.

KAREN: The opposition thought that just because Vaughn got in as chief that the women would leave the band office, but we didn't.

GLENNA: Since he was my cousin, I'd been the one to tell him, even before he got in, that if we didn't get help, we wouldn't leave. I said, "It's not going to solve anything, just you getting in." He was very understanding and I said, "It might hurt you, but we have to keep on protesting until we get some help." It was before the election I told him that, and he said he would still support us, even if it meant him losing the election. We had thought his supporting the women might hurt his campaign, but I guess it helped.

KAREN: Then things weren't any better after Vaughn got in because he had difficulty administering the band after having taken over from the old chief. So he got hassled by some of his own supporters, with them saying, "When are you going to do things? When are things going to start looking up?" Well, he tried.

BET-TE: Then some of the old council was still there—some of the old chief's councillors. Also, the old chief had influence down at Indian Affairs in Fredericton, so they all were working against the new chief. Vaughn was getting threats and it was a strain on his family.

JUANITA: I remember coming all the way from the hospital in Saint John just to vote for the new chief, thinking there would be a big change!

They were building houses galore for men, and there was my

sister, Marjorie, living in that dingy trailer with her floor caving in from rot. I told her, "There's no need of this. We're going to move you into that new house next to your trailer." She was scared, said, "I don't want anybody to have any bad feelings for me." I said, "Well, cripes, you had better do something to force their hand." So we went in and occupied that house.

I went up to see the chief, Vaughn, for some reason, and he was talking on the phone with his back towards me. He was telling the owner of that house, "We're going to kick her out of there in the morning. We're going to take the RCMP over and drag them out if necessary. We had a band council meeting last night and signed a band council resolution giving you a certificate of possession for it."

I just sat there watching him and thought, this is the s.o.b. I supported and he has the same attitude toward women as every other chief has had. I said to him, "You son of a bitch. If you had opposition before, mister, you don't know what opposition is. You're going to know it now," and I left.

The women here, the same women that were supposedly fighting for women's rights wouldn't come and support my sister; they wouldn't even sign a petition for her. It just so happened that there were a group of Indians here from other reserves, and I told them what the administration was going to do the next morning. They stood guard all night with us, and when we saw the police cruiser coming in the morning we had blockades at the doors. They said, "We only want to talk," so they came in and, after first threatening my sister, they promised to build her a house if she moved out.

She moved out and they did build her a house, but it took that much. I don't know how many times she had tried to get one before. She had five children and was on the road, living from house to house, sometimes in a basement, for eight years. By the time she got that house her youngest was twelve years old.

GLENNA: I know we split up with Juanita and Marjorie right in the middle of that time, but I don't remember why now. Then later on we sort of got back together again.

BET-TE: I know Juanita stopped protesting and wouldn't have anything to do with us for a while, but now I honestly don't remember what had happened.

What I remember is that some of us stayed in the band office after Vaughn got elected, for one thing to make sure our grievances were met. Also, some like myself had no place else to move.

GLENNA: The election was at the beginning of October and we stayed on in the band office until December. Then just Bet-te was living there and the jail was nice and comfortable so we moved Sandra into it. They never got rid of us right away. In fact, they never did get rid of us. (laughter)

We more or less ended the occupation when Blockman (Vaughn's nickname) actually took over from the old chief in November. The councillors were talking to us and we were promised that something was going to be done. Vaughn obviously was trying hard to help us.

BET-TE: Everybody else had gone and I was the last person living in the band office because I didn't have no place to go.

The band office was running normally during the day and I just had one room upstairs that I slept in at night. The office wanted me out of there, so I said, "Okay, find me a place to live." That's when they looked around and found Gookum's old house which was in terrible condition. They fixed it up so that it would be more-or-less liveable for winter. There was no heat registers or furnace, but it had an old wood stove. I didn't really have any furniture, but they put some new stove pipes in, and I didn't mind it. I got a washer through welfare and that was good enough for me.

I stayed there through the winter and then me and Barb (Nicholas) went to the States on The Longest Walk (a walk by Indians that converged on Washington, D.C. to publicize their grievances).

It was around that time—a little less than a year after Vaughn got in—that he finally had to resign. He was getting a lot of static and I think the strain was too much for his family.

JUANITA: He couldn't hack the pressure; the same kind of pressure he tried to deal on us, we just reversed on him and he couldn't take it. He quit and back in went the old dictator.

KAREN: I personally was so disappointed when Vaughn resigned. He'd finally quit because he didn't have any money to work with, so then they had to have a by-election.

GLENNA: Vaughn *was* concerned about how the people felt. He wanted to help people and it really bothered him that he couldn't. He quit only after he cleared up all the left-over debts from the previous administration.

KAREN: We were so disgusted when the old chief got back in. And less than a year later. We didn't even want to think about that election, and we didn't get very involved in it, did we?

GLENNA: No, we didn't. Then there were too many running against the old chief and it split the vote.

KAREN: Oh, were we mad. I can't remember what happened then; I think we just stayed quiet.

GLENNA: We were already beat. We brought it up a few years ago when the chief and his supporters were beat by our candidate, Dave Perley. They were making all kinds of noise and we told them, "Accept defeat gracefully like we did." That is what we'd done; the old chief and his gang were in so there was nothing we *could* do.

BET-TE: The same thing started all over again; we were right back where we started. The chief has still got it in for some of us real bad. *Still*.

CHAPTER FOUR

ON TO OTTAWA: THE YEAR OF THE WALK

AFTER THE FALL BY-ELECTION of 1978 in which "the old regime" was voted back into power, the Tobique women were extremely discouraged. However, rather than giving up their struggle, in the spring of 1979 the women launched a new campaign which would draw not only regional, but national attention, to the injustices faced by Native women in Canada.

As evidenced in the following dialogue, the Tobique women's anger became the catalyst for the Native Women's Walk to Ottawa of July 14-21, 1979. Caroline Ennis, who assumed responsibility for much of the walk's organization, laughs now that, had she not been so naive at the time, she never would have taken on such an enormous task.

Although the Women's Walk to Ottawa was a success in so many ways, the women saw the $300,000 it brought into Tobique Reserve for women's housing, reaching hardly any of those most in need; in their view, the money was used instead to the political advantage of the band administration. Hence, the Tobique women's struggle against grinding daily injustices continued....

CAROLINE: As soon as the old chief got back in he fired the band manager—who had run against him in the by-election. When only a couple of the councillors challenged the chief, we knew he was going to be able to do what he wanted again. One good thing about that election, though, was that my husband, Dan, got in as a councillor. See, the band had applied for having one more councillor, so the by-election was for chief plus one position on council.

GLENNA: When the old chief got back in, we knew we were going to have to keep protesting.

KAREN: Some of us were on The Longest Walk in the United States, so we had gotten the idea of one for ourselves. But we only talked about it in the spring of 1979; before that we weren't really serious.

GLENNA: After the old chief got in, we were still having problems. Different women went to him individually with their requests. When we went to talk to him, we made sure he knew other women were outside supporting us. I was still in the trailer and fighting for a house. Sandra was living in the jail and Bet-te lived with me a while because she couldn't find a place, then moved into a cement shack.

BET-TE: When I came back from The Longest Walk and from some travelling through the Dakotas and Montana, I couldn't find accommodation and Mom and me were fighting at the time (laughs), so I lived with Glenna at her old trailer for some of that winter. It didn't work out too good, though, with all her kids *plus* me. When I had had it at Glenna's and it was too much for her, I thought of that little cement shack out in the park. There was electrical wires going into it; no toilet or water, but I'd lived without that stuff before. Glenna got some guys to help move me out there.

At times the snow was hard enough that I could go down to a spring in the river—about a quarter mile—to get water. I'd lug it back up, which is very steep. If there were storms or I wasn't feeling very good, I just went out and got snow and melted it. For laundry, I'd lug everything down to some place on the reserve, then pack it all back up.

Towards spring when it started melting and the snow was getting softer, I'd start falling through the crust of snow when I tried to get water from the spring, so living out there was getting too much for me. Then I had my little boy, Ne'Pauset, in early May.

YC: You were with me when you started into labour, because I got you to come and stay with me near to the end.

BET-TE: We made up. (laughter)

CHERYL: I was still having a hard time getting help from the band, too. The house I lived in had been condemned when I'd moved in a couple of years previously. I had just had my second child; she was sickly, and that house had no insulation. I got so fed up with taking my little one down to the hospital, and asking and asking and asking for a bit of help at the band office.

Then in the spring of 1979, the band council's housing allocation meeting was coming up, and we heard that some of us women, like Glenna and me, were finally going to get houses.

CAROLINE: See, as soon as Dan got elected to the band council he went and got all the information he could at Indian Affairs—the role of a councillor, where authority lies—and one of the things he found out was that all council meetings were public. When he told us, we started going and listening to them. You see, it was a process of finding out what our rights were. The traditional accepted way around here was that council meetings were only for the chief and council, and everybody including myself *assumed* that's how it was until Dan was elected.

The chief and *his* councillors tried to keep that housing allocation meeting a secret from Dan because they knew he was helping us, consequently the chief called a meeting in Grand Falls and they never told Dan about it till the last minute. Meetings were *never* held off the reserve, and Grand Falls is about forty miles away, so that tells you the lengths the chief would go to. Dan came up to the meeting anyway and also notified us about it, so we chased them all up to Grand Falls.

GLENNA: And the councillors agreed to let us in the meeting. We knew it was a public meeting, but when we walked in the chief told us to leave. I said, "Well, we might as well stay right here," and we waited outside in the lounge.

CAROLINE: We were mad because Cheryl really needed a house, and so did a lot of other women, and the only woman to get one was Glenna—because Glenna lobbied for about a year to get that house. We'd written to Indian Affairs, to members of parliament, to everybody, for Glenna's house, and the councillors knew if they didn't vote her one they'd have to answer some questions.

KAREN: I think Glenna got a house to try and keep us quiet.

GLENNA: There were eight votes and I got seven. I think only the chief didn't vote for me. It didn't shut us up though—we kept protesting.

CAROLINE: Ever since that Longest Walk from California to Washington, D.C., every now and then Glenna would mention our doing one. We started talking about it more after the old chief got back in, but I guess we weren't serious about it until that meeting in Grand Falls, when they turned Cheryl down. That's what set it off. I was mad enough to do it. (laughter)

We wanted to raise public consciousness about Native women's problems, and mainly the walk was over housing. We wanted the public to get angry that such conditions should exist in Canada.

KAREN: Caroline did most of the outside organizing for the walk, and Glenna most of the inside, explaining to women what it was all about. Over forty women and children from the reserve went.

CAROLINE: We decided to have it in July just in case walkers were forced to sleep out in the open. We started the actual organizing about three months before, which was good because at first I had a hard time. I was lucky, though, that I got the New Brunswick Human Rights Commission to let me use their telephones, otherwise we never would have been able to do it.

Glenna started talking to people on the reserve. She talked to everybody about actually doing this thing, and at the beginning they didn't think we were serious. Originally we were going to walk right from here. How stupid we were. (laughter) We had a hard enough time getting the one hundred miles from Oka Reserve, Quebec (near Montreal) to Ottawa!

My first intention was to lobby and bring the walk to the media's attention. Finally I got coverage in *The Globe and Mail*, but it took a long time. It seemed once we were publicly committed and other people heard about it, things took off from there. But we didn't have any money and I was getting desperate.

Finally it was getting *really* close to the time of the walk; we didn't have any money for the bus, not one cent. We hadn't received any donations yet and newspapers said it was against their policy to publish appeals—that if they did for us, everybody would want the service. Although one woman reporter did manage to get an appeal and a post office box number printed in her paper, until the walk nothing came in and *that* was when we needed funds.

The New Brunswick Advisory Council on the Status of Women had collected donations so that a few of us could make a couple of trips to Ottawa for advance planning. While in Ottawa I went to Indian Affairs and talked to Rod Brown, the assistant deputy minister, who used to be the regional director for this area. Indian Affairs had some consultation funds that he thought they could give us and he got that money to me in really short time. I was amazed how quick and easy it was, once they set their mind to it. Then I had to fly back and get the money to the coach lines, since they needed cash up front before they would come with a bus. That was *two days* before the walk. It was really a mess; everything was last minute.

We used the Indian Affairs money to pay for the bus and driver, which we had for over a week. Then we used the other donations for food, sneakers, foot powder, Pampers (laughter), and all that. Amazingly, we still had a little bit left over when we got home. But I think Rod Brown either got transferred or fired over the money he gave out to us. The Conservatives were in power at the time of the walk, but I heard when the Liberals got back in, they gave him trouble over it, and pushed him out.

SANDRA: Caroline, Pat Paul (Caroline's brother) and I were in Ottawa a week early to figure out the route, set up meetings, and find places to stay. We were so busy!

CAROLINE: Fortunately Pat was living in Ottawa at the time; I would never have been able to do it without him. We had a thousand and one details to take care of—I was completely exhausted even before the walk began—arranging for places for people to sleep, getting the necessary permits for the walk. White women were helping us, too, raising public awareness and getting donations.

We also managed to contact other Native women's groups and individuals, so we had people joining the walk from British Columbia, the Yukon, the Northwest Territories, as well as Ontario and Quebec.

We attracted attention from the RCMP, too. As soon as we started planning the walk, our telephones were tapped. You could actually hear a strange sound in the background, it was that obvious. They even answered my phone once. They told one of our supporters that our number was no longer in service. I know the RCMP kept an eye on us during the walk, too, to make sure they had nothing to worry about. But really. What threat could we be to the country anyway? (laughter)

We got denied help from Catholic priests along the route. When we were looking for accommodation, they refused to put us up in church facilities, even if they were nearly empty. That's why some nights we had to stay in campsites and sleep out on the ground.

SANDRA: When we started out on the walk, getting on the bus here on the reserve, you should have seen the men. They were standing outside laughing at us, saying, "You fools. What are you going to accomplish?" Oh, we were angry. That is when we were determined to do that walk because they were going, "Ha-ha-ha. Look at them stupid women. What do they think they are trying to do?"

We took the children with us and stopped at all the reserves along the way to see how many of them wanted to come along with us. We had contacted them ahead of time. I'll tell you, there weren't a great many. It was mostly women from Tobique on the bus. I think the others just thought, "Well, somebody is doing it. Why should we?" They might have been afraid, too. A woman from here got beat up by her husband for going.

CAROLINE: The bus got into Oka Reserve on July 13th and we met with some French-speaking reporters through a translator. We had thought we could stay overnight at the Catholic school or some kind of retreat house where they had all kinds of room, but the priest wouldn't let us. We ended up sleeping on the floor of a little town hall right in Oka. But it was so hot, the floor was so hard and there were so many flies, that I ended up taking my youngest son, Jimmie, and Karen's son, Spencer, outside with our little pieces of foam to sleep on the lawn.

The next morning when we woke up I was soaking wet with the dew. It was cold during the night; my whole bed-roll was wet; my hair was wet.

I'll never forget that hectic first morning at breakfast. We filled the whole restaurant. Everybody with us was on welfare and we had to feed them, so every morning Glenna and I would have to get up ahead of the crowd, after walking all day and then meeting till all hours of the night. With about two hours of sleep, we'd get up early and try to find breakfast for everybody. Sometimes there was no restaurant and we'd have to buy rolls, juice and stuff like that and bring back tons of it. Every day I went out and found a drug store to get more bandaids and foot powder.

By noon of that first day, most of the older women and the children were forced to ride in the bus because of the heat. The temperature went up to almost 100 degrees Fahrenheit. The younger women walked, though, even the ones without proper shoes.

LILLY: Oh, it was hot, but most people walked all the way. I was sixty-two when we made the walk. I think I was "the oldest walker." (laughs) After we hadn't even walked very far, people came out from their homes with cakes and cold drinks for us. I thought that was nice of them—they were French people. It was good because it gave you a lift to go on in all the heat.

GOOKUM: We never got much support in New Brunswick, just from a few white women's groups. But when we got to Quebec, oh, we got a lot of support. People putting out our lunches, providing accommodation. Gee, from there on people gave us a good reception. Some women had to sleep on the bus or outside, but most of the time people along the way tried to find places for us.

CAROLINE: That second night out we had some problems with a

few of the young women. We had told them before we left, there's going to be no drinking, no drugs.

GOOKUM: The second night some of them had a party in the park and a lot of the kids were crying. I told Glenna, "We should stop this right off because, can you imagine the publicity if people see us staggering in a town somewheres?" The next day there was a case of beer in the bus, so I told Glenna and Caroline, "We'll have to get out and talk to them women." We were having lunch and Glenna put the beer on the picnic table, said, "Who owns this?" Nobody wanted to claim that case of beer. Glenna said, "Well, we'll throw it in the garbage." She said, "If anybody wants to drink or smoke up, we'll pay your gas fare back home."

CAROLINE: When Glenna talked to the women who had been drinking, two or three agreed they weren't going to do it again, that they would just wait till we got to Ottawa. A couple of the younger ones talked back, though. They wouldn't listen, so Glenna put them on a bus back to Tobique, and we had no problems with any of the rest after that.

CAROLINE: The second day out, we started walking at nine a.m., and it was another hot day, but we still walked till mid-afternoon. It's a good thing Kathleen Jamieson (who wrote the book *Indian Women and the Law in Canada: Citizens Minus*) had an air-conditioned car, because the stupid restaurant where we finally stopped had no air-conditioning and I couldn't cool off. I asked Kathleen if I could sit in her car. She said, "Sure, come along," and she and her husband took me for an air-conditioned drive. It was just in time because my body had started to throb and I thought I was having a sunstroke. By the time we'd got back from getting some supplies at a drugstore, I was alright again.

LILLY: Oh, but our feet. At one place it was so hot and we had to stop because our feet and ankles were swelling up. Somebody got powder and we washed our feet right on the street. Reporters were taking pictures of us putting on the powder.

GLENNA: When we passed this one reserve, people had sandwiches for us. They knew we'd be walking by there around noon-hour, so all these women got together and had lunches out along the road. I'll never forget that.

CAROLINE: Each day some more people would join us. Jean Gleason from the Yukon walked all the way from Oka with her kids. Native women from a lot of different reserves joined the Walk. It was good—we needed a lot of encouragement because by the second day out, personalities were clashing, people had headaches, sore feet, quick tempers, aches and pains.

KAREN: I think I heard Glenna say one time that she hated everyone during the walk. (laughter) Which is true. Everybody hated everybody. Everybody talked about everybody. But we did it— we kept going. We were all so tired, the heat, the kids, everything. We weren't sure—"Why are we doing this? We're crazy." I used to like to walk with Sandra because we'd walk at the same pace, with our shorts and knobby knees. (laughter)

GLENNA: There was the men supporting us, too. Pat Paul and Karen's husband, Carl, accompanied us—also quite a few spiritual leaders. It was so nice to get a group of men to believe in us because, except for our relatives, men were afraid to come out and openly support us on our own reserve.

That third night we stayed in Hawksbury, Ontario, slept in a hockey arena. The management let us cook supper in the cafeteria and let the kids swim in the public pool and rollerskate while the women were being interviewed.

KAREN: We had meetings and meetings. Walking during the day and meetings at night. We'd have meetings to decide whether we should have a meeting. (laughter)

SANDRA: That's why I hate meetings. We had a lot of interviews, too. Caroline and I had an interview with Gordon Fairweather (head of the national Human Rights Commission), Danny MacIntyre, the black guy who used to work in St. John for Human Rights, and others ... all kinds of reporters.

CAROLINE: I think that was the night one of the reporters asked me if the government was going to meet with us. I told him, "We invited Joe Clark (then prime minister) and his wife, Maureen McTeer, to meet with us, and they said they couldn't, but I'm sure he'll change his mind." See, when we wrote the invitation, we had insisted on Maureen McTeer coming too, because we knew she supported women's rights.

A couple of the kids coughed and coughed all night long—they sounded awful, like they had bronchitis or something—so I said to myself, the minute I wake up, make sure those kids get to a hospital. The next morning it was misty and damp, but didn't rain, so we had a break from the heat. I got somebody to take the kids to the hospital, but the hospital gave them a hard time because they had band numbers and no Ontario medical coverage. It ended up that I had to go and argue for them and catch up to the walk later on. Then we had to go and buy medicine for those kids out of our walk funds.

At our lunch stop some television cameras showed up and we were on television that night. We got more and more media coverage as we went along, and people coming out from Ottawa to walk with us. When we finished walking for the day, besides visiting and doing interviews, some of us also were working on a position paper to present when we got to Ottawa, though we didn't know exactly who we were going to meet with yet. But we did get word that evening that the minister of Indian Affairs, Jake Epp, was coming out to meet with us the next day.

By now I was getting totally exhausted from so little sleep and being so busy. Also, my youngest son Jimmie was getting exhausted and all night long he'd be talking in his sleep and having nightmares, so I was feeling guilty because I knew I was neglecting the little guy, too busy with everything else. That night I decided, he's going to get some sleep even if I have to go lay down with him. As soon as we got in, I fed him, didn't bother to eat myself, went and took a shower—cold by the time we got to it, had Jimmie cleaned up, and went and slept in the dining area away from the gym because the kids were noisy all night long. It was the first and only good sleep I had that whole time.

The next day, July 17th, was a real scorcher again. Fortunately we didn't have a long distance to be covered that day, but we still had one case of sunburn severe enough to need medical attention. It was at our over-night stop in Rockland that we got a letter delivered from the prime minister's office saying Joe Clark and Maureen McTeer were going to meet with us after all. They must have changed their minds when they saw we were getting so much publicity.

Jake Epp, the minister of Indian Affairs, arrived that evening with a crowd of reporters and television cameras, so it turned into more a public forum than an informal discussion—though he'd said he wanted to talk to the women informally about their problems. The television cameras made some of the women reluctant to talk. The minister met with us on his own initiative; we didn't even ask him. See, all the media coverage was forcing everybody to pay attention to us.

When we started getting on national television, people at home who'd thought we were crazy or something really changed their attitude toward us. Somehow I guess being on The National (the CBC's 10 p.m. news-in-depth program) made the walk legitimate.

The publicity was forcing everybody into making some sort of statement because Gordon Fairweather sent out a press release saying the Human Rights Commission supported our walk; and the NIB (National Indian Brotherhood) kept getting enquiries from the press about, "How come you're supposed to be representing status Indians in Canada and you're not saying anything about these women?" Finally they must have felt pressured enough to send some NIB people out to see us, and after that, on the same evening as Jake Epp came out, a guy showed up from NIB trying to strike a deal with us. To this day, that guy hates Sandra. (laughter)

Anyway, he came out and said to us, "If you'll back our position on the (Canadian) Constitution, we'll back your walk." He had a copy of a proposed press release they would issue supporting the walk, but warning the government about the dangers of changing the Indian Act. I was so mad, I said, "Who the hell do you think you are? If you people were doing your job we wouldn't have to be walking. Why should we make deals with you? We're in the driver's seat now—we have the cards in our hands at this point." He went away mad, but he was back the next day, so the NIB *must* have felt pressured.

KAREN: That guy even brought a paper over about their proposed deal and wanted us to sign it. See, I think what happened is that we were outside of Ottawa and the NIB was on the inside. They knew what kind of impact we were making on everybody—all the publicity—and they thought, "Oh, wow!" The prime minister was going to meet with us; the minister of Indian Affairs was coming to see us.

KAREN: We told people a lot about housing, of course. Then reporters started asking Sandra about 12(1)(b) and sexual discrimination in the Indian Act.

SANDRA: It all happened on the walk. Somebody mentioned that I was there, so reporters would come and talk to me because of our taking my case to the United Nations. See, Canada was dragging its feet on its defence, not answering the U.N.'s questions, so the press wanted to know more about it. So I'd do interviews about that part, and other women would do interviews about housing and so forth. At first I was there to support the women on housing, since I couldn't get a house myself, but since I was there, the press made an issue out of non-status and 12(1)(b), too. So that is how I got more involved and got more publicity.

KAREN: Sandra had interviews even before the walk because of the United Nations case, but then even more afterwards. Remember *Canada AM* (a national television morning news show)?

SANDRA: Yes, Caroline and I went to Toronto for that. They warned me beforehand what kind of questions I'd be asked, then I just answered with what I knew about it. We always made sure that they knew our leaders didn't back us up. The fact that they were against us always was brought up because interviewers would say, "Well, don't you have leaders to represent you?" We'd have to say, "No. If we had leaders to represent us, we wouldn't be going through all this."

CAROLINE: It was actually the media who started putting in the thing about non-status women during the walk. In the process of walking we drew up a position paper, and one of the issues that came up was the non-status thing. Another was the fact that there was really no national Native women's organization. There was the Native Women's Association of Canada, but it couldn't really function because those women weren't getting any funding. Those were two of the things we talked about in our paper; funding for the national organization and the non-status issue. On the issue of status, we decided that it would be best to ask for reinstatement to the first generation since to go beyond the children of women who had lost their status would take too much power away from the bands. After all everyone in the band could remember who had married who, who had lost their status and who were the children of these women.

Each night we would work on the position paper. Anything we wanted the government to do was in that paper, all our complaints. Altogether we listed twenty-one concerns, ranging from housing and education to health and the right to be buried on reserves. Theresa Nahanee who is a writer lined it up really nice to present to the prime minister and the minister of Indian Affairs.

That fifth night of camping out we were fortunate because the mayor of Rockland, Quebec was so generous to us. Him and his family and all the townspeople greeted us so warmly; he arranged for us to use the arena and all of its facilities; provided lifeguards so we could swim in his private pool.

KAREN: The last day of our walk before arriving in Ottawa, the women from the NIB offices came and joined us. They were all in their high heels, fancy clothes, the kind of fancy tee-shirts the NIB used to give out, nail polish on their fingers. And here we were, grubby and sweaty. (laughter)

CAROLINE: The women's tee-shirts had *National Indian Brotherhood* on them. The NIB wanted to be seen there so that they wouldn't look like fools in the parade. We could have pointed that out to the press, but that was the last day before the march into Ottawa, and by that point I didn't care. We already had enough problems and I just wanted to get everything over with. But I knew that they were just there to make the NIB look good.

KAREN: At the end of the walk it was another terribly hot day. We were coming up the hill and all the news media were coming down from Parliament Hill, getting ready to greet us. A whole crowd of people was applauding while we were walking. Oh jeez, it was emotional. Tears coming down our eyes, crying. I hadn't realized that we had made such an impact, but we did. I'd thought, here we are walking all this way and nobody cares, but they did.

SANDRA: We really didn't think anybody would listen to us, or that we would accomplish anything. Just getting there was emotional.

KAREN: At the outset we wondered, are we just wasting our time here? But there was such a reception. News media, TV, women's groups, even the gay liberation and some people who are not very well liked—Marxist-Leninist—(laughter) but they were there and they supported us. There were all kinds of signs and placards like, "Feminists Support Tobique Women" and "Marxist-Leninists Support Native Women."

I was surprised we had so many people supporting us there. I was thinking, I wish Indian Affairs would listen to us the way the press are listening to us. I knew it wouldn't help whatever Indian Affairs was told, but the press did a lot for us. They were always so surprised by what we had to go through.

We'd tell the reporters what to ask the Indian Affairs minister and officials. They did; the press kept calling up Indian Affairs and interviewing people, and Indian Affairs was afraid of them. Sometimes we would get our white supporters to phone for information, too, especially when we were getting the run-around. Often it worked, and Indian Affairs officials would give them information they wouldn't give out to us.

GLENNA: Of course we had all our kids with us, too. It was The Year of the Child and I've got a picture of my youngest daughter, Tiffany, from the walk. It says something like, "Indian Children Need Help Too." It showed the kids bare-footed. (laughter)

LILLY: When we'd started out on the walk there were about fifty of us, but by the time we walked into Ottawa there were four or five times that number. Some of them weren't even Indians and they were supporting us. French and English. There was a big rally when we got up to Parliament Hill, speeches, television cameras. People had hotdogs and hamburgers, cold drinks for us.

GOOKUM: On the walk I couldn't actually walk far because I couldn't stay in the sun that long, so I rode ahead with Carl and Pat. I walked the last part though, and when we were up in front of the Parliament Buildings, I looked back to see all them women come walking up. They looked so determined.

BET-TE: I got chills, seeing that.

GOOKUM: I felt like crying; that was the happiest moment. I kept looking back and there's these cement benches there. (laughs) I tripped on one and fell, hit my knees. Wayne (Nicholas) picked me up, said, "Gookum, are you hurt?" He was so worried about me, he was almost crying. Holy ... I could hardly walk that day, kept sitting down every chance I got. My poor knees!

Boy, that was gratifying, though, all these women coming to support us. Even from the Yukon. From all over, everywhere *except* New Brunswick.

CAROLINE: We had Native women's groups from several provinces, the Voice of Women, the Advisory Council on the Status of Women, the National Indian Brotherhood, labour groups, feminist groups. At the rally in the afternoon on Parliament Hill, we held a press conference. David MacDonald who was Secretary of State then, and Jake Epp, the minister of Indian Affairs addressed the crowd. Flora MacDonald (who was then Indian Affairs critic for the Conservatives) couldn't be there, but David MacDonald spoke on her behalf.

By the time we got to Ottawa, I was a walking zombie. Here Andrea was talking on national television, and we had all these people talking and listening to us. It's like I didn't have any feeling; I think it must be like when you have a nervous breakdown, because I didn't hate anyone, I didn't love anyone, I couldn't get mad, I couldn't feel happy, nothing—it was blank. I think I was just plain exhausted. Here everybody was listening to Andrea and tears going down their faces, and I'd look around and be amazed—how come I don't feel nothing? But I didn't. I couldn't stop yet, though, because the next day we were meeting with the government officials.

Our meeting with the officials was at the Government Conference Centre. Besides Joe Clark and Maureen McTeer, there were minister of Indian Affairs Jake Epp, Health and Welfare minister David Crombie, and Secretary of State David MacDonald. Part of the meeting was open and part was in-camera.

SANDRA: I had to meet the prime minister and I was so bashful, I really didn't know what to tell him at first. That was the first time we had really "done something"—met officials—so I was really scared. We talked to Maureen McTeer and she was really supportive; asked us a lot of questions, said she would do what she could with the people around her.

KAREN: That was my first time in Ottawa, and what an introduction. It was a big, fancy place and was I impressed. Here we were, meeting in that big conference room in Parliament with the prime minister, cabinet ministers, cameras, translators. It was the first time I was exposed to all that ... earphones for simultaneous translation.

SANDRA: Karen was listening to French instead. (laughter) We were all impressed. Karen kept taking pictures. One of the older women said, "Gee, I wish I could go up there," so Caroline made arrangements for her to go sit up there with "the big shots"—Joe Clark, Jake Epp. Boy, that really made her day. Joe Clark told us they were going to begin revisions on the Indian Act so we could get our status back.

CAROLINE: He told us that it was the National Indian Brotherhood that was responsible for the Act not being changed, but that his government was going to go ahead on it whether or not they had the NIB's consent. Jake Epp gave us his approval in principle of the brief we presented, and David MacDonald promised he would get funds for Native women's organizations.

GOOKUM: After we met with the prime minister and all the VIPs in Ottawa, Caroline said to the women, "You're on your own now." One of the girls from Montreal told me, "We went to a bar then, had only two drinks and I was drunk!" (laughter) She was so surprised, but it was because she'd had nothing to drink all during the walk.

CAROLINE: The next day was Saturday and we didn't schedule anything, just let everybody rest up. Then on Sunday there was an open air church service in a park and in the evening we held a diplomats' reception in a church hall. We wanted diplomats from other countries to know how Canada was treating its Native women.

SANDRA: Caroline and I went to all the foreign embassies, too—all we could get into—and they couldn't believe what was happening to the women. They would always mention that Canada was so proud that they weren't discriminating, and here they were still discriminating against Native people, and letting our leaders discriminate against their own women.

Joe Clark assured us something was going to be done—that they were going to introduce legislation to end sexual discrimination in the Indian Act. Then that all fell through because his government was defeated by the Liberals soon afterwards.

All the time Trudeau was prime minister, he never believed in our cause. One time I heard him say, "How can they call themselves Natives? I'm a native here too—a native of Quebec." I don't think he believed Native women were having so many problems on reserves. He only listened to the men's organizations saying, "Those women are just trouble-makers, just radical women wanting attention."

CAROLINE: We did get $300,000 extra housing money on this reserve because of the walk. The Native Women's Association of Canada got a major increase in funding, too, as a result of the walk, because that is one of the things we insisted on. Those

Conservative cabinet ministers did follow through on their promises. I'm pretty sure they would have come through with changing
the Indian Act, too, if they had been in power long enough.

With the non-status issue, though, once *we* put forward our
position in the brief, we felt we had to keep pushing it. With the
old chief back in power here we still had daily problems to deal
with on the reserve, too.

BET-TE: Less than a month after I had the baby in May, I moved
back to that cement shack in the park. I got the chief's administration to deliver me water out there, and they did for a short
while, then quit again. Shortly after that I went on the walk to
Ottawa with Ne'Pauset. At three months old he was "the youngest
walker."

When I got back from the walk I asked the chief's administration to fix the cement shack up and they wouldn't. Also, they
refused to deliver water and by now it was getting on towards
fall.

So I bundled the baby into his carriage and hid a rifle in there. I
was going to go down to the band office and take the chief hostage;
make him live under the same conditions as me—having to wash
in a basin, shit in the pot and stuff like that. On my way down I
stopped at Glenna's place. Barb (Nicholas) and Glenna were there
and they took the rifle away from me—which is really a good
thing, I suppose, because I probably would be put in jail, away
from my kid.

GLENNA: You would just have gotten out this year. (laughter) But
you were so desperate at the time.

BET-TE: I went down anyways, after they took the gun away from
me, and walked with the baby right into a chief and council meeting. I told them, "You guys won't deliver me water any more, so I
want you to find me and my baby a place to live." I told them, "I'm
not leaving here until you find me a decent place. I want you to
promise me a house, and I want it down in writing and signed by
all of you."

The chief and council said verbally, "Yes, we'll give you a

house when one comes in." When I got that paper later, they had switched it around and said they'd build me "a unit," which turned out to be this apartment I'm still living in (one side of a duplex). Originally they had promised a small house, which is all I wanted—I didn't want a great big fancy house.

Instead they moved me into the jail, since by then Sandra had found other accommodation. We lived in the jail for quite a while until they moved us into this unit. They started another apartment too, but never finished it.

This apartment isn't even finished yet—several years later, but it's a lot better than living in that cement shack. If I'd been smarter I could have stayed out there, I suppose, and had them build onto it, but I was pretty desperate for a place with running water and a toilet.

GLENNA: The chief's administration allotted me a house in April before the walk, but they didn't start building it until the end of August. See, houses normally are started in the spring so they can be finished before the cold weather in the fall, but they kept delaying mine. The chief was giving me a hard time; for some reason he didn't want me to build up here.

CAROLINE: No matter what we tried to do, the chief's administration gave us a problem. When we tried to vote, they'd give us a problem; when I went for a job they'd sit in the selection committee and I wouldn't get hired. They did everything they could to get at us. Every damn time an election comes up they complain about Karen's husband, Carl, (who's in the RCMP) because he's the present chief's brother. Ever since Dan was on the band council, they haven't liked him either, because he's kept helping the women.

I don't know how many times we challenged the way they were running band elections. One year I was a student so I was living off the reserve temporarily but eligible to vote. The chief and his buddies knew for sure I would vote against him, so they prevented me from voting. I think that was the same year they broke open the ballot box after it was sealed. They said a non-status woman had voted, so they broke it open and had everybody come back and vote all over again.

There were a lot of election irregularities, and when we didn't get any results from notifying Indian Affairs in Fredericton, we contacted Ottawa, but they still didn't question that election. It held and the chief had won, so somebody at Indian Affairs was right in there helping him.

One Indian Affairs official who for sure was good friends with the chief—always partying with him—was Jack Vater. Eventually Indian Affairs got rid of him, but only after a guy published a letter in the *The Telegraph-Journal* about Vater up here in his government car partying with the chief all weekend—using that company car on his personal time. A newsclipping of the letter was sent to Indian Affairs in Ottawa, but Jack Vater kept his job for the longest time. It was only recently they got rid of him.

GLENNA: That election in the fall of 1979, when they wouldn't let Dan vote, the old chief got back in. That's when they were stalling on building my house and refusing to help me winterize the trailer. The furnace was always breaking down and the water kept freezing up.

Cheryl was having a hard time too, and Bet-te was still living in the jail. We were all getting desperate, especially knowing the chief was going to be in power at least two more years. A lot of times some of us women would go into the band office together. Other times one woman would go in with her grievances, and we would keep calling the band office, or keep going in every so often to let them know she had support. The main thing was to make sure the chief and them knew we were supporting each other.

Finally at the end of November we occupied the band office again. This time it was me, Cheryl, and Bet-te and our kids, with other women coming and going like Barbara (Nicholas), Sandra and Bet-te's mother, YC. But it was always me, Cheryl and Bet-te.

We were in there a week and getting a lot of threats. Then on the weekend things started getting out of hand. On Friday night an Indian Affairs official called me and said that the RCMP riot squad was waiting downtown; if we needed them, all we had to do was call. We didn't need to that night, but the next night things got even worse.

CHERYL: Some of us were inside and a crowd was pelting the building with bottles and stones. They broke about six windows, a street light, and did a bunch of damage to the outside of the building.

BET-TE: There was nearly a riot. It started with a lot of shouting back and forth, the opposition antagonizing kids who were supporting us. Mostly it was the teenagers supporting us against kids from families on the other side. But some of the chief's councillors and their white wives were there, too—they were instigating things from the background. Everybody was worked up and kind of panicking because there were rumours of a riot squad coming in. About six police cruisers had showed up already—we didn't call them, they just showed up.

GLENNA: People were smashing windows and threatening to burn down the band office. I got scared and was afraid the teenage boys would get hurt. I know it had started to bother my kids; they were so nervous. That was when I decided to move out. Barbara and Bet-te didn't want to—they said, "It looks like we're giving up"—but I said, "No, we're not. If Indian Affairs sees the danger we're in, then they'll finally do something." We didn't want to cause that kind of trouble—there was enough problems on the reserve already.

So I called Raymond Tremblay who is from here and was working in Fredericton as district manager, and told him what was happening. I told him it was too cold to move back home, so would Indian Affairs put us up at the Galaxy Motel in town? I told him, "I'm afraid for my children and I want to get out of here."

Shortly after that Raymond Tremblay and Alex Dedam who also worked for Indian Affairs had a meeting with us and okayed it for us to move down to the Galaxy. Those two guys really helped us out, but both of them got demoted over it. Alex Dedam had been right up there in Indian Affairs before that, and was stripped of his authority afterwards.

CAROLINE: The chief and them got very leery of the press after a while. By the time Suzette Couture came to do the story for *Today Magazine*, they literally were running away from reporters. One time we had a film crew by the chief's big, new house. His brother was building a garage or some sort of addition onto it, and came out yelling, "Get out of here!" I think he would have gotten a gun if they hadn't left. It sure scared the camera men, anyways.

GLENNA: We stayed at the Galaxy for about three weeks. The kids were going to school from there, but we were having a hard time getting permission for them to take the school bus. Then the snow started; I got sick and ended up in the hospital for a while. It was all tension, I guess—I started feeling sick and having really bad headaches.

I'd get phone calls, "We're going to burn your house down," usually late at night. After I moved in people would drive by really slowly and call me names, or they'd dump garbage in front of the house. This kind of thing was going on and some people on the reserve don't even believe it. I was afraid for the kids, but they held up pretty good. Every so often the objectors would say something about me to my kids, and that would bother me. It was getting so bad, and I hated to keep talking and complaining about it.

If it wasn't for my father, the house would never have gotten finished, because every pension cheque he'd buy me a few sheets of sheetrock. Then I'd put that whole tax rebate—$90—into the house. Meanwhile the men were getting help with their houses, and they were working. I kept the receipts of money I spent—almost $4,000.

There were two prayers we used to always say together. One was of Saint Jude who is supposed to be a saint for the hopeless—something like, "the hopeless cases." (laughs) No wonder the kids felt discouraged. The other one was the Infant Jesus prayer, "Ask and you shall receive, knock and it shall be opened to you." Then when we got a house I said to Tiffany, "See, your prayers are answered." She said, "Yeah, but that's just one." (laughter)

My grandmother always believed in dreams; some of them, it

really happens after you dream of certain things. But this one, I didn't expect. I dreamt that the whole reserve was like a circle, and I saw all the people that were fighting. They were stabbing each other on the back, spitting on each other, calling each other names. It was like Tobique was a circle and it was going around.

I tried so hard to get off it. I wanted to get off so bad, but every time I wanted to step down I'd see this puddle, this water. The circle went around three times, then the last time I did make it off; I stepped into the water and it was full of a lot of twigs. When I looked down I saw this man face down in the mud puddle where the twigs were. I know it was the chief, I didn't have to see the face, but one side of his face was covered with blood. He was face down and he wore that shirt he always wore a lot. I knew it was him.

I looked at him and just stepped over his feet. I didn't feel sorry for him, I didn't feel hatred for him, I didn't feel nothing. In my dream I said aloud, "Look at this man. There's so many people around here and nobody's trying to help him." I looked at him and I walked away.

After that, when I woke up it was like, even if I tried to hate him that day, I don't think I could have. But it made me realize that it wasn't me to judge him or punish him. It would be somebody else.

The dream must be like now; nobody cares for him, like in the dream, nobody cares one way or another about him now. In the dream I walked away and let it be, and that's how I felt the next morning. It must have been a message that I should just let it go. He'll have to answer to somebody else. So after that I could even talk to him. I can even dance with him now. (laughter) I wouldn't *vote* for him, but I danced with him at our reinstatement celebration. It shocked so many people; they said, "I thought you hate him." I said, "Not anymore."

SANDRA: The band office fire was after we had all moved out and there was going to be an investigation into the band administration's books. We got news of the investigation, and that's what we wanted, so we moved out. That's when it burned to the ground and all the files got destroyed in the fire.

GLENNA: His nephew burned it down. That night I dreamt a big building was burning, and when I got up the next morning I saw fire trucks leaving the reserve. Wanda's little boy called me, said, "Glenna, did you hear about the fire?" I said, "I bet some big building burned." He said, "Yeah. How did you know?" I said, "I dreamt about it," and he told me, "Yep, the band office burned right down."

KAREN: The chief's nephew got charged for it; he got convicted and served time, but he's out now.

SANDRA: There was a lot of gossip. Especially when there was going to be an investigation *the next day*, and all the files were burned. So no investigation. (laughter)

We could always get a bunch of women together for something really important, but it was always the same small core that kept at it.

YC: After the band office burned down, things were about the same until Dave Perley got in as chief in 1983. *Some* women got houses, and we got it so that houses were in both the husband's and the wife's names. The women were still struggling, though. If you'd go up to the band office and ask for anything, forget it.

BET-TE: After the fire was when we really got involved in the status thing. Women's organizations and even some Indian organizations started coming around and asking us to go here, go there.

The status thing was kind of a repeat of what happened with the chief. All he had to do was meet with us and work together to get decent housing for women; all he had to say was, "Okay, let's try this." But he didn't want to do that. He caused all that shit on himself. It's just like the status thing. It could have been handled in one day, but no. It took years and years.

CHAPTER FIVE

LOBBYING

As THE TOBIQUE WOMEN'S PROTESTS became publicized, they began to receive speaking invitations outside the reserve. Here Eva (Gookum) Saulis and Bet-te Paul recall their participation at Indian Rights for Indian Women (IRIW) conferences in the late 1970s when that national organization was in existence.

BET-TE: Women's organizations had started coming around and asking us to go here, go there. We went out and talked to these organizations so that they would apply pressure on the government. That was when me and Gookum started attending Indian Rights for Indian Women meetings. We also met with Jake Epp, who was minister of Indian Affairs when the Conservatives were in power, and even before that, with Jean Chretien when he was Indian Affairs minister for the Liberals. While we were going out, there was always women here at home holding the fort, backing us up.

When Gookum and I started going out, that was before the non-status thing. It had to do with housing and we took our placards from the demonstrations with us.

GOOKUM: Glenna and I were invited but she didn't want to go, so Bet-te went with me.

BET-TE: First we had tried to accomplish what was needed for people's survival right here on the reserve level, but when that didn't work and we were invited to Indian Rights for Indian Women, we tried that path.

We didn't know what to expect. We found out we actually had

representation—Native Indian women from New Brunswick on IRIW—and we never knew anything about it. Native women sitting there on the board and they never contacted us the whole time of our occupations. I think they got reprimanded.

We'd never been outside the reserve to meetings before, and that first one was in Edmonton. We were put on the agenda at our very first meeting and we didn't even know about it. We weren't at all prepared to speak.

GOOKUM: It was a big assembly of women, and the first morning there Bet-te read that we were on the agenda for ten o'clock *that morning.* I was so nervous putting our placards up in front. One was of a man with a bottle in his hand kicking his family out of their house. I started speaking but my voice was shaking—I was just about to cry—so I told Bet-te in Indian, "You take over." I couldn't speak, it was so emotional. We were tired, too, since we'd got there late the night before.

BET-TE: I was so scared I almost started crying too, but I just explained what was happening at Tobique with housing and why. I told them we weren't getting anywheres with Indian Affairs or chief and council. It's frightening looking out over a big assembly; I was scared shitless. (laughter) I remember wanting to reach over and tell Gookum, "Hold my hand." We were pretty emotional, too, because I think we realized how important it was to tell those people. Especially when that Noel Starblanket stood up and really didn't want to hear what we were saying.

GOOKUM: Starblanket [then president of the National Indian Brotherhood] got up on stage to speak right after us. He told everybody, "I don't understand what's going on here. I'm not going to support that muck!" Then Pat Paul, Caroline's brother, called out from the back, "You're the person who should understand. You're the one that represents all the Indians in Canada." Pat was told to shut up.

When Noel Starblanket stopped speaking, Jennie Margetts (president of Indian Rights for Indian Women) got up and said, "The national Indian Rights for Indian Women support the Tobique women one hundred percent!" and everybody got up and cheered for us. Gee, that gave me tears.

BET-TE: Me, too. We got a standing ovation. I think that was the first time our cause became nationally known, and other groups got involved in it.

GOOKUM: I told Jennie Margetts, "I feel so useless. I don't even talk or anything." She said, "Don't ever feel like that. We need your moral support. We need elders here, too; just being here is enough." She said, "Don't worry. We've been at it—talking to big assemblies—for ten years, and we still get nervous."

BET-TE: You were good at talking to people afterwards—you did a lot of lobbying. We went to three or four major conferences together, once to the Chateau Laurier Hotel in Ottawa. I took the baby with me that time. The executive was being pressured to have a younger woman, and they asked me to run. I was at the learning stage of politics, so I didn't want to take it on, but was pushed into it.

Then when I did get into the executive, I found out they never really wanted to hear anything I said, and when I got back home I never received any information or was called for any decision-making, so I figured it was just token bullshit. Consequently, I resigned from that position and told them the reason why—"If I'm supposed to be on the executive, then you've got to let me know what the hell is going on."

GOOKUM: When Indian Rights for Indian Women started, they were fighting mainly for the rights of Indian women—like property rights—on reserves. It was later on that they included the non-status issue. Well, it was for *all* Indian women, regardless of status, but only later on did the status issue become more central. Mary Two-Axe Early from Caughnawaga (near Montreal) always pushed it, but not too many others—not until Sandra's case.

BET-TE: Going out to IRIW conferences, we made connections with other groups. Newspeople would talk to us, too, and white women's groups.

GOOKUM: Indian Rights for Indian Women is where we met Mary Early and a lot of cabinet ministers and senators. Once I said to Flora MacDonald, "I'm Eva Saulis from Tobique," and she said, "Oh yes, you're the woman with the big problems from the small reserve." (laughter) She was always very supportive to us, ever since she was the Conservative Indian Affairs critic in the mid-'70s.

Caroline Ennis was instrumental in pursuing Glenna Perley and Dan Ennis' idea of taking the case of a non-status woman to the United Nations. She recalls that this was initially a *strategy* to put pressure on the Canadian government in order to make officials address the concerns Native women were raising.

The Tobique women's strategy of going to the United Nations did exert tremendous pressure on the federal government to change the Indian Act. On December 29, 1977 the complaint of Sandra Lovelace against the Canadian government was communicated to the United Nations Human Rights Committee in Geneva, Switzerland. Because of delays by the Canadian government in responding to the Human Rights Committee's requests for information, the final verdict was not made until July 30, 1981. That decision found Canada in violation of the International Covenant on Civil and Political Rights. Canada was in breach of the Covenant because the Indian Act denied Sandra Lovelace the *legal* right to live in the community of her birth.

The Canadian government was embarrassed by the publicity the Sandra Lovelace case was receiving. Even prior to the United Nations final decision, government officials began issuing press releases announcing that the Indian Act would be amended *within a year* to end discrimination against women. A story, "Indian Women achieve full status next year: Ottawa," in the December 11, 1980 edition of *The Toronto Star* opened with the statement, "Canada has told the United Nations it will bring in legislation next year to change laws which discriminate against Indian women, despite statements by Indian Affairs minister John Munro that such action might be delayed until 1985." In actual fact, 1985 was the year the Indian Act finally was amended, after a long struggle between those, such as the Tobique women, calling for change and those resisting it.

Once Sandra Lovelace agreed in 1977 to be the woman whose

case would go to the United Nations, she became the logical and most recognized Tobique spokeswoman for the non-status issue. Glenna Perley has never liked travelling, so most of the lobbying trips to Ottawa and other centres have been made by Caroline Ennis, Sandra, Sandra's sister, Karen Perley, and from the early 1980's, Shirley Bear. In the following conversation, Sandra and Karen recall their "early days" of lobbying.

SANDRA: Even from the time of the walk we had a position on reinstatement worked out; immediate reinstatement for women and children—that is, former band members and their first generation children. We figured we would just handle that present problem, and then if something else came up later, then the women who were reinstated could help us deal with it. Reinstatement was something we always talked about and always wanted—full reinstatement to the bands.

KAREN: It was the end of 1977 when that complaint was sent to the United Nations and it wasn't till the summer of 1981 that a final decision was reached. The Canadian government kept stalling— they would never answer the questions the United Nations was asking. Remember, Sandra, often when there was a change in your case, you wouldn't even know about it?

The media would know first and tell you. They'd ask, "What is your reaction to this latest development?" and you'd have no idea what they were talking about. (laughter) Well, they were right there in Ottawa or some city, and we're out here in the sticks. I remember your case being discussed at university and I was proud.

SANDRA: When I moved back here I still travelled for the issue— went to Copenhagen for the United Nations women's conference. Caroline got me there, because Canada had already chosen a lot of white women, and she called the Secretary of State, said, "How come no Indian women are going?" We found out Mary (Two-Axe) Early was going, but Caroline said, "I think Sandra should go because she should tell the world what is going on with the Native women, too."

So that's how I ended up going to Copenhagen with Mary. I'd gotten to know her at Indian Rights for Indian Women meetings and ever since then, at anything important I'd go to, she'd be there too. It was at Copenhagen, though, that we got close, because we shared the same room and I'd help her around.

We went to Copenhagen, but we couldn't speak formally because it was too late to get on the agenda. What we did was go lobby with women's groups there. We had a speech with the Canadian delegation, NAC (National Action Committee on the Status of Women). They were shocked. Shocked at what was going on. Some of the Canadian women didn't even know anything about 12(1)(b). That's the time Canada signed the U.N. charter saying they wouldn't discriminate against *any* women.

So I came back and told people, "Canada is still discriminating against women—Native women, anyway!" All this time we were out doing our lobbying, the (Native) men's organizations were lobbying against us. For that matter, they're still lobbying against us. Every time somebody asked me, "How come the men don't do anything to help you?" I'd tell them, "Because most of them are married to white women and they don't want to jeopardize their wives' status." If the male leaders cared for their own people, their own women, they would have fought *with* us to end the discrimination but instead they fought against us.

On top of everything else, we were getting a lot of harassment at the border, too. See, when a woman moves back from the States, you have to report at the border saying you are moving back. Then they raise questions of your children. They didn't know I was back till they saw my name in the newspapers; that's how they got hold of me. I asked them, "What are you going to do? Take my child away from me?" They said, "No, we just want you to sign this paper saying he is a Canadian citizen." I said, "No. What if he chooses to be an American? Besides, he is living with me, and wherever I live, he lives." Finally I'd swear at them when they came around.

But then customs started harassing other women and their children. I told those women, "Just tell them to *#&¢# off! Don't pay any attention to them." At that same time a white woman was living here from the States with her child, and she was not harassed at all. She came from Maine to live with an Indian guy on the reserve. Her child was going to school here; got free books and everything. All this while Indian women born here can't get any of that. That really pissed me off!

Christian did attend school here for a while. The band administration had to let him because they'd signed a band council resolution for another woman's kids and they couldn't refuse me. However, Christian started getting harassed at school for what I was doing—kids telling him, "Ah, non-status, you don't belong here. Go back to where you come from!" Sometimes he'd come home crying. So I transferred him to school in town, but the kids from here still gave him a bad time. Because of what *I* was doing, they took it out on my son. I felt so sorry for him; it wasn't his fault.

When we started off with the lobbying, some of the women I'd grown up with would say, "Hey, you don't belong here. Get out of here. You're non-status ... a troublemaker." But I didn't really care as long as I felt what I was doing was right. I wasn't about to stop for nobody. I didn't care if they liked me or not.

Being gone all the time would cause marital problems. Also, your children suffer when you have to go away so much. When I went to Copenhagen my little girl, Chkwabun, was only six or seven months old. I swore at the time I would never leave her again because when I came back she started crying, wouldn't leave me out of her sight. I felt so awful. But then something else came up and I said, "I have to go."

I couldn't afford to take my kids along when we went out lobbying, so my mother babysat for me. She believed in the cause—was non-status then herself. She'd say, "I might not be able to go out there myself, but if you need to go and need somebody to take care of your kids, I'll do it for you."

KAREN: After the walk we did stop going out to lobby for quite a long time, I think because we thought, wow, something is going to be done; they really are going to change the Act. We waited and waited and nothing got done. Then Joe Clark's government fell and we had to start all over.

SANDRA: We had to start lobbying and giving out interviews again. We saw interviews as our chance to tell the public about our situation. Remember when the United Nations finally ruled against Canada? July of 1981.

KAREN: We were living in Fredericton and had a big party because we were so sure the non-status were going to get reinstated. It kept getting announced in the newspapers, but ... just more empty promises.

SANDRA: The Liberals were embarrassed in the international community, so they said, yes, they would end discrimination and amend the Indian Act. Then we waited and waited. We never gave up, though. We got to know more and more women who were fighting for the same cause. We all kept in contact and when something important came up, would scrape together some money and go.

KAREN: Like Union (of New Brunswick Indians) assemblies, we always got together and went to raise the issue of reinstatement. We went to Native women's assemblies, even white women's meetings, like that New Brunswick umbrella group of women Shirley (Bear) was involved in starting up. We'd bring up reinstatement everywhere we could.

> While Tobique women were working for reinstatement nationally and for better housing locally, Shirley Bear was initiating parallel struggles over housing on her husband's reserve in north-eastern New Brunswick. Then in 1980 when women from Tobique invited her to help plan a provincial Native women's conference, Shirley's acceptance soon led to her joining their reinstatement campaign. In the following interview Shirley recalls her time on Big Cove reserve, her growing consciousness of sexism and racism, and her memorable experiences of lobbying with Caroline Ennis.

SHIRLEY: In the late 1970s I had more knowledge of external women's issues than issues on the reserve level. I hadn't really looked at what was happening to women on reserves because I was so happy in my own little world. Before we had Ramona, Peter and I decided to get married, basically because we'd been living together and thought, why not? (laughs) I had been sick, had had two miscarriages. I think mostly we were afraid of more medical expenses and I hadn't given 12(1)(b) much thought— Peter is status, so marrying him meant getting my status back. Actually I was afraid to get married again, after going through it once, but Peter was so sure. We got married, and along came Ramona.

Then in 1980 I was approached by a woman who was being kicked out of a house in Big Cove, even though she was Indian and from that reserve. She was pregnant and had been deserted by the man she'd been living with, and it was just before Christmas. The man had left her, gone to work in Fredericton, forgot about her and found another woman, but he said she could live in the house because by now she was carrying his child. This man has children all over the place. She had no place to move except her mother's which was already overcrowded.

The chief and council was selling the house to a teacher at the Big Cove school, an Indian person—and he wanted to move in by Christmas. It was a beautiful house built by CMHC and Veteran's Allowance with a guaranteed loan.

This woman had not married a white man. She belonged to that reserve. I asked her, "Would you be willing to stay and fight?" and she agreed. I said first I would find out if the house was owned by the band, and what a hell of a time I had trying to find out. But one good thing was that they'd never heard of me so they didn't know to be suspicious of me and ended up giving out a lot of information.

Armed with that information I went to the woman. I said, "It's a band house. You don't have to leave if you don't want to. If they're selling it, then they're collecting the money for something else, or they're just saying that they're selling it. The band owns the house—it's as much yours as anyone else's."

She believed me—and she didn't believe me—because in the mean time the RCMP and the band councillors harassed her. By now it was around December 23rd, and the chief had not yet gone to see her. I said, "What do you say we go to the band and *demand* you—and not anybody else—gets that house?"

By then some women came to me and after a lot of talking we'd agreed on what to do. There were about fourteen of us. We announced that we were going to demonstrate, and it was all over the radio. The reporters were hounding the chief already before we even got there. The minute we arrived, didn't those buggers in the band office lock up and fly away? They were driving over snow banks to get away, because we'd made a blockade. They all left so here we were demonstrating against an empty building that they'd locked up. (laughs)

We had counted about twenty-five families on Big Cove who were very, very bad off; about fifteen or twenty who were very, very well off; and the rest were so-so. It's the first time I ever looked around at the woman's situation on the reserve. I'd go home and literally cry.

I went to see other people. In one house they had their mattresses leaning up against the wall during the day—a small house. No sheets, no blankets—literally no blankets—and the mattresses stained like anything. I said, "Jeez, where're your blankets?" The woman started crying, said, "We had to sell them." I said, "You had to sell them?" She said, "Well," and she named her husband, said, "We were partying and he needed something else to drink."

At that point I said to myself, it's not even *his* fault. That's when we—the women who had organized—started raising money for Christmas food baskets. We went to the chief and said, "We're asking for $50 donations from people who can afford it." We figured he would reach into his own pockets. Here's a fellow with four snowmobiles in his yard, a yacht, a big, luxurious camper, and Lord knows what else, a beautiful, big house. The chief said, "Okay, how much do you need? $50? I can arrange that."

He picks up the telephone and calls Fredericton, Indian Affairs, Welfare Department and asks the woman there if she would send a voucher for $50. I stood up and said, "What?!" He said, "Just a minute," to the person on the phone. I said, "You mean to tell me you're going to get it from welfare?" He said, "I'll call you back" to the welfare department and asked me, "Well, don't you know what you want?" I looked at Evangeline and said, "You talk with him. I'm leaving," and I walked out. I called CBC, said, "I want

you to do a story , and I want it done right. I want it 'biased'!"
(laughs)

So we had three or four meetings with CBC for a story on
housing. They even went in and tricked the chief into an interview. The guy was beautiful. We exposed how the office was set
up; the housing situation; the poverty and *who* was poor. In Big
Cove the band government hadn't changed for sixteen years, so
who was poor sixteen years ago was still poor and their children
were poor—the non-supporters of the chief and people who
basically weren't able to help themselves, never given a chance.
Their children were the same way—generation after generation.
The whole thing happening over and over again.

The day of our housing demonstration, the chief and councillors called up their wives—even the police constables called up
theirs—and all of them came and demonstrated against us. They
followed us around and tried to intimidate us with their vehicles,
coming really close and not stopping. Peter took photographs.

Never in my whole life had I been hit with paranoia from
people as I was then. One woman kept yelling at me, "You don't
even belong here. Why don't you go back to Tobique where you
belong? You Tobiquer. All you Tobique women are trouble-
makers." After a while you don't even hear them. But I *did* hear,
"If you don't f___ing get out of here, we'll take you out in a
box."

We went down to the RCMP detachment and the captain wasn't
around but I left a letter which in effect said, I'm letting the division
in Fredericton know about the situation and I'm sending a tele-
gram to Ottawa, that if anything happens to me or my family or
any of the women listed below, it'll be on the chief's head. I would
blame him because he is the one responsible for having those
people threaten us, and he's the one responsible for all this ugly
situation.

Nothing did happen, but the paranoia. Then in the spring
when CBC aired their piece on national television, again people
started driving back and forth on the dirt road *behind* our house—
where no one ever drives. People forced Suzy Lewey off the
reserve—they were throwing rocks at her house, threatening her

kids—because she and I were organizers of the opposition. They ran her out, and they ran the woman out who attempted suicide because of her situation.

The woman who we initially started the protest over, finally got a new house because she refused to move. The house they were trying to get her out of had a fire place, and I said, "The only reason they want you out of here is because that teacher can see himself roasting his nuts in front of the fire place Christmas Eve!" I'll bet you that was true. (laughs)

We'd raised our own money for the house and built it our-selves. On Sunday afternoons when we were working on it we'd get carloads of people asking, "Do you mind if we look?" Finally Peter would say, "She's washing the floor." I said, "We're going to have the reputation for having the cleanest damn floors on the reserve!"

Around that time—late 1980, early 1981—I got a call from Andrea Bear Nicholas. I had associated with her in art circles, and she's a relative. Andrea said that she and a few other women from Tobique were planning a big conference that might reorganize the New Brunswick Native Women's Association. The association was like a little daughter group to the national Native Women's Association in Ottawa, really just two or three women and they never discussed 12(1)(b). Andrea was getting worried things were going to go down the drain before New Brunswick women did anything.

At the time I was totally immersed in our local housing issue, and in fact, I'd gotten in touch with Glenna (Perley) because by now she was the central person for Native women's issues in New Brunswick. She already had that reputation. (Alma Brooks, who actually still is president of New Brunswick's Native women's association, was also involved). As far as I know Andrea was para-noid about some of the women involved and wanted me there as "protection." (laughs)

I had the feeling that we needed a provincial conference be-cause of what I knew already from Big Cove, and because Native women in New Brunswick knew beans-all about women's rights. I saw that starkly in Big Cove; it's a man's world. So I agreed to help and we started meeting in Fredericton to plan the conference.

It was a "first" in this area. We had it in the spring of '81, got funding from Secretary of State. Glenna and I had to go to the bank and get a loan on the strength of a letter from Sec State, since they were late with the money. We must have had honest faces. (laughs) Fredericton, where we got it, is a very prejudiced, white, middle class town. We got $1,200 from Sec State and did the whole conference on $1,800. That's with about 250 women there for three days.

We got a real good deal from Keddy's Motel and also used a band hall in Fredericton; paid all the women's expenses; had good speakers, including Marlene Pierre who was president of the Native Women's Association of Canada and NAC representatives. Jim Manly, the NDP Indian Affairs critic came, and that's where we met his wife, Eva. Madeline Leblanc (chairperson of the New Brunswick Advisory Council on the Status of Women) and some Voice of Women representatives came. So did Premier Richard Hatfield. We even had Steve Sacobie—a real chief. (laughs) *And a lot of women.*

For many women there, it was the first time they'd heard about 12(1)(b), the first time that they realized they were discriminated against as women. We had workshops; a Native woman from Quebec, Monique Souie, came in to MC for free. She's fluent in English and French. We just told her what we wanted, and she went and did it while the rest of us went crazy. You see, we only had a limited budget and more women kept arriving. Everybody was "hyper;" nobody had organized a conference like that before. I guess a lot of credit is due Andrea for being a real fuss-budget— fussy to the point of making everybody angry. (laughs)

It was a really good conference. We worked our asses off. What came out of it for me personally was the major lobbying effort to abolish 12(1)(b). For most other women it was a good infor- mational meeting—and that's what we called it—on this wrong law that women were living under. A law they had accepted to the point that if they married men without status, they weren't Indian anymore. At the time the issue wasn't *defined* as reinstatement yet; we just wanted to get rid of 12(1)(b).

We elected an executive, gave them the mandate to address 12(1)(b), and promised we would stand behind them. That was the founding of the New Brunswick Native Women's Council. The women were so impressed with our organizational ability that they were ready to elect us immediately, but none of us wanted on the executive because we had other lives. I'm afraid the women who were elected that first year were manipulated terribly by individuals who, though they didn't want the responsibility of the power, still wanted the power.

After the conference I got myself appointed to the Advisory Council on the Status of Women in New Brunswick. The first issue I raised was my *per diem*. It was something like $75 a day and I was on welfare so didn't know how to deal with it. If we went by the Welfare Act I was only allowed $75 extra *per month*. The chairperson had said, "You're going to represent all the native women in New Brunswick by your seat in the council," so I got worried because I didn't have the money to do all this travelling and telephoning, to be in touch with everybody.

I had to make a report at every quarterly meeting so I hit the council for a travelling grant. They don't normally give such things. I fought like hell for that. I said to them, "I'm on welfare. I can't even afford to keep my *per diem*." A lawyer who was on the Council was appalled at what I was going through. Madeline wasn't really willing to deal with it but another member said, "We've got to do something about this. What does it really mean?" So she got in touch with welfare, not even mentioning my name, and found out that I wasn't entitled to my *per diem* under the welfare. Yet every goddamn one of them could even use theirs as a write-off for their income tax.

I talked to the welfare people in Big Cove and they said don't worry about it. The *per diem* was a gift, as far as they were concerned. The Council gave me one trip around the province which I could do the way I wanted. So I hit all the reserves in New Brunswick; I got to visit and talk to the women who were involved in things on every reserve. I had a nice big long report. (laughs)

The good thing about being on the Advisory Council was that I saw Native women were in the *same* situation not only all over

New Brunswick, but in Nova Scotia, in Prince Edward Island, in Quebec. I heard many really horrible stories from the women who had married out.

At the Kanawake Reserve in Caugnawaga, Quebec I saw a whole bunch of things happening. There were those who claimed as traditionalists that there was no such thing as non-status—as far as they were concerned the women were still Indian, Indian, Indian. Then there were people in that same community who believed that the Indian Act was right and that the women knew what they were doing when they married out.

There were also people who were kind of border-line—yeah, the women should get their status back, but the white men can't move back with them. Yet a lot of white women were living there. Then, the radical ones—the ones considered "radicals," and the ones who were right—believed the women should come back and if white women could live on the reserve, why couldn't white men? Just is just. Kanawake is a huge community, and granted, they can't accommodate any more than are already there. But that should not be *their* responsibility—that should be the government's responsibility. It took away their land.

In Nova Scotia, the Union (of Nova Scotia Indians) works pretty much with the provincial Native Women's Association, and it believed the women should get their status. In Truro I know they were giving women their status like in Tobique. Still, I don't think there was anyone who was bold enough to say, "Heck, we are a community. We can make our own by-laws and what the hell if the government doesn't give us additional funds? There must be other ways we can get additional funds as a community." We Indian people lack a lot when it comes to investigating for resources; we are always looking to the government too much.

After the Native Women's Council was formed, Caroline (Ennis) and I put a lot of store to other Native women getting involved. We also found we had a similar interest in fighting 12(1)(b). She and Dan and Peter and I used to meet a lot, either on the road or in Fredericton.

One time Peter and I were talking and I said, "Things aren't moving fast enough. Here it's 1981 and Canada is going to ratify that U.N. Convention (on sexual equality) and Sandra Lovelace's thing should be coming into effect." He said, "Why don't you start a petition campaign?' We discussed it and decided, no, there's been petitions. But he said, "Don't stop at New Brunswick. Go national. Go international." I said, "Why not? We could take it all over the world." The more we talked about it, the more the thing just snowballed.

The next time Caroline called I said, "Why don't we start a campaign to abolish 12(1)(b)?" She said, "Good idea." We talked about some pretty drastic things to do. One was a walk all the way across Canada, dressing someone up as Trudeau (then prime minister) dragging a casket with "Native Canadian Woman" on it. (laughs) We had a whole bunch of ideas, but I do think that one would have been effective. Then Caroline came up with the idea of a pamphlet—"We'll have a big mail out."

I was in the Advisory Council, so we thought that my council position could be used as "campaign headquarters." We didn't realize the council was a government bureaucracy and that you don't use government bureaucracy in that way. (laughs) But we were naive. We thought, gee, a women's representative, of course she's going to do this. But we did manage to talk Madeline into giving us so-many-thousands of photocopies and mail-out service.

Also I talked with the Kent county MLA and he agreed to do mail-outs for me. I went to see him, saying, "I am a representative in the Advisory Council on the Status of Women. I have this problem and what could I expect from you?" He said, "Of course I'll do whatever I can. What do you need?" I said, "Well, I need photocopying and I need mail-out." (laughs) He said, "Shirley, I really don't have that kind of money, but I will do one major mail-out for you." So I gave him this great big thick package of information on 12(1)(b).

Now, Caroline's aim after the 1981 conference was to be on NAC. By now we had gone to a NAC national assembly. That's where we met Mary Thompson Boyd, Shelley Finson and Eva Manly. Caroline got up to talk and she ended up elected as a regional representative. (laughs) We had already gotten the Saint John women's political action committee to print up "Support

Sandra Lovelace" buttons. So we had those connections and Caroline said, "I think we could convince NAC to fund the publishing of this 12(1)(b) pamphlet.

So we met at Howard Johnson's one day—had lunch with Dan, Jimmie (Caroline's son), Peter and Ramona—and developed the pamphlet over about an hour and a half. We ordered a big meal so we wouldn't feel guilty about sitting around so long. (laughs)

NAC got us in touch with Marilyn Keddy in Nova Scotia who was director of the NAC trust fund. She and some other women in Halifax invited Caroline and I down to do some primary lobbying and get the pamphlet in order. We spent the weekend at Marilyn's house—she was single and free-wheeling at the time. They invited three sets of women to come to three different meetings. Plus we did a session with Alexa McDonough the NDP provincial leader. That was Caroline and my very first together-effort in lobbying a political figure.

The pamphlet was printed by the University of Mount Saint Vincent in Halifax in 1981. They did it for practically nothing. We got NAC to fund the printing; they promised us $1,000 if we could do it within that amount. So NAC paid for our trip to Halifax. At the time I was selling paintings so I wasn't really strapped. Marilyn Keddy fed us—she has this cushy government job as women's health director. We were there three days; did a lot of phoning from her office; found a place to print; one of the women in her office did some of the lay-out; I did the art work. We did one in English and one in French.

It was classy looking, a good pamphlet. The first run went like hotcakes and we did a second printing. Then rather than a third printing we had people photocopy them. Caroline and I were both getting swamped with phone calls and letters asking for them—"Send us 1,000 ... Send us 500."

That pamphlet was a good strategy. We were getting requests from women's groups, lawyers for their conferences, Native women from across Canada. In those days Rose Charlie (president of the British Columbia Indian Homemakers Association) was working steadily on 12(1)(b), but between B.C. and us there was hardly anything. Indian Rights for Indian Women was going down the hill. The Native Women's Association of Canada had been in operation for many years, but they weren't doing anything to address the issue.

After the pamphlet, it didn't seem like things were moving fast enough, and that's when we started going to all the conferences we could, doing workshops. The sad part of it was every couple of weeks we had to run off somewhere, and Ramona was small. She would cry her head off, and Peter looked like he was ready to cry too—"You're going again?" Ramona would get on her play phone and say, "Yes, we're having a meeting. Seven o'clock is a good time." Or she'd go, "We're having a meeting today. Bring your lunch." (laughs)

The first lobbying trip Caroline and I went on together was to Sackville in 1981, to the Maritime Conference of the United Church. Somebody told us, "The United Church has a lot of money." (laughs) We figured we would hit the church with the most money because the Roman Catholic Church wasn't willing to do anything. Somebody had suggested that we hit all the big conferences and get them to sign petitions and pass resolutions to change 12(1)(b). The reception was so good.

The president of Conference spoke personally with us; asked what we wanted and I said, "Money." (laughs) Eva Manly got us in touch with a woman lawyer from Amherst who tried to get us on the agenda, but couldn't. We were pretty upset. That's when a minister, Bonnie Barnett, latched onto us—she was part of the planning committee—and we got a chance to talk to the committee. They said, "We can at least have you to speak on the floor of conference at some point," and that's what they did.

Caroline spoke and then answered questions. She had done it before and had taken political science, so was testing out her wings. (laughs) There were a few typical attitudes like, "If we make this resolution the Native men aren't going to like it," or, "We white people shouldn't meddle into Native people's affairs." They never looked at it as a justice issue. They were looking at it as a traditional cultural thing, and we caught onto that pretty fast. Dan Ennis was with us and he is sharp at picking those things out. We'd caucus with him and Peter. Dan would say, "What are they doing? It's a justice issue. What's it got to do with culture?" So you learn fast.

Caroline and I went to Ottawa several times. What is memorable from those trips hasn't to do with lobbying achievements, but with being so hungry. (laughs) When there was that North-South conference—the one the "have" nations had about the "have nots" in Ottawa in 1981, the socialist and environmental communities held an alternate conference. All the lobbyists stayed at the same place as the foreign press so that they could get their "propaganda" out. We somehow got invited to do a workshop on Native women. Caroline got hold of it and told me, "They want us to go to this alternate conference."

My son had an apartment in Ottawa but was in England so we stayed there. His cupboard was bare. We had no vehicle and Caroline didn't bring any walking shoes. She had these fancy new little shoes. In order to stretch our money we walked around a lot the first day, but then drank a lot of Perrier water. (laughs) Caroline ended up with blisters on her feet, and her feet are so tiny she couldn't fit anybody else's shoes. Oh God. We were there for five days. Forty dollars and five days just doesn't go.

We gave the workshop and it was very good. Our main message was that we wanted the whole world to start pressuring Canada to stop the discrimination against Native women, to change 12(1)(b). The National Indian Brotherhood was there—that was before they found anything wrong with being the "Brotherhood" (laughs) —and we publicized that—"the *brother*hood." A young fellow who was the press agent for the NIB kind of latched onto us. He helped me put an information package together and he and I ran all over the place with it. He was distributing NIB material and said, "Come and tag along!"—paid for all the taxis.

But it's hard when you're doing something and worrying about food. I met some people from Moncton who knew my art work, and they set up one meal. We ended up going to the Native Women's Association for a ticket back to the airport. Otherwise we would have had to walk or hitchhike. That was memorable. Anything you would do to that extreme is pretty darn memorable. At the time, though, all my energy was going to informing people about Indian women, so I never thought of it as a hardship.

After that we got on the tail of the National Indian Brotherhood; wrote letters, "How do you call yourselves 'the brotherhood' when you're also supposed to be representing women?" I used to call them periodically just to "harass" them; ask them what they were doing with 12(1)(b). (laughs) I'd try to get on the agenda of their annual assemblies. Once, I got on the agenda, but then they would never let me know its date. They did things like, "Why don't you come, but a few days early and we'll get together and talk. We can't put you up but you can stay in my room." Wicked. So I never bothered going. I didn't think there was any point, after people who had known about the issue for so long never did anything about it.

Around that time I started going to NAC meetings we wanted to push them to take up the issue of 12(1)(b). After all white women are voters. They are the ones the Canadian government is going to listen to. But then I found it almost futile because they'd always complain about Caroline not putting anything down on paper. They wanted us to be just like them. I got to some of the white women's conferences, like "The Feminist Connection" in Winnipeg and a women and religion conference in Thunder Bay (sponsored by the Women's Inter-Church Council). Now, *that* was an interesting one. (laughs)

I was amazed when we got there. They had a list of workshops to choose from, and a Native woman I knew went in just ahead of me. She identified herself as Native and gave her name. The registration woman replied, "Oh yes," and put down "poverty." So the Native woman took me aside and said, "They're going to put you *automatically* in 'poverty' because you're a Native woman." I said, "They'd better not because I have my eye on something else." They had things on power and I was interested in learning more about the power struggles women go through.

Sure enough, when I signed in I'm obviously Indian, and the woman at the desk said, "Oh yes, poverty." I said, "I've already marked off the workshops I'm going to attend," and passed her the paper. She said, "Well, the Native women are going in the poverty one." I said, "Really? Is that where you keep Native women?" She got all flustered, said, "But we were informed...." " I said, "By whom? I never informed you." They went whispering around. I went and talked to two Christian feminist women I knew quite well, and they got really angry. The organizers *assumed* the Native women would be resource people on poverty.

We were sitting there talking about it, getting very upset, when a woman from Latin America overheard us and asked, "Did they put you in poverty too?" I said, "Yes." She swore in Spanish and said, "It's not right, what's happening. Let's meet in my room later on." So we attended the speeches but my stomach was churning too badly to concentrate on anything good that was happening. That afternoon we started getting together—three or four Native women, a Cuban woman, and my two feminist friends. We must have talked for four hours, and decided to approach the organizer—the big shot—to change the agenda the following morning.

We tried to meet with the organizers that night, and they were all very sympathetic, but you know, *we* were being too sensitive, and the whole damn bit. We decided that the following morning we were going to go in there and stand up in front of the whole assembly before anything happened, even before the opening prayer. We were going to say what's happening; that we're feeling powerless because you are over-ruling even where we can go in workshops.

We had agreed on who was to talk and then when the time came that woman didn't do it. I was feeling worse and worse. However, the night before we'd gotten Rosemary Brown (an NDP member of the Legislative Assembly from British Columbia) out of bed to tell her how we felt. So when she was having her work-shop that day she invited women to come down and talk about it. Through all of that Rosemary finally got them to change the agenda.

The sad part is that we changed the agenda, we had our say, but the following day we still got the same lousy treatment from the woman organizing the conference. She was still matronizing. But what was good for me was, I saw it all coming together—the power—

and I thought, you know *we've got power*; it's just in how we use it. Use it without abusing it.

Later when I addressed them, I talked about 12(1)(b) and about women's powerlessness; that we didn't wanted to fight with Indian men over 12(1)(b), but the government. I told them that they, themselves, were perpetuating that unjust law, too, because they voted the government in. I spared nothing. I never do when I talk.

I told them about 12(1)(b) and about what they could do, because that's what people always ask, "What can we do?"—that they should start lobbying the government, sending telegrams, letters, and to use their votes. We passed our pamphlet around. I also talked about my perceptions of the little myths we all have to live with as far as men are concerned; the very basic man-woman relationships.

The really significant thing for me was realizing the *power* that people have and the *conflict* that Native women have within their little systems ... and how to work towards eliminating or at least making those conflicts softer. It's harder even to change Native women's attitudes than non-Indian because Native women have an awful lot more to work out ... more at stake, it is so personal.

That conference was worthwhile, too, because both the immigrant women and I got good resolutions passed, and it got me in touch with the more radical of the United Church women. That is where I made my connections, besides Mary (Thompson Boyd) who I'd met already. From there we got a lot of assistance from the United Church Task Force on Christian Feminism.

When the Canadian Constitution was patriated in 1982, a series of five annual First Ministers' Conferences on Constitutional Aboriginal Matters were initiated for the purpose of defining aboriginal rights. Because the Tobique women had seen how the Indian Act was exempted from the Canadian Bill of Rights, allowing for legal discrimination against Indian women to continue, they were convinced that equal rights for Native women must be clearly entrenched in the new Constitution.

Even federal papers on the issue of 12(1)(b) stated that the Indian Act had to be amended by April of 1985 when Section 15 of the Canadian Charter of Rights and Freedoms came into effect, since the charter guarantees equal rights without discrimination on the basis of sex or race. In fact, this did prove correct in that the Indian Act was amended shortly after the charter came into effect. However in 1987, the struggle continues for entrenching an equality clause strategically *within* the aboriginal rights section of the constitution. The Tobique women see this as necessary in order to prevent Indian leaders from using their constitutional aboriginal rights to continue the discrimination against their women (an argument some chiefs already have used).

Shirley Bear, Caroline Ennis, Sandra Lovelace, and Karen Perley have attended the First Ministers' Conferences to lobby for a sexual equality clause, utilizing their connections with the New Brunswick government to gain access to the meetings. In the following conversation Shirley, Karen and Sandra recall those times.

SHIRLEY: At the initial First Ministers Conference in March of 1981 we went to Ottawa precisely to change 12(1)(b) *before* Indian self-government could ever come about. The women who are active in this area agreed that there should not be any self-government without a sexual equality clause for Native men and women— because otherwise you are starting off discriminating against a whole group of people—women—to begin with.

I was on the Advisory Council and in discussing the sexual equality clause with Madeline Leblanc, she felt sure (premier Richard) Hatfield would support it because he is an advocate of women's rights. I knew then that he wasn't going to support aboriginal rights period; he has come around since then, but at the time he didn't feel that Indian people had any special rights and he as much as said so in the newspapers. I figured with his connection with women, we could at least talk about that.

Periodically Hatfield came to our Advisory Council meetings because we had a direct advisory line to him—there were no in-betweens. Madeline used to encourage me to use that. At one meeting he asked me, "What do you think of aboriginal rights?"

I said, "Well, what I think of it would be in disagreement with what you think, but beyond that there is the whole thing of justice and of Native people being treated as fourth or fifth class citizens because they are a non-entity." I said, "People have to start supporting that they be the same as everybody else."

Hatfield said, "We'll make an appointment and you come see me at the office about this." My God, there was about ten of us that went up to his office, mostly from Tobique, plus Alma Brooks (president of New Brunswick Native Women's Council) and her executive. We were lobbying for him to fund a number of women to go to that First Ministers Conference, *and* for him to support the abolition of 12(1)(b), *and* that self-government should not happen unless women got their rights back first.

Just prior to the conference, the Yukon aboriginal group phoned and asked us how we were faring, and what we thought they should say. Mary Simon was working for them then. We told them, If you're going to learn anything from this whole damn thing with 12(1)(b), put in sexual equality right off the bat. See, in the north they didn't have 12(1)(b) legislated down on paper like we do in the south, but it was being practised as a discriminatory thing in some instances, like health and educational rights. The Yukon did support our position.

SANDRA: I remember when we got to Ottawa, going to a briefing at the Native Women's Association of Canada (NWAC) office. I asked them about 12(1)(b) and the woman speaking looked at me, said, "12(1)(b)? That's not our first priority." They had mentioned everything but, so I said, "What about reinstatement?" When she said, "That isn't our first priority," again, I asked, "Wasn't that why this whole thing [of Native women organizing] started? To fight for reinstatement? For all the women to get together?" She said, "No." They were so worried about their funding and which men's group to join, that's all they thought about.

SHIRLEY: As far as we knew, Jane Gottfriedson who was president of NWAC was supposed to address the issue. Initially we never intended for anybody in our group to address it; we just wanted to be there to advise Hatfield. Jane had been assured by the Native Council of Canada (NCC) that she had a seat at the talks, and when the question of women arose she could go up and speak. In fact what actually happened was any time the question of women came up, it was Saul Sanderson, George Erasmus and Del Riley who spoke on the subject of women. *None* of the women spoke.

They wouldn't let Jane speak. Duke Redbird, Smokey Bruyere and Harry Daniels from the NCC (the non-status organization) spoke. The men all kept saying, "We don't agree with discrimination, *but ...* " At that time NCC supported the sexual equality clause but the National Indian Brotherhood didn't.

When the issue of "women's rights"—as it was called at the time—was brought forward, Hatfield was not well-informed at that point so he fumbled around with it. We got busy right at the end of that day's session and lobbied with Hatfield to have Sandra move up front and address the issue on the second day.

Then after Sandra gave her speech, Levesque (the premier of Quebec) had Mary Two-Axe Early speak. Then Ontario Premier Bill Davis gave his seat to Donna Philips (president of the Ontario Native Women's Association). Women spoke from Saskatchewan and Manitoba, too.

SANDRA: That was when we got to know Gail Stacey-Moore and the Quebec women, They asked, "Would you be interested in meeting with us?" so we ended up having meetings every night. We found that we agreed on most things, so we all stuck together. After that, if there were important meetings they wanted us to show up for, they'd pay for our hotel room and food. That's how we got travel funding for things, them plus the United Church. Sometimes we'd get our welfare cheques ahead of time to have a bit extra money. (laughter)

KAREN: The Quebec women (Quebec Native Women's Association) have a big organization and funding. Mary (Two-Axe) Early had a lot to do with it, too. She was so committed to 12(1)(b).

SANDRA: And the Quebec women were dedicated to Mary. Because Gail once told me, "Mary passed this on to me, and I'm doing this for Mary"—for herself, too, but it was Mary that got her started.

SHIRLEY: I remember that conference so well because I lost fourteen pounds that week, I worked so damn hard. (laughter) I was going from 7 o'clock in the morning till way late at night. I didn't care to go the bar, so everybody else went, while I lobbied around, went to extra technicians meetings.

It ended up, though, that the NIB negotiated for themselves on the weight of the women's issue, and they refused to do anything, so no equality clause. They even stated that, "It is *our* tradition and *our* culture if we want to discriminate against women." (laughter)

The following year, March of 1984, I didn't go but I heard basically the same thing happened as with the first conference.

KAREN: Caroline, Sandra and I got to that one, Mavis Goeres, too. The first day the women's equality clause was just brushed aside; it wasn't really dealt with at all.

SANDRA: Then right after the first day's session, that NAC lady from Montreal, Liz Kennedy, came and found us in Mavis's hotel room at the Chateau Laurier—Mavis had a room right there because she was a delegate for the New Brunswick Women's Council. Liz told us, "Hatfield's down in the lobby. Come on down and catch him!" so we ran down and he said, "Do you know what happened?" I said, "Yes," and he asked me, "Do you want to speak to the issue tomorrow?" I said, "Yes," so we all went out for a drink at that place Indians go to in Hull and made out the speech—me, Karen, Caroline and Mavis. We kept saying, we have to go back and do the speech, then somebody said, "Why don't we do it here?" (laughter)

KAREN: The next day we all got right into the conference meetings. Hatfield started right off by making them go back to discussing the equality clause, and (prime minister) Trudeau had to—he was chairing the meetings—though he didn't like it. Trudeau would have been even madder if he understood Maliseet. We didn't know how to translate "prime minister" so we just said words that mean "biggest head in the country" or the "big head of the country"—which he was. (laughter)

SANDRA: Trudeau said, "Next time, bring an interpreter." I said, "I am just making a point. People are saying we're not Indians, but we speak the language."

SHIRLEY: Basically the same thing happened as with the first conference. NWAC gave their voice to the NCC again. They were co-opted by the men. Now it was "equality for everybody; reinstate everybody." It sounded even worse than the first year. But Hatfield was a little more sophisticated and knowledgeable by then and took on Trudeau. (laughter)

> Along with these national lobbying efforts, significant developments also were taking place locally on the Tobique reserve. In the fall of 1983, Dave Perley was elected as chief, defeating the old chief. Once again the women, and a significant number of men, occupied the band office. The occupation was an act of support for the new chief; they wanted to ensure that office records, containing evidence they believed to be incriminating to the old administration, were not taken and destroyed.

KAREN: Dave got in as chief and we were so pleased, but most of the councillors who won were from the old chief's former administration. Dave had been trying to get an investigation of the books to see where all the money had gone. Because of that, some of the councillors refused to sign the band council resolution for the band budget.

My God, we didn't have money for any services on the reserve for the longest time—no school, no police protection, no fire truck, no social service, no garbage collection. People were volunteering for some things, but it wasn't enough. The situation was getting really bad, really tense. Nothing was moving. That's when John Munro, the minister of Indian Affairs at the time, came to Fredericton.

SANDRA: It was the Union (of New Brunswick Indians) annual assembly, so we all went to try and help Dave with the problems he was having with the councillors. Munro said, "Sandra, is this about 12(1)(b)?" and I said, "No." Right away he figured we were there to lobby for 12(1)(b) and we weren't; we were lobbying for the chief. (laughter)

KAREN: Munro was certainly no help that time. To me it sounded like he said, "Go back to your reserve and work things out your-selves." He was such a jerk. The same with Indian Affairs; nobody would support the investigation. It was so frustrating. And all those things with housing—people not getting repairs, blatant favouritism, money spent and not accounted for—had been go-ing on for years and years. So depressing.

The Tobique women kept working for better conditions locally at the same time as they carried on their lobbying campaign to change 12(1)(b). Both the local and the national struggle had developed out of their daily life, and both concerns continued be a part of their everyday life together. However, after Dave Perley became chief and the situation on the reserve gradually improved, the women could turn more of their attention towards reinstate-ment, that is, having the Indian Act amended so that women and their first generation children would be reinstated to their bands.

By now, every few months the federal government was issuing press releases that legislation *soon* would be introduced to amend the Act. The Assembly of First Nations which is "the most power-ful of the Native men's organizations"— as Native women call the AFN and the Metis and non-status organizations—fought against any changes. It argued that no part of the Act should be changed until an entire revision was made which they approved. In what follows, Shirley, Sandra, and Karen recall a few of the more memor-able lobbying experiences of 1981 and 1984.

SHIRLEY: In the spring of 1981 we were again working to come up with some strategy to change 12(1)(b), and I think that is where we actually started talking about "reinstatement." Caroline, Karen and I went to Toronto to meet with Mary Thompson Boyd and some of her "radical" women friends. (laughter) Mary and the United Church task force on Christian feminism gave up office time and space, and we did a national telephone lobbying cam-paign from the head office. Mary's group of women helped us do some strategizing, plus the telephoning to get women across Canada to lobby in their own areas.

We found we were doing a lot to involve women in New Brunswick. We were already able to encourage Native women in

Nova Scotia to be very vocal about 12(1)(b). They were lucky because the Union of Nova Scotia Indians were sympathetic to the cause and were helping the women. Truro was the first band across Canada, I believe, to apply to Munro (the minister of Indian Affairs) for a moratorium after he gave the directive in 1980 that bands could suspend 12(1)(b). The moratorium meant that women marrying out from then on wouldn't be taken off band lists any more. Truro's applying was largely through the efforts of Clara Gloade, the president of the Nova Scotia women's organization, who worked in the Millbrook band office.

On that telephone lobby we did in Toronto, we also got in touch with women in British Columbia. We found out that Rose Charlie (of B.C. Indian Homemakers Association) was making a lot of noise about 12(1)(b). In fact they were dealing with a number of issues, all on not much money. Some Indian women had even been to jail for occupying the Indian Affairs offices in Vancouver. (laughter) Rose told us she was going to do a lot more. Finding out all this was exhilarating for us.

We also got in touch with some Winnipeg women who were going to work, but never really did. We contacted Indian women in Saskatchewan and Alberta, too. Jennie Margetts (the past president of the national Indian Rights for Indian Women) decided it was a good time to jump on the wagon again. And it was good in spite of all that happened after—it was good that Jennie got in—because she was extremely vocal and already well-known.

When Caroline and I sat down to talk, we knew what was wrong and what was needed, but we didn't know how to say it in white women's terms. So in Toronto we had a workshop with Mary's bunch. One of the white women, Linda Mulhull, did a little number on flip charts and it helped the other white women understand the issues in 12(1)(b). After that it was easier at other lobbying sessions for us to put "the package" together.

See, we knew what we wanted and what had to be done. In Toronto we were trying to figure out number one—who was the culprit? Why is it taking so much time to change this law? Who is wanting and not wanting it to happen?

We figured out it always went right back down to money and

what we had to do was find a way to say, "That's not the *point* and we shouldn't even be discussing how much it's going to cost the taxpayers to change this law because it is a *justice* issue." That's what we came down with. And the fact that people were always saying, "the men ... the men." Yet we could have counted several thousand Native men who also wanted 12(1)(b) changed.

At that point somebody said, "Once it's changed, who gets to be called an Indian?" That's when we really began discussing reinstatement. In fact, we called our little lobbying group with Mary and Linda and the Toronto women, the "Ad Hoc Group for Reinstatement." The group itself didn't go very far, but we started introducing those words and before you know it those words were coming back to us. Through the Quebec women, for example, and the Native Women's Association of Canada; they started saying reinstatement. Before it was "12(1)(b)" and we shifted it to "reinstatement."

When we talked about the situation more seriously we realized the government wasn't going to reinstate everybody. We wanted women reinstated who were born with status and lost it through marriage, *plus* their children, the first generation. We weren't going to bother with men and all the other discriminatory clauses. We wanted to narrow it down, and that's where we ended up.

In Toronto we also got in touch with women's organizations and some individual women in the United States—to start sending letters to the Canadian Embassy as a pressure tactic. A number of women from the States did that. My sister in New York is one of them. Women from Texas. We touched on women we knew here and there. I even wanted to call England and Greece. Why not? (laughter)

KAREN: I was disappointed at the lack of response from those American women's groups, and famous women like Gloria Steinem. I thought, I don't believe this—they're supposed to be so pro-women and they didn't even have the decency to phone back or write. It didn't phase them a bit, maybe because Canada is a foreign country. I guess Canada is not very exciting ... and Indian women. Woop-de-doo! (laughter)

SHIRLEY: Mary funded all that phoning through her church office. She is one fantastic person. By now the United Church funded most of our lobbying—they were very supportive. I don't know of any other church that gave us as much. The Roman Catholic Church wouldn't help—they're too paternalistic. Caroline called the Jewish Congress and they agreed that 12(1)(b) was unjust but they wanted some major thing from us before they would directly lobby.

It was around that time when Jim Manly (The New Democratic Party Indian Affairs critic) started turning and supporting a watered-down version of reinstatement palatable to the Assembly of First Nations. You know, I wondered, "Why Jim?" He'd done a lot for Native people—not a hell of a lot for *women*, but a lot for Native people. I think the AFN must have got to him.

KAREN: Remember that lobbying trip to Ottawa in the spring of 1984? Caroline, Janet, Sandra and me?

SANDRA: We didn't leave here driving till 7:30 at night and stopped at Grand Falls about thirty miles away for coffee. I said, "Let's buy some postcards to send home. We've made it all the way to Grand Falls!" (laughter)

JANET: We got in about five o'clock in the morning, couldn't find Caroline's relatives' place, tried to phone them from an all-night donut shop, got directions from a policeman, threw pebbles at the windows to wake them up, got in and slept for a few hours, then went lobbying members of parliament.

KAREN: We went to Lynn McDonald's office (a feminist New Democratic member of parliament), Flora MacDonald's office, so many MP's offices I can't remember them all. More and more rumours had been flying around that legislation was to be introduced at any time. So we went to lobby for our position and it was right around that time when the Liberals introduced Bill C-47. We supported it because it was going to give women and their first generation children back their status.

SHIRLEY: By 1984 it seemed a lot of other women were on the move with the reinstatement issue, too. White women's groups through NAC and the United Church task force of feminism. More Indian women's groups were getting involved. But in May of 1984 the national women's organization, NWAC, went in with the AFN on a "consensus" position that called for "everybody" to be reinstated to a "general band list," and for the bands—chief and councils—to decide who would get back onto their band lists. Of course, that meant a lot of women would never get back their band membership and that anyone with one drop of Indian blood could be an Indian.

Then the AFN and NWAC fought together against Bill C-47. Just like at the First Ministers' Conference, NWAC wanted to "reinstate everybody," but now they went from being in with NCC (the non-status organization) over to being in with the AFN (the status organization). At the First Ministers' Conference they got co-opted by the NCC men and this time they got co-opted by the AFN men. Both the Quebec women and us disagreed with the consensus position and kept fighting for immediate reinstatement for women and their children. We didn't want any "general band list" which was really a "general list" that would be filed away somewhere in Ottawa and would put people in limbo.

Bill C-47 was passed by Parliament in June of 1984, but then it got "killed" in Senate by Charlie Watt, a Native senator, the day before summer recess. Then John Turner called a federal election, and the Liberal government fell, so Bill C-47 "died." We got some shoddy treatment from the national (NWAC) at their annual assembly that autumn over the whole thing—they were afraid of an open discussion about why they had opposed C-47 when it would have fully reinstated both women and children.

SANDRA: We weren't allowed to speak because they said we weren't paid delegates. Every time one of us got up to speak they'd cut us off, and they tried to make us sit at the back. They said we were already represented. Actually they never even discussed 12(1)(b) or immediate reinstatement. Obviously most of the women there didn't know what was going on. It was always us that pushed to talk about it, but they silenced us. After a day or two we gave up and formed a new coalition, the Aboriginal Women's Coalition. After women there saw what was happening, they'd told us, "Let's have a meeting and hear what you Tobique women have to say." A lot of them joined—women from British Columbia, Alberta, Quebec, Nova Scotia, all over Canada.

During the federal election campaign in the summer of 1984, a party leaders' debate on women's issues was sponsored by NAC and televized nationally. During the debate Brian Mulroney pledged that, if elected, the Conservative government would amend the Indian Act quickly and reinstate women. After the Conservatives won the election, David Crombie was made minister of Indian Affairs, and promised to introduce legislation as soon as was possible.

In February of 1985, as Indian leaders were preparing for the third First Ministers' Conference on the Constitution, a memo from Crombie's office was leaked which called the Indian Act an "embarrassment." It urged the Cabinet to remove sexual discrimination from the Act and restore Indian women's rights. David Ahenakew, then president of the AFN, immediately and vehemently opposed Crombie's proposal, setting off what would become the final struggle to shape the long-awaited and long-debated legislation, Bill C-31. In the following conversation, Sandra, Karen, Shirley, along with Caroline Ennis, look back to that lobbying campaign.

SANDRA: In the spring of 1985 we made several trips to Ottawa. In February Caroline, Checker (another Tobique woman) and I went to try and get funding from Indian Affairs for us to meet with the House of Commons Standing Committee on Indian Affairs. We were there for over a week; lobbied to appear before the Standing Committee at their Bill C-31 hearings. We got an appointment with Indian Affairs, but they wouldn't give us any money; they said there was no funding.

Even before we left the reserve, we didn't have no money and Checker and I had to get our welfare cheques early. I had to borrow money from my mother. Dave Perley, the chief told Checker, "Now if you girls get stuck, we can get some help for you." Well, we did get stuck. Quebec Native women were picking up the tab for our hotel and meals, but only temporarily. We needed money to stay in Ottawa and lobby.

We'd get in touch with Dave Perley, who was meeting with David Ahenekew (president of the AFN)—it was just before the First Ministers' Conference—and Dave would just say, "I'll see what I can do." It seemed like he was trying to avoid us, so we thought, oh no. Dave is changing his position; he's listening to Ahenekew. A bit later we saw Dave in Ottawa and straightened it all out, but in the meantime, we had no money.

Then we got a meeting with the minister of Indian Affairs, David Crombie, and Crombie said, "Write up on paper how much you need and I'll get it to you tomorrow." He gave us the money right away. We didn't even have to account for it or nothing, because he knew we were there lobbying and what the money was going for. He'd known us ever since the women's walk to Ottawa in 1979.

At that meeting Crombie told us how the legislation was going to go. He said, "I know your problems—the problems of Indian women. I can't please everybody, but the women will be reinstated right to the bands." He said, "Now, about the children, I'm not too sure yet."

So we figured then that the children wouldn't be fully reinstated to the bands, but that they would get their Indian status at least. He didn't say that children's membership was going to be up to the bands; he said he had to have more meetings with the people. But he did tell us there was going to be reinstatement. That was the *first* time we got a meeting with Indian Affairs. Before that when Caroline and I used to try, all we would get was the run-a-round.

CAROLINE: Theresa Nahanee was an aide to Crombie, and she was always supportive to reinstatement. She was on the women's walk to Ottawa with us.

Gail Stacey-Moore from Quebec and Rose Charlie from British Columbia Indian Homemakers Association were in Ottawa, too, and we had an Aboriginal Women's Coalition meeting.

SANDRA: I had so much faith in that coalition when it started. It really sounded good and it had important women, but once money got involved. Some of the head women got funding and were spending it on this and that, so we—the Tobique women, Quebec, and Rose Charlie from B.C.—got angry about it. When we weren't meeting about the hearings, we were meeting about the coalition problems.

If we weren't having meetings, we'd be on the phone, trying to set meetings up. (laughter) We got an appointment with the Standing Committee for the next week, so we came home and went right back again. We had to pay for our own way there again, but got refunded later from the Committee.

CAROLINE: That second trip we were in Ottawa for a week—me, Sandra, Shirley, and Cynthia Gaffney (also a Tobique woman)—went. We were there for a week because we had to write up the brief. Our lawyer, Don Fleming (from the University of New Brunswick Law Faculty), was with us. We told him basically what we wanted in the brief. We argued amongst ourselves over some of the points. Cynthia and Shirley almost got into a fist fight at one point. (laughter) I don't know what they were arguing about, but Cynthia said, "Leave me alone. Lay off me!" It was late at night and we were all tired. I was sick. Don would listen to us, go away and write up what he thought we wanted, then come back and we'd argue amongst ourselves some more. He didn't argue with us—*we* argued. Then he'd leave again.

SANDRA: He wrote it in big, fancy lawyer words we couldn't pronounce. (laughter) It came out the way we wanted it in the end, though.

CAROLINE: Whoever was reading kept stumbling over the words, so we finally said, "Let Shirley read it," so Shirley ended up reading it.

KAREN: That was like at the First Ministers' Conference. Sandra was in Cynthia's room trying to read our statement and she finally said, "These words are too hard. Let's go back to simple words."

CAROLINE: We worked day and night to finish that brief. We'd lobby all day, then work until one o'clock in the morning, to the point that we were sick of one another, cooped up in one little room with no money to go anywhere, do anything just to get away.

SANDRA: While we were working on our brief in Ottawa, we *also* were trying to get hold of Hatfield. It was just before the 1985 First Minister's Conference and there was a big preliminary meeting going on in Toronto. We heard that they weren't even going to discuss sexual equality at the conference because all the men leaders were against it; they saw the issue as a "nuisance." But Hatfield said, "No way. We have to speak on sexual equality." He was the one pushing for it to be on the agenda because he was listening to us women.

SHIRLEY: We were already in Ottawa so we did get to that third First Ministers Conference and Hatfield said outright, "No Indian self-government without sexual equality." Again the men wanted sexual equality to be first on the agenda—I guess to get it over with—and again they haggled. You see, when they went to that Toronto meeting to prepare the agenda, AFN, NCC and the Metis Association got together against all the provinces, right?

The men's organizations found Mulroney warm to aboriginal rights when the Conservatives first got back into power in 1984, so they were pretty confident. And by now Hatfield is supporting aboriginal rights but he wants equality for women before *anything* happens. At the point during the pre-planning meetings in Toronto where the men eliminated sexual equality from the agenda altogether, Hatfield said "no conference" without it. Even though none of us were in Toronto, he pushed the issue on his own. By then we'd also gotten to know Dan Horsman, the fellow Hatfield's got for Indian relations, who is an all-right person. Dan even got us extra delegates to the 1986 First Ministers Conference. See, though Hatfield got sexual equality back onto the agenda, they farted around at the conference long enough that it didn't get discussed adequately. The men's organizations never got anything out of that 1985 conference, either. But in the meantime we got reinstatement!

Then on March 14th we presented our brief to the Parliamentary Standing Committee. It was titled, "Bill C-31: A Comment on the Elimination of Sexual Discrimination in the Indian Act." When we made our presentation, I was surprised that we *commanded* so much power of the audience; that the media would pick up so much on what we were saying. Big Cove women could have been there, or the New Brunswick Native Women's Council, and they wouldn't have gotten the response "the Tobique Women" got.

I guess I had built up a phobia about the reception we'd get, especially after seeing a national organization like NAC being attacked like dogs. Keith Penner, the Liberal big shot on the committee, was literally chewing them out for what he perceived as "white women's meddling into Indian affairs." Even though Mary (Two-Axe) Early was there supporting them. Jim Manly, the NDP Indian Affairs critic, was very *picky* about NAC's presentation, saying, "It doesn't deal with real issues." The panel kept trying to trip NAC up with stupid little things like, "What kind of policies do you think reinstatement *specifically* will require?"

I was sad that Chaviva Hoesak, the president of NAC, even answered the last question. I couldn't help myself, and sent her a little note, "That's not the issue—what policies are made are beyond your scope. You're just addressing reinstatement and the abolishment of discrimination within a completely discriminatory Act. That's it."

By now Mary (Two-Axe Early) stepped in. She did a real impacting-type performance, throwing her hands over her head on the table, saying: "Oh my God! Again and again and again! Am I going to die without ever seeing any justice done?" Everybody went very quiet. (laughter) Oh, you know, that kind of drama really slapped everybody.

We were on for the following day and the chairperson, Stan Schellenberger, gave us a great, big *compliment* for the best presentation to date.

But Schellenberger had talked with us prior to that. He'd said,

"I have seen a letter from a Tobique woman and I have to share it with you." It was from one of the women I had talked with two weeks earlier and given an envelope, said, "You don't need a stamp. Just write to these people." I said, "You don't have to be a writer; you don't have to use any big words. Just tell them how *you* feel and what you think should be done." She's a fairly simple soul. She just wrote, "Would you please stop 12(1)(b) and reinstate Native women to being Indian again." That was it. And she signed her name.

Schellenberger was so impressed by that very simple letter. He said, "Do you know her?" and I said, "Yes, of course I know her." I was pleased because I spent three or four days hitting every house that I could, leaving five or six envelopes and addresses. This was one woman I thought would *never,* ever write, and it had such a powerful, personal impact on the chairperson of the Standing Committee.

Already he was proud of us before he went up and took the chair. There was a woman on the committee who was real flowery and pretty and then she'd stab. She was like all the males I've heard throughout our campaigning, and she claims to be feminist. And Schellenberger cut her off. Whenever somebody was negative about our presentation, he'd cut them off. (laughter) He liked us. Maybe that letter showed him how much ordinary Indian women across Canada wanted the Indian Act changed.

Also, the letter was from a status woman. I told them, "Put down if you are status or non-status." See, it wasn't all non-status women who wrote. This was a woman who always had her status, living on a reserve. She didn't give a damn if all the non-status women started living on the reserve; she just wanted the injustice addressed. A lot of the women and men from Tobique did write. Jim Manly (then New Democratic Party Indian Affairs critic) had nothing negative to say about our presentation and neither did Keith Penner (Liberal MP, influential as past-chairperson of *Indian Self Government Report*).

SANDRA: Then at the beginning of April we had to go back to Ottawa to appear before the Senate Legal Committee. One of the questions they asked was, "Aren't you represented already?" I said, "If we were represented already, I wouldn't have to be sitting here telling you our problems." Caroline told them, "I think she represents any non-status woman that wants to live on her own reserve or that wants status for herself and her children."

The Union (of New Brunswick Indians) had sent a telecommunication just that afternoon saying, "We want this bill stopped right away." The Union was telling the committee, "You don't have the right to change our laws. We can discriminate against women if we want to." We were just ready to go on, and that telex was being passed around the room. One of the committee members came over and asked me, "Did you know anything about this?" I said, "No."

Then during questioning, the committee said, "Your leaders don't want this bill passed." That's when we told them, "If we were properly represented—if our leaders were for women or didn't discriminate—then we wouldn't have to be here."

The woman senator from New Brunswick, Brenda Robinson, turned out to be very helpful. I'd said, "She'd be a good person to start educating." She didn't know very much about the issue but we talked to her, and gave her a lot of literature. She told us she'd talk to a friend of hers about our position who *as it happened* was chairperson of the Senate legal committee. I think that helped us out for the hearing.

The black woman senator, Anne Cools, came after us about representation, too. See, they were all worried about representation. Of course, with the Toronto *Globe and Mail* article, that's written history. They did a story on our brief and the cross-examination afterwards, and Caroline got on the front page *Quote of the Day*:"'Why aren't you the prime minister of Canada? Because you're the wrong colour and you're a woman.'—Indian spokesman Caroline Ennis answers a question from Senator Anne Cools with one of her own." (laughter)

After Bill C-31 went to both the House of Commons Standing Committee and Senate Standing Committee on Legal and Constitutional Affairs for hearings, on May 6 it was tabled, with amendments, in the House of Commons. While it then remained "at

Report Stage" until mid-June, MPs could move amendments to the bill. Lobbying continued right up through that amendment process, with the various interested parties pressing their own positions to any sympathetic MPs.

Then, when Report Stage ended in June, the House of Commons voted on the amendments and Bill C-31 moved to Third Reading for passage. The final bill still gave back full Indian status to women who had been born with, and lost, it upon marriage. In fact, it gave full status back to anyone who was born with it and subsequently lost it for any reason. All that was required was the completion of a relatively simple application form. This meant that no chief and council could bar former members from the full rights of band membership. All the lobbying by the Assembly of First Nations and others to allow bands to *deny* women their full status had not swayed David Crombie and the Conservative government to back down on this fundamental point.

As in the initial bill tabled in the House of Commons, first generation children would receive back their status, but each band would be given two years to develop its own membership code. In other words, Bill C-31 would give bands *for the first time* the right to determine their own membership, with the exception of reinstating former members. With the new bill, no person—Indian or white—who presently had status would lose it.

In late June Bill C-31 passed successfully through the House of Commons, on June 26 it was approved by Senate, and on June 28th, 1985 it was scheduled for Royal Assent, or signing, by the Governor-General of Canada, Madame Jeanne Sauve. For the first time in 116 years, sexual discrimination against Indian women was no longer the law in Canada.

The Tobique women's struggle for reinstatement began as a strategy to bring the problems of all Indian women—status and non-status—to the attention of the Canadian public. What began as a strategy became a full-fledged campaign. Though their goal of that campaign finally has been achieved, the women are too wise politically to imagine that *legal* change is going to solve Native women's problems overnight. However, the fact that, against tremendous opposition, the Indian Act was amended to give back women their full rights, is an historic achievement which cannot be overestimated.

Here Karen and Sandra remember their initial reaction to the news that Bill C-31 had passed its final hurdle.

SANDRA: When we started out, reinstatement always seemed so close. Whenever we came back from a lobbying trip, we'd all believe, it's going to happen, it's going to happen. Then, nothing … we'd have to start right back at it again.

When I'd be interviewed later on in the 1980s, the reporter inevitably would say, "I hear it is finally going to happen," and I'd say, "I'll believe it when I see it. I'm not going to count my chickens before they hatch." (laughter) I couldn't believe it when Caroline called me in June, said, "Sandra, it's finally over." I said, "Over? What's over?" I was just getting out of bed. She said, "No more. The bill's passed." I started crying.

I went over to my uncle Louis' place, where everybody gathers for morning coffee. When I went in I said, "Didn't you hear?"

KAREN: You were in tears, so I asked, "What happened?" I didn't know if it was good news or bad news. (laughter) Then you told us we got reinstatement, and everybody started saying, "You all did a good job," and congratulating Sandra.

When you told us, I still wasn't really sure, though, because we hadn't heard anything official. I had the same reaction you had—I'll believe it when I see it. Maybe I expected a little bit more, like, so it happened, so where's the fireworks? (laughter) It must have been all those *false alarms*.

CHAPTER SIX

RETROSPECTIVE

GAINING REINSTATEMENT WAS a major milestone for Native women in Canada, especially for the women of Tobique Reserve who worked so hard for it. During my interviews with the women, as well as talking about specific events, they reflected on their past frustrations and hopes for the future; took stock of their accomplishments and assessed what is needed at this stage in their struggle.

In this closing chapter, several of the Tobique women each share a few reflections as they look back over their campaigns, and ahead to the future.

LILLY HARRIS

It was a long struggle, but it was worth it. We would probably never have got back in—been reinstated—if we hadn't gone on the women's walk or demonstrated. Before the walk nobody ever listened to us—you had to do something outstanding so that people would take notice.

I always thought we had a good cause and that people needed to pay attention. We went to so many meetings! When the women were going—like to New Brunswick Native Women's Council assemblies—I always went, took my car with four or five women. Yes, I supported them all the way. Well, I was non-status myself.

Oh, I can't describe how it felt when the change (to the Indian Act) finally came through. Especially after it got put off so many times, but I kept praying. I didn't think it was going to come through that quick at the end. All you can do is pray, pray, so it will happen. Finally it did, and thank God for it!

EVA (GOOKUM) SAULIS

We've been at it for so long. Those times during the occupations were so emotional, so nerve-wracking too. We had misunderstandings, rumours going around; we'd get on each other's nerves. Of course we couldn't always agree on everything. We had a hard time.

Once I told Bet-te, "I don't hold any grudges, because we're working for one purpose only. I don't care what anybody calls me or what they say in the newspapers." Our one purpose was for the women to have their rights, then later on we included the non-status. I almost got into a fight with a woman once; I told her, "I don't want any pat on the back. Before I die I want this 12(1)(b) eliminated."

Some people argued that "it's traditional for Indians to discriminate against their women." They pointed to those old pictures of an Indian family moving from one place to another; you'd see a man walking ahead with his bow and arrow and the woman walking behind with small children, hauling that *travois*. It looks like she's doing all the hard work.

I heard remarks about that by white women, "I don't want to be your squaw. I don't want to work hard like that." But there is a reason for why that man walked ahead. It's because he had to protect his family against animals and enemies. It wasn't that the woman walked behind him because she had to do everything. Like when the women had to look after the family, it was because the men went away to provide for them by trapping or working in the woods. "Being a squaw" wasn't a worse or unequal thing. Everything had a *purpose*.

There is so much more I could tell you in my own language, but it's impossible to translate. So much more. I told my sister-in-law, all the people who speak our language up and down the St. John River should get together. We should have a gathering and just talk Indian. The younger ones could listen in. It's so interesting when we get together. My sister-in-law said, "We'd better hurry up. We're not going to be around much longer!"

MAVIS GOERES

So we've had a long, hard struggle. I think what kept us going was our heritage and our sticking together. Maybe we didn't have all the same ideas, but we all had the one main goal in mind—equality for the women. We're just as good as the man. I think what really kept us going is our determination to seek what is rightfully ours. And that *is* our heritage. We all knew that no government agency—be it white or be it Indian—was going to tell us we were no longer Indian, when we *know* we are Indian.

Here the Canadian government was making instant Indians out of white women. You might as well say they were trying to make instant white women out of us Indians. And it cannot be, because being Indian is our heritage—it's in our blood. I think that is our determination right there—it's because we are Indian. We were fighting for our *birthright*.

We had the demonstrations, the occupations, the women's walk to Ottawa. We got some housing for unwed mothers, but the band administration started giving that housing we got on account of the walk to unmarried men. Political promises. But still, we got something started, and we realized we'd been discriminated against for so long—Indian women in general—not just status or non-status ... because I never liked that word, "non-status."

I knew I was Indian—nobody took the Indian blood out of me. Therefore I think all of us women decided there's this whole discrimination thing going on, and it's all geared against *the women*. The women had no rights. Yet the man could do whatever he wanted to do. He could bring a white woman in, have children by her, and she had status. She had more to say than the Indian women did themselves. That's when the Tobique women *really* got involved.

We had obstacles along the way. Sadly, we had problems with Native organizations. I really feel that money has a lot to do with all these organizations—AFN, NCC, Métis, NWAC, even the New Brunswick Women's Council—straying from their original purpose. When they first organized it was to get Native people together, but then they would get monies which they were told to use for this purpose and this purpose only. But the money was coming in, people were getting paid—good pay that some of them never had before—and they forgot what they originally were going for. They got strayed.

I got an application from the New Brunswick Women's Council just yesterday to sign and send in my $2.00 as a member. I can't do it. I'm sorry, because I was on the executive and on the board of directors. I went to the First Ministers' Conference with the province under the women's council. I was fighting for equality and for the women, but once they started straying away from that objective, I gave up on that organization completcly. I saw we weren't going anywhere.

A lot of those organizations were corrupted by money and greed and power; they really went down the drain. The difference with us was that, what money we had was donations. Nobody had control of us, nobody got any pay. We were lucky sometimes even to have a place to stay. In Montreal the other fall at the NAC meeting, there were five of us in one hotel room; whereas, the other organizations all had rooms, meals provided. We ate at the Y.W.C.A.

Even on the women's walk to Ottawa, they were all donations. We slept on the bus or outside, let the elderly or sickly stay in whatever was offered. In Ottawa we even stayed in a jail that was turned into a hostel. A lot of us had blistered feet, but we went on. There was many times we'd be so discouraged, some would want to turn back—and some did—but most of us all kept each other going. The encouragement was there. It seems when everything is against you and you think you can't go on any longer, there's something that comes from within—something inside—gives you the added strength to go on some more.

Oh, it was a long, hard battle, and I pray there will be nothing standing in the way now to disillusion our happiness. Now that we've got our women's rights back now that the Indian Act is finally changed. I don't think Tobique will have any problems as far as reinstating their women, but I feel for other reserves, because I think they *are* going to have problems. We are okay here with our present administration, but with the wrong administration we could be in trouble again, too.

When I look back I see that we became more and more aware of the Indian Act standing behind a lot of our problems. Something I don't think other people are aware of, though, is the *hurt* that comes with it. No white woman actually came up and said anything to me personally, but there is one married to a man on this reserve that came up to my friend, Lilly Harris. Lilly had got up to say something at a band meeting, and this woman said, "Aw shut up! You non-status don't have nothing to say here." That hurt.

Another thing that hurt me regards my youngest daughter, Susan. She is very, very active in sports, very good in teams. When it came to Indian Summer Games, they said, "You can't play because you're non-status. You're not an Indian." I said, "My God, she's got as much Indian in her as a lot of them here." That's when I really got mad. I think the anger and hurt is what pushed us on, too. It wasn't only happening to my daughter, but to other women's daughters *and* sons. I protested and the *Toronto Star* did a story on my Susan and on Mary (Two-Axe) Early, showing how 12(1)(b) affected both their generations.

That Indian Act and the discrimination against women had such far-reaching effects—on relationships between people and on little day-to-day things. It's a good thing no white woman came and called me "non-status" like they did Lilly, because I would fight them—physically, I mean. Nobody ever has, thank goodness, because I don't want to fight, but I wouldn't back down from one, either. I would fight for that because I am an Indian, an Indian through and through. I wish I could sit here and talk to you in Indian because the meaning comes out so much better, so much stronger.

Now that we've got the Indian Act changed and the women back, our reserve will be so much the stronger for it. Because Indian people will off-balance all the whites who have married in. Not just whites, either. Do you know that even Indian women from other reserves who married in, feel they have more right to voice their opinions than our own women? But they don't have the same feelings for this reserve we do—that were born and brought up here. They don't.

We that grew up on Tobique know what the reserve used to be like. As an Indian person born and living here, you don't like some of the things that have been happening. But when you remember, then you can see that, yes, it can be different again. When you have twenty-two grandchildren like I have, and many live here, you want a better future. It *can* be better. That's what I mean when I say, now with the women back, our reserve will be so much the stronger. I know it.

JUANITA PERLEY

I think the strength for the future lies in our grandchildren. That is where the hope lies. The present generation is disinterested in our traditional ways. I started getting involved in Indian spirituality about fifteen years ago, and began going back to the old ways. When I was growing up I thought I was a little cuckoo maybe— that all of my marbles weren't there because of the way I thought. Everybody else just went to church, so I thought I should straighten out my thinking. I read religious books, trying to get back into the Catholic Church, until 1971 when we had a huge Indian gathering here that my sister, Marjorie, co-ordinated.

Traditional people came from all over Canada, and talked about the Indian way. I thought, well, I can't be all crazy because these people think like I do. I began doing research and talking to Indian elders, and gradually I found it was meant for Indian people to follow their own way. I used to have a few run-ins with the priest. One time I told him, "I never argue religion with my own people. If they want to be Catholics, fine. I don't care what they want to be." I have a lot of friends on this reserve and we never argue about religion—politics, maybe, but never religion. (laughter)

The priest felt threatened by the growing spiritual movement. The final straw for me was when a woman died, and everybody went to the funeral; nobody cares what church you are from.

Again, the priest started preaching hatred, only it was worse. He said, "You shouldn't even let anybody who isn't Catholic into your home. You shouldn't talk to them on the street."

I was really furious and went down to see the priest. I'd written to the bishop, put in a complaint on him preaching hatred in the church. At first the priest denied it, but he convicted himself, because he tapes his sermons and we listened to it on his small tape recorder. Everything I accused him of was right there. He said, "Well, I never meant it that way." Finally, though, he straightened up. We have been working in co-operation, I guess after he found he couldn't scare me.

The priest was really good when my son died. We didn't have a religious leader here, so he did the sermon and helped bury my son. I thought that was pretty good. He even let us have a traditional ceremony in the graveyard. I was going to have the ceremony anyway, but I thought, just to save trouble, I should ask him, and he said, "That would be nice."

I especially have hopes for Dave Perley, this chief in now. He had good ideas when he started out, but the council wouldn't buy it; they don't want to give the people power, which is what the new chief wanted. Dave wanted direction from the people, but the old council didn't, and some of them are *still* there today. The chief will do fine if the people don't get impatient, if they give him enough time.

But as I said, the generation here now is really disinterested. I don't think they care one way or another about anything, because of disappointment about the way the world is going, and the easy accessibility to drugs and alcohol. I don't think it has much to do with their not having anything to *do*, because if anybody was going to be alcoholic, it was our generation—we had nothing, not even sports. So I don't think it is because we don't have huge activity centres here—I think it has to do with them being *lost*.

They don't have an identity. Hardly anyone wants to be an Indian anymore. They don't teach culture in the school here, only beading. They don't teach language and Maliseet should be the first language in that school. And I think after a while, the young people didn't know who they were. The conflict that goes on inside them is that they may be brown on the outside, but everything they've been taught is white.

Once in a while you're going to get a taste of discrimination wherever you go. The darker ones really had a hard time in the school downtown. The kids are sensitive, and not too many graduate. I try to tell the parents not to break the tie they have with their children. The kids are gone from 7:30 in the morning; you don't see them till 4:00. They have their supper, study and go to bed. So the influence the parent has with them is gradually being taken away. The kids changed when they started going to school in town—from obedience to aggressiveness, to being disorderly.

Before going to school downtown, you never heard kids sassing back their elders, and the younger they went down, the worse they got. What Indians need to know is this tie that we have first to the family and then to the earth. Now that tie is severed before the person is ready. To survive in a society that is foreign, the Indian tries to be part of it, but every so often somebody closes the door and reminds us, "You're an Indian." Then we realize, I know everything white people do, and they still don't accept me.

Then with spirituality, our children are not taught their own Indian way, so a big part is missing out of their lives. Finally I kind of gave up, said, "The hell on them. If they want their kids to be white, let them be white," and I stopped fighting for a better school on the reserve.

We will lose our language, though, if people don't wake up. It's hard. I only spoke to my oldest three in Maliseet. Then when they hit public school, they came up against the language block, so I thought, I'd better speak to my kids in English first, and I can always teach them Maliseet later on. So I spoke just English, and the next bunch did better in school, but they couldn't speak their own language! (laughter) So I have to teach them Maliseet now, but they are really shy when they're older. I laugh easy and some days I laugh when they mispronounce words. I don't mean to laugh *at* them; it just comes out funny. I do notice that they talk Indian more to their kids, with whatever little Indian they have.

I still think there should be better laws to protect women and their children. What bothers me most today is kids who are stuck because the mother won't leave a bad situation. I think the Canadian government should make better laws to protect children. Some children are battered pretty bad, but very seldom does the law go out and arrest the parents. I often wonder about how much anybody really cares about kids. Most of the law-makers are men who don't have much to do with raising kids. They are upper-class, anyway. They don't even raise their kids—have nannies and day-care.

I really don't think reserves are going to exist much longer. What I see is something that has been coming since that White Paper of Jean Chretien's in 1967, doing away with reserves altogether. The men think that idea is dead, but it isn't; it's coming about in small sections at a time. Indian money is gradually being filtered through other agencies like Canadian Mortgage and Housing. Instead of the money coming to us directly, it is being handed over to provincial programs. I told the chiefs that once at an all-chiefs meeting in Redbank.

I said, "Indian Affairs is holding you with a noose around your neck—they've got you with just your toes on the ground—dangling that money over you. You're being drawn to that money, when you should be saying no." I said, "Your people are just as responsible because they keep demanding more, like more expensive housing. In my time we didn't just get a house, a man had to build it. Now the young couples get houses built. Why aren't they encouraged to be the same as we were? The only people who should get houses built for them are the old, disabled or widows, women and children who don't have homes. But able-bodied men? No."

I told the chiefs that all those programs are part of the government's plan to eventually municipalize Indian reserves. Their aim is to make us municipalities. That will accomplish just what the White Paper was about. The White Paper policy was to eliminate reserves by 1987; erase the Indian Act and make us municipalities. They wouldn't be chiefs any more, but mayors and town councils. But the title would suit most of them better, anyways! (laughter)

One of the things about that White Paper was that when they

were given self-government and administered their own funds, they would have to tax their own people to subsidize what Indian Affairs wasn't sending anymore. It would probably be like a white community with certain monies coming in and the tax payers keeping up everything—roads and education. It would probably end up the same way. I told those chiefs, "Don't think we'll always have Indian Affairs looking after us!"

I think people would be frightened to death by anything very different from the way things are now. We have become so *dependent*. My solution would be to claim a decent-sized land base, declare *sovereignty* and nationhood. If you look at our land base traditionally, you don't just stop at the reserve as our territory; our territory is a big strip running right up the St. John River into Quebec. That's our traditional land base. A certain amount of Irving (the $600 million empire of New Brunswick industrialist K.C. Irving) and them's tax money should be coming into Indian funds. Also, a certain percentage should be coming into the Indian Nation from the hydroelectric dam, because it is on our land.

Then you could invite other people to come and help set up industries here, like salmon and trout farms, maple sugar. Blueberries could be revived again. You could smoke and can the fish. The present chief thought it was a good idea but the people are scared because some guy came around and told them nobody would be getting any money then. I think people would feel a whole lot better if they were earning their own money.

Those are our (the traditionalists') plans now. We have a land base and our Nation House set up. We'll have a few cabins built in the next few years; plan to farm and fish, dry food the old way. We want our children to still go to school, but also learn their culture and the old ways, so when they are older they'll have a choice. We're getting a lot of support from other places, though it is a slow process and sometimes I feel like screaming and pulling my hair out! (laughter) Some of my kids and grandchildren come out and want to have their homes there. They like it, probably because they taste the freedom they lack here.

I used to worry about the way people on this reserve were going, but I've slowly matured to the point where I've learned you can't change people's thinking, you have to let them go. But it is hard watching young people waste their lives; especially watching the weekend tragedies. I agree that the way people live now is easy. Going back to the old ways requires a lot of labour. Maybe as the present generation gets older it will see the benefits, though.

We as Indians have given a lot. The whites have been here over two hundred years, and when they came we treated them well. They would never have survived if it hadn't been for the Indians nursing them along. Then as the years went by, Indians gradually felt more like outsiders in their own land, because of the encroachments. We have adapted a lot—mastered the white language, education, technology, but for what price? We live in push-button houses but have polluted rivers; fly in airplanes but have polluted air. We have mills that make paper and kill the fish, then the white people turn around and tell us Indians not to fish! There is no end to it.

People call it all "progress" but to the Indian it is a set-back. We can't hang onto our values and live this new way too. Eventually you have to chose. You can't be traditional and live in the white man's system at the same time because you are helping to destroy the earth. Even me, sewing with my sewing machine, I'm partaking of that dam! When I cook supper on the electric stove, there's a hidden cost. Eventually we have to get away from that dependency—I do for my sake, anyway, though I don't know about the younger generation. They might find it too difficult. I was raised in very poor conditions so it doesn't bother me if I don't have fancy eating.

I guess we tried to give our children more than we had, and in the process we gave them more of the white man's way of life and less of the Indian. So we created our own little monsters! (laughter) I hope to see this reserve try for sovereignty, for nationhood. I've always thought that, if anybody could do it, it would be us because we're a big enough reserve to pull it off. There are a lot of aggressive people here, a lot of educated ones, too, if we could all pull together.

BET-TE PAUL

I became more aware of how important our language is when I was travelling around, visiting Plains Indians in Montana and the Dakotas. The culture is in the language so much. We've lost a lot of our culture, but now we have to keep the language; we've got to pass it on. A lot of us have travelled, been involved in other Native political struggles besides our own. I think that seeing other situations and the *power* people can have by holding onto their values, their convictions, their beliefs, has given us added strength.

Out west there's been people killed in their struggles. I met women on The Longest Walk who'd lost their sons at Wounded Knee. They have warrior societies out there because they're more male-oriented. It's been mostly the women that are the strongest here. Like the men's reaction when we first started out protesting—their reaction was shock that women had *the gall* to stand up and say, "This is *wrong*," when the men themselves didn't, yet they knew it was wrong, too. I think in that way it humiliated them, and that is why they got so angry with us at first. But how long can you let something that is wrong continue?

We didn't come from a male-dominated society—it was matrilineal. Some of us have been digging to find out our old culture, and one document about relationships shows there was a special relationship between the elder women and the young girls. Also, the elder women were the ones to hold places in council and to guide the men. We had chiefs, but the elder women were behind the men; they were listened to and held in high respect. The young maidens didn't have any say, really. The married women looked after the families, and had a say in anything that concerned the community. The males were the hunters and warriors, but the women took care of the village, the encampments.

As far as clans went, the bloodline went through the woman— that's down on paper in the archives. The blood comes from the mother, not the father, which is exactly the opposite of what the Indian Act imposed on us. See, that's what the government wanted to destroy; the women were the bearers of the children, so they wanted to destroy that concept of togetherness, and what better way than to label somebody "non-status" once you married out? What better way to break up families and communities?

You see a lot of blond-haired Mohawks in the States, but you never consider them "non-status" like in Canada. They see themselves as Mohawks and so does everybody else. Their identity comes through the clan, and if the woman married a white guy it didn't matter; the child would be whatever the mother was. It was the same way for us traditionally and obviously the government wanted to break it up.

But we believe now that membership has got to be restricted somewhere down the line. That is only common sense because, if you don't restrict it, after some point you wouldn't have a drop of Indian blood in you. We have to make our blood-line stronger, and instill in our children a pride in our culture.

Maybe there are memories of strong women built in us through the generations; that strain of standing up for what you believe in; fighting for your children, saying, "Stop! This is wrong. You can't keep doing this and getting away with it." If we didn't, we'd still be like we were in the old chief's administration. But we did stand up, we did fight back.

When I see something wrong, people being treated unfairly, no matter who—man, woman or child—if somebody needs help, I have to do something about it. Even some of the women who used to throw rocks at us and threaten us, there's been times recently when they've needed help and we've come through for them. We didn't hold a grudge so much that we ignored them. They are a woman in need and you put your personal feelings aside.

When we started something, like the occupations or the non-status campaign, we never strayed from it; we've been going after the same thing all these years until we finally got it. There were times people tried to sway us, get us involved in all this other crap—like with the AFN or the Union (of New Brunswick Indians) or NWAC—and we said, "No way! We're going to keep fighting for this cause."

We've been ostracized and that didn't stop us. The Union opposed us, undermined us—lobbied against us in Ottawa, but we kept going. A lot of discrediting there. Like the time in the fall of 1984 when a couple of guys from the AFN had taken the NAC press relations person out to dinner and tried to pressure her, telling her not to listen to us and that we didn't represent anybody. AFN was telling her, "Keep your nose out of *our* Indian business"—that kind of thing. We had to straighten NAC out, tell them, "This is what we're saying. Don't believe what anybody else is saying about us." We told NAC reinstatement was a women's issue and they could be a pressure group, too. It is more important than any nationality when it concerns helping each other out.

Those guys are wary of us because they don't know exactly what to expect. They know we aren't going stand by while they are trying to pull off something that's sleazy—we're dog-determined. They couldn't buy us off with funding, because we never had any—what we got, we scrounged. (laughter) We never depended on any government funding. We got money from here and there, used our own, had cake raffles or bake sales. But we always found a way to get where we had to go.

We learned a lot along the way—a lot about lobbying and working with the media. We helped start up the New Brunswick Native Women's Council, but now we've come to the fact that we're just going to be the "Tobique Women's Political Action Group." That's all we ever were, you know. We never wanted to be like how the AFN is, or the Union. But a political action group is always what we were—a number of women—it was never one woman that pulled it off, but the effort of a group of women. One person never does it alone. And of course it wasn't only us that got reinstatement. Even at the beginning, you have to look to Mary Two-Axe Early and the Quebec women. Indian Rights for Indian Women, too, even if maybe they went off the track a bit.

It was different women from all over the country. I do think that the media attention we got sort of got women moving again, though, because at that time not too many women were involved in 12(1)(b). We were saying something to the world. But "Tobique Women" was always a group effort. Some of us would get burned out and others would take over, but there was always a group behind the women that went out to lobby. Maybe someone would go off the track a bit, but we'd always have meetings and say, "Hold it, this is what we're going for." When somebody said something, it was for the group. We trusted each other enough to know what our aims were and that way, if we were speaking we always thought about the rest of the women and how everybody felt. It was never just one woman's opinions.

Our struggle was always *for the children*—to have a decent home for our children. Any parent wants that for their children. Like here's a woman whose husband is living with a white woman in the family home, while she's living in a trailer that's small, leaking, falling apart, where the toilet doesn't work half the time, and she's the one trying on welfare to make ends meet for all the children. *That* is what we fought to change.

Looking back, it amazes me how the kids maintained through all the protests and occupations. Times they'd be so tired, and scary times they'd scream with fear. With us women, there'd be times we wanted to give up, but we just had to keep going, to support each other. Some would get grouchy and others would sit down and talk with you. Each other's support kept us going in the hard times. Plus the sense of right and wrong; that it wasn't right, the treatment women and children were getting.

We've made a few advances. We have a foot-hold with dual-ownership of homes—the certificate of possession is in both the husband and wife's name now. Some status women have been getting houses, and now with Bill C-31 passed, some former non-status women are to get houses, too. People's attitudes have changed over the past few years; there is a little more respect towards the women now than there was before. More women are being hired for jobs. Some of the men want to see women as band councillors.

I think people here respect the *determination* we've had. They know there are people outside the reserve who respect what we've done. If you talk to most Indian people across Canada—not necessarily leaders, but *people*—they'll say, "Yes, Indian women's birthright should never have been taken away." Yet it took us and all the people fighting for reinstatement this long to get it. Now that people see what we've accomplished, I think they respect us for it. But there is being a fear built into people, too.

I think the government and some of these chiefs that have had control on reserves for so long, are trying to instill a fear into people—fear that there's going to be hundreds and hundreds of women coming back, "and you people are going to get less money." Yet look at what was happening here—the band administration keeping names on the band membership list and collecting money for themselves with those names. Well, now that money will have to go to the people who it rightfully belongs to.

A former non-status person will have to put their name on the housing list, just like anybody else. Most have been living here all this time, anyway, so it's not really anything different. The women who made their lives and put down their roots elsewhere aren't going to uproot their whole family, leave their jobs immediately, and rush back to the reserve. That's unrealistic. All the women wanted was their birthright back, which was rightfully theirs in the beginning.

JOYCE (YC) SAPPIER WITH BET-TE PAUL

BET-TE: One day Ramo and I were driving downtown and looking at all the new houses going up on our land—even the town of Perth is on our land—being debated right now in our land claims. I said, "Look at all these houses here. All these white people are paying taxes to the government where they should be paying taxes to us because that's our land they're sitting on." It's documented that they've been squatters for generations. The government let them get away with it all these years and now the white people think it's their land.

The government and their laws! They took our land and they took our rights. Like with you, Mom, they took your rights, tried to make you "white." That's why, when you came back to the reserve, I told you, "Don't ever let anybody tell you you're not an Indian."

YC: People tried to label me "non-status." I'd just tell them, "Once you're born an Indian, you'll always be an Indian." I'd throw up the white women on the reserve at them and say, "If those honky women belong on this reserve, then surely to God I do."

BET-TE: So many of the councillors fighting against us were married to white women. Their women have had a lot of power, a lot of influence, and they're threatened by Indian women getting back on; they've rubbed our noses in it for so long. Probably that's why the *resistance*.

YC: The old chief resisted reinstatement, too. He always could use non-status as a reason for not helping women. No wonder he didn't want the non-status back! They would never vote for him.

BET-TE: For sure that was a factor, because those are the same people he went against, and sent people against. That feeling doesn't leave you; of course you're not going to vote for him if you get your band membership back. It's probably the same with chiefs right across Canada, because they've stayed against the women for so long, denying them their rights.

YC: All the while collecting money for them, and telling them, "You're not an Indian anymore."

BET-TE: White women here were getting help left and right. While huge families, single mothers were asking for repairs or a house—people really in *need*—it was the white woman getting repairs. Shit, we didn't take that for very long.

YC: See, the houses have never been allotted according to need. The chief and council choose and they think about their own families first. That's what you see.

BET-TE: Because the band council is choosing, they've got the power and they feel that power. Favouritism. If we were in a matriarchal society like traditionally, boy, those guys would be in a hell of a lot of trouble. (laughter) Indian Affairs still has its clutches in there, too.

There isn't a housing committee yet, but we hope it's coming around now. Some of us women wrote a letter to council stating that there should be an independent housing committee. There should be criteria for who gets a house, and the criteria should be based on *needs*. The councillors are supposed to come through on it, but it has taken this long, this much struggle.

YC: It has been a long struggle. Jeez, I remember the day Ray and I got married. We got married just in time for me to vote in the band election, because the administration then was so against the non-status. We were trying to vote the chief out of office, and Ray scheduled for us to get married right on election day.

I guess there was a whole mess of people waiting for us outside the band office and it was getting near closing time for voting. They'd been waiting and waiting and all of a sudden heard car horns honking. Everybody started yelling, "Here they come!" We walks into the hall and they clapped and done a circle, dancing around us. You should have seen the chief and the band manager shaking our hands, congratulating us. (laughter) But of course they knew which way we were going to vote!

BET-TE: And all the time, trying to get it so that you couldn't vote— that you hadn't been married to Ray long enough.

YC: They tried to block me from voting, but Ramo (Ray) told Jimmie, the election guy, "She's voting. She's got my band number." Jimmie wanted to see proof, to see the marriage certificate. Ramo said, "You open it yourself; it's right here." So Jimmie gave me a piece of paper and said, "Go ahead and vote." You should have seen the people hollering. They made us kiss right in the voting booth before I put my ballot in. (laughter) They said, "Come on, Ray, kiss the first non-status voting!"

But I kept fighting the chief and his administration because I still identified with the non-status women, still supported the women. I didn't feel right even though I was status again.

BET-TE: Sure, she got married, but so what? She was always an Indian. Now she'd got a band number. What is it? You're an Indian just because you have a band number? Big deal.

YC: I didn't feel like I gained my status just by marrying Ray. I didn't feel right until the reinstatement went through. That's when I celebrated, "Yahoo, I'm an Indian once again!" (laughter) That's why I drank and partied that night we had the big reinstatement celebration here. Oh my God, was I sick the next day!

BET-TE: A lot of people were. (laughter) Glenna danced with the chief. His wife came over to me at the dance saying, "Doss (affectionate Maliseet term for 'daughter' or 'girl'), you did such a good job!" I said, "No thanks to you." (laughter) She said, "My husband and I supported you." I said sarcastically, "Oh sure you did." I couldn't get over it.

CHERYL BEAR

Back before we started protesting, it was always the same situation for women. If a woman was alone with kids she had to fight. Juanita had to fight. Marjorie had to fight. Sometimes I think you weren't considered a person unless you had a man in the house. You had to be married. If a single woman with kids went and asked for help, they'd say, "Why did you have children?" (laughter) Oh, I'd love to shove that down those men's throats. I'd like to ask them, "Why did *you* have children?" There's no difference.

Looking back, I can see some changes. I think attitudes themselves have changed. It might have been the way people were raised, but it was expected women were supposed to take it—punishment or abuse—from the man, and not retaliate. I used to see that often, but now a lot of women don't accept abuse anymore —their attitude's changed. Women have expectations of their own and they don't see why they can't have a home of their own. Why can't we have the same *choices* men have? And jobs? Everything, really.

There's women now that are getting houses. I know that a lot of men don't like it. Some of them will come out with ignorant statements; others know enough not to say anything, but you can tell the old attitude is still there.

Things haven't changed much over the years with the towns-people. There's still no Indian people working down in Perth, except for one who's a hairdresser. Nobody else. Pretty well every-body has to go over across to the States for work. Some people won't even go downtown to shop. They go to Grand Falls or over across. I was told if we ever get land claims money we should boycott Perth-Andover; take that money somewhere else.

People are trying to start a co-op up on the reserve; that way we wouldn't have to bother with the shop-keepers downtown. I think they'd lose a lot of business, because I know for myself, I spend a lot of money down there.

There's still problems with the schools downtown, too. Every so often my little girl comes home with a complaint of white kids calling her "squaw." A couple of months ago we had meetings with the principals about our complaints, and they said some-thing would be done, but it never is. I suggested that they have a Native RCMP or somebody like that talk to all the kids on Career Day, and let the white kids see that we work, we're individuals, we're human. The teachers agreed with the idea at the time, but I never heard about it since.

CAROLINE ENNIS

In 1977 when Noel Kinsella agreed with taking Sandra's case to the United Nations, we weren't actually looking for ways to settle the problem of the non-status women. We were looking for ways to put pressure on the government to listen to us. It was still mainly the issue of housing. We saw going to the United Nations as a way to pressure the government and bring our problems to national attention. But then people—media and any white people we talked to—kind of latched onto that, because it's such an obvious discrimination.

I think the 12(1)(b) campaign did serve its purpose, though it wasn't the issue to begin with. The reinstatement issue finally sunk into the Canadian consciousness—enough to have the Indian Act changed—but the thing went on and on. Our walk to Ottawa was in 1979 and the Act was changed in 1985. It took that long for it to sink into the Canadian consciousness.

We didn't get one bit of help from the Liberals, all the time they were in office nationally. In fact, at a NAC lobbying session in the early 1980s, Pierre Trudeau said to an Indian woman, Pauline Harper, "You mean to tell me you non-status women want the right to go back to the reserve and collect benefits for your kids that my kids can't get?"

When I heard about that, I said, "My God, if he thinks he is missing any benefits, I'm sure I can talk one of the women from Tobique to send her kids to go and live with Pierre Trudeau—live in a fancy house like Justin or Sasha does. We'll bring Justin and Sasha up on the reserve and then they'll be able to partake in those benefits their father thinks they're missing out on. (laughter) I was actually going to write Trudeau and tell him that. It made me so mad, but the women got a laugh over it. "The child swap."

We had a lot of opposition along the way. The Assembly of First Nations gave us a hard time. They used the argument of self-determination to hold up reinstatement. We were never against self-determination, but the AFN used self-government as an excuse. It is dangerous, too, when most chiefs aren't able to handle the little power they have now *responsibly*. It's really the government's fault, though, because the government has never asked for *accountability* from the band councils or the provincial organizations like the Union, or the national.

There's nothing—or very, very little—to prevent rip-offs or the trampling of human rights. We certainly learned that Indian Affairs doesn't bother about complaints made to their officials. We found out their way of dealing with complaints is to send the complaint to the person it's made against. Some accountability!

How many bands are still like we used to be here, with nobody going to band council meetings, because they think they aren't allowed? Not too many people even go here, except the women who want to know what's going on. There was always a "gentlemen's agreement" amongst the councillors that, "Once we get out of this meeting, we're not going to talk about what went on." And most councillors are still *men* on all the reserves I know of. I can only think of two women here ever voted in as councillors, Pauline Nicholas and Suzy Bear.

Glenna told me that her son, Sterling, didn't want to watch that CBC television dramatization of Sandra's story, "Where the Heart Is" on *For the Record*. He had nightmares over the occupations. Then Bert MacKenzie, the Director of Operations for Indian Affairs asked me when that show came out, "I didn't get a chance to see it but some of the chiefs were telling me, 'It wasn't as bad as all that'!" The nerve of them! I said, "It wasn't as bad as that; it was *worse* than that!"

The things that were happening here then are still happening on other reserves now. People are starting to speak up and stand up for their rights, though. Those chiefs saw us as a threat because we'd give *their* people ideas, and I guess we did.

GLENNA PERLEY

I see the changes we made, like with the housing lists. Now there's always some women that get a house, like my daughter Kim with her two little girls. If it wasn't for the occupations, I don't think she would have had a chance. The other thing we changed is that the council doesn't completely ignore the elderly and the veterans like they did before. We made the public aware of what was going on, so that the administration had to change some of its ways.

There's been more houses allotted since we began to protest. I don't think the housing problem will ever be solved until we get an independent housing committee, though. Dave, the chief, made out a band council resolution to set up a committee, but I don't think the councillors will sign it. Some of the men are still selling the houses that they've gotten from the band. I don't think the problem will ever be solved unless the women have some say in it.

When things would slow down with the reinstatement campaign, we would tell each other that we shouldn't let the discrimination go. I don't like the idea of flying, so I don't go out to lobby much. Mostly what me and Bet-te did was talk to the women here and explain to them where things were at with 12(1)(b), and convince some of the men that it was wrong—make sure we still had support on the reserve.

When we started protesting, everything happening was so new to people, but they soon learned. It woke up a lot of people when we started protesting, and I guess they started thinking, things aren't the way they should be, and there could be a change. I think a lot of people realized that, but there's still a lot that won't speak up. Like just a few years ago, at a band election rally I was sitting back listening to all these men complaining. I just kept thinking, "Why did it take so long for them to wake up? Or why did it take so long for them to do something about it?" I felt like saying it, but I didn't. (laughter)

Instead I said, "Now you know what I was talking about five years ago." They just looked at me. It was sad for them to wake up after so many years. But at least enough people woke up to vote Dave in for chief.

Something I've thought about often is that, of the women who gave us such a bad time during the occupations, four or five are separated now themselves. You see, they laughed at us back then—thought our situations were so funny. We put one sign out, "Don't Laugh, It Can Happen to You." They tore it up.

They're not laughing now, and I think one of the reasons those particular women don't come to us for help is that they remember what they did. Our grandmothers used to tell us that if you made fun of another person or you hurt another person, it usually falls back on you. Like YC said, "Yeah, you wait a few years and see where they are!" and sure enough, they're having the same problems now. But at the time they had it so good with the old chief, they didn't care about anybody else's problems. A lot of them were just being used, but they didn't realize it.

I was saying to Bet-te and Kim recently , "Until the day the women start realizing that their own brothers, their own fathers, uncles aren't going to help us—they're going to keep helping the men—nothing will change." When the women start realizing that, and selecting women for band council, then there will be a change, but not until.

It's not that women haven't run for council—they have. I have, but I didn't campaign. Next time I would campaign more. It's not that I would only help the women; I'd try to be *fair*. I know the problems. Pauline Nicholas and Suzie Bear were councillors. They had a lot of relatives to vote for them. I don't remember when Suzy was in, but Pauline was good. She got tired, though; had a lot of kids and her husband was away working, so she didn't run again.

Even with women getting back their status, there still will be problems. I'm not looking forward to self-government too much. I don't think we are ready for it—because of the way things still are, with only men in council. Nothing really will change until we have equal representation. Not just five men and one or two women; that's not going to be enough. I think they should make a band council resolution where, if we need eight councillors, then there should be four women and four men. The problem is, of course, getting the men to do that. (laughter)

Another good thing would be to have an election for chief every four years rather than every two. With only two years, there's not enough time for any kind of a change. Vaughn didn't have a cent to work with, and some of the people were turning against him, instead of trying to understand what was going on. That was happening with Dave at first, too. Also, the same old councillors were trying like hell to make it look like Davey's fault. Things will never change as long as the same men keep getting in. I just hope the women will get reinstated in time to make a difference in the next election.

Last night we were talking about women getting back on the band list, like Wanda, my aunt Idy, her daughter Norma, and Norma's daughter, Tina. Not Davey, but all those chiefs who were so against reinstatement are going to keep the women off their band lists, because they *know* those women coming back won't vote for them. So the chiefs that fought against us are going to keep fighting against us, I'm afraid. It's important for women to keep working, because the struggle isn't over yet.

I think some of the men are just starting to realize how much "power"—I don't know what you'd call it—how much "pull" the Tobique women have. The men don't want to admit it, but they are beginning to. For example, the men held a protest a couple of years ago over the administration hiring a French guy—I guess they felt the Frenchman was taking their job. They blocked the roads, but only lasted for two or three hours. There was only three men out there, and they asked the women to support them. I said, "Yes, I support you, but I'm not going to stand out there. I don't have the jobs—you do." I said, "I'll make coffee or sandwiches, whatever you need, but you have to be out there and do it on your own." I wanted to sit back and watch them do it. It only lasted a few hours. (laughter)

The men never realized what it takes. They would have to really believe in the cause. All the occupations we had—and some went on for months—took a lot of commitment. They caused disruptions to families, households. And you can't just do it and not explain it to the children. I had to explain to my children that it was for their own benefit I was out there protesting; if it wasn't for them, I wouldn't have to do it.

I asked my youngest daughter, Tiffany, "When you grow up, are you going to go out and protest if you don't believe in something, or if you need something?" She said, "No, I won't have to, because you're doing it for me now." (laughter)

SANDRA LOVELACE SAPPIER AND KAREN PERLEY

SANDRA: We got into a lot of arguments with the chiefs about the reinstatement issue. They said things like, "You've made your bed, now sleep in it"; "My (white) wife is an Indian because the law says she is."

KAREN: They *believed*, the government says you're Indian, so you're Indian. Therefore the government tell us we're not Indian, so we're not Indians.

SANDRA: Then we'd start arguing. Heavy arguments! (laughter) "I was born an Indian," that's what I'd tell them.

KAREN: If they believed that, where is the reason in all of it? Sometimes your own flesh and blood would say, "You're not an Indian any more. That's the law; that's the Indian Act." See how law-abiding Native Indian people are? (laughter) So we'd have these chiefs telling us, "It's our *right* to discriminate."

SANDRA: A few chiefs supported us. Davey, of course. But most of them are chauvinist. They'd say, "You're only a woman, so what do you know? Go watch your babies, clean your house." That's the attitude.

KAREN: Maybe the men will start changing now that the law has changed, though I don't think some of them realize yet that it has really changed. The other day a guy from here wanted to register his white bride. The band office said, "No way," and was he mad. See, that's how "aware" they are. The guy kept arguing, still trying to make her an Indian. What nerve!

SANDRA: Another argument our so-called leaders used against us was, giving women their status back would "dilute the Indian culture." How could it? I teach my children my Indian culture; the white women teach their kids their *white* culture, because the men are out working. It's mostly the mothers that teach the kids. My children are surrounded by my culture, my language, so how can we dilute it? I think Indian women coming back will *improve* it.

When you hear some of those guys, you get really angry. Then you go out there even if it means scraping together your welfare pennies to do it. If they are going to treat my child different from theirs, that makes me angry. Plus, I have two daughters and I don't want them to have to go through the same thing.

All that lobbying we did! The most devastating experience for me was when Joe Clark's government fell in late 1979. That was disgusting because we knew we were so close; Clark had promised the change. We were so sure. Then we had to start from square one with the Liberals all over again, and we already knew what asses the Liberals are. (laughter) They listen to men.

KAREN: There were so many frustrating experiences, I can't think of which was the worst. The Liberals, Indian Affairs. The Union (of New Brunswick Indians) so much against us, telling the media, "If there is reinstatement, there's going to be violence"— well, there hasn't been any violence yet.

SANDRA: Graydon, the Union president, told the media there was going to be violence if the women were reinstated. Who is going to doing the violence? The Union? He said people would burn any houses the non-status get. I doubt it. I don't think anyone would dare do that here, because the women would stick together.

KAREN: It was so frustrating when those guys talked so nice to our face, then went against us behind our back; also when the Native Women's Association of Canada wouldn't fight for the same things as us, when it should have been their fight too.

One thing I wish didn't happen was all the tension and bad feeling right here at home during the occupations. God, it was awful. You could feel the hate. Honest, it is just this year I started talking to some of those people—and it is an election year! (laughter) I won't be talking to them for long; things start getting dug up again.

SANDRA: The really painful stuff was right here at home. Plus strain on marriages and relationships because we were always gone lobbying. Especially towards the end, it started happening to all of us—"Gee, you're going *again?*" But we'd all go. (laughter) Because we knew it was important. We had to get it done and reinstatement was so close.

KAREN: I think we came up with some good strategies along the way, like getting white women's groups involved, writing letters and sending petitions to Ottawa. Some of those organizations were really big, like the United Church and NAC. The women's walk to Ottawa because it was women and children—we knew that would get to people. Getting to know the women MPs and senators. *They* did a lot of lobbying for us. Flora MacDonald, Lynn McDonald. Like in 1981 the women in parliament and senate from all the parties held a press conference and issued a joint statement calling for an end to 12(1)(b).

Then there were the strategies here at home. The petitions. Ninety-five percent of band members signed in favour of reinstatement, and we could tell people outside about that. Another good strategy was near election time when we thought, who can we get in here for chief that would support us? That's when we came up with Dave Perley.

SANDRA: At first he wasn't interested, but then individual people talked to him, "Come on, Davey, go for it." He did and after that, it always helped to tell the media, "Our chief supports us. He backs us up and accepts us." I always made sure I mentioned it, because it would make the other chiefs look bad for not supporting their women.

KAREN: Another thing, I think Glenna and Caroline were talking about, and honestly, I was just waiting for it to happen; having all of our sons marry the non-status women just so they could become status again. We were going to plan a *mass wedding*, like my son would marry Mavis or Pearl, and so on. (laughter) It sure would have gotten a lot of press! I was kind of looking forward to that. But we didn't have to go that far.

Another effective strategy was Sandra's case to the United Nations. That's what got the media attention. I mean, it's *history*; it will be in history books, "Sandra Lovelace." (laughter) Once when we were at one of those cocktail parties in Ottawa, Sandra said, "I'd better take it easy. Tomorrow it might be in the papers, 'Sandra Lovelace fell on her face'." (laughter) All those trips to Ottawa. We would leave home, drive to Fredericton, get on the plane, then get in a cab. We'd say in Indian—well, it's really hard to translate into English—"Here we go, our heads bouncing off to Ottawa again!"

KAREN: The lobbying part, we'd kind of laugh over. What was your most memorable experience?

SANDRA: Mexican food. (laughter) I don't care about the hard work, as long as I can get Mexican food.

KAREN: With me, I was still kind of nervous when it came to talking with people; I was always afraid I'd say the wrong thing, or I wouldn't understand what they were saying. (laughter) I never had to go through being interviewed for the press. I never said too much. I would tell Caroline, "Why should I go? I never really say anything." She'd say, "Yes, but you're very good at remembering things and writing stuff down."

SANDRA: There have to be people who watch and take notes.

KAREN: That's right. You sit and watch what's going on in the background while the other person is busy talking, and you learn a lot of things.

SANDRA: Even if we went and relaxed over a drink, we'd talk about it all the time; going over what had just happened, deciding what to do the next day. That's how we *lived*—it was our life.

KAREN: Another time, way back during the walk, somebody— Glenna, I think—called a cab. It was her first time in Ottawa, and she didn't know where anything was. We were on Parliament Hill and she told the cab driver where we wanted to go. A bunch of us women climbed in, and the guy drove around the corner and stopped. (laughter) The place was right there.

SANDRA: We had our disagreements, but we never disagreed on the most important issue. Our goal was reinstatement and we all agreed to that.

KAREN: If a couple of us disagreed over something, we'd just stay away from each other for a while, and by the next meeting everything would be all right. We never let anything break us up or stand in our way.

I think we were the first group of women to ever stand up to a chief and council on a reserve. We are amongst the reserves I know of. Maybe—I hope—some are doing it *now*. Why us?

SANDRA: Strong women. Stubborn, too.

KAREN: Strong, political-minded people, I think. Like Glenna is a very strong woman. Gookum. They were the two that started it.

My mother was politically minded. When election time came around, she got into it—on the reserve and federal elections, too. We were exposed to politics at an early age.

Another thing is that we all lived in the States and travelled a lot. Maybe if you stay on the reserve all your life, you don't see anything. I mean, you live in a small, little world. But when you leave, and then come back, you see the difference.

SANDRA: You start asking, how come things are happening here that aren't happening anywheres else?

KAREN: And the ones who haven't been anywheres else were the hardest ones to try and convince to change.

Another thing with Tobique is that we've kept our language, whereas other reserves around here haven't so much. Maybe some of the matrilineal stuff and the strength of the women has been passed on, too.

SANDRA: A long time ago, before Christianity got in here, I think the men and women lived together equally. There was no discrimination. It was the women who chose their leader traditionally, because they were the ones raising the children; they knew who was strong.

When the men argued that they didn't want reinstatement for fear of the white men coming in and taking over, I think it's really us women they were afraid of. I think that is the main reason the chiefs opposed us so much. They know we are persistent. If we believe in something, we will fight, we'll keep at it until something comes of it. Maybe the men are afraid of the competition. (laughter)

That's why they want self-government without sexual equality. I never wanted self-government before the women got their rights back. The men have to work with the women to accomplish anything, and the sooner they learn that, the better *everybody* will be. I told a guy in Ottawa, "Listen, if you men would only work with us in *unity*." See, they were the ones always talking about "unity," but they didn't even want me back on the reserve and I was born here. I said, "If we all worked together we could have a lot of things accomplished. We could get Indian self-government, but we have to work together and be equal." He said, "You're right." But do you think they would do it? Not yet.

SHIRLEY BEAR

Looking back, one funny memory is of Caroline and I running around Ottawa at the Parliament Buildings trying to get $5.00 from somebody for lunch; or trying to have somebody buy lunch for us without being too obvious about it. My God. We were so damn poor. (laughter)

Also, the process of our getting to know each other. Caroline's really different from me; her values are different, her dealing with people is entirely different from mine. It took a lot of *honing* for us to be able to work together. Yet when we were doing workshops you wouldn't know there was that much difference between us.

I found Caroline very enjoyable to work with because she believed in the issue so much. I tend to go one hundred and fifty to two hundred percent over something I believe in. Peter put it to me one time, "If you went at your art the way you go at 12(1)(b), you'd be famous by now!" (laughter) It's true, too, because I put my whole heart and soul into the damn issue.

I would come home and say, "I'm not going on any more trips," then a while later the phone would ring and Peter would look at me, "Are you answering it?" When I answered, sure enough, there would be Caroline on the other end, saying, "Shirley, we just *have* to go to Ottawa. There's this really important thing happening."

One of the things I had a hard time dealing with was that Caroline would get an urgent phone call and would not take notes. She'd end up saying to me, "We need to make reservations. We're going." I'd go to work, make the reservations, only to realize that I didn't know where the hell I was going, beyond our main destination. Beyond that, *no information*.

That's when I'd call Caroline, and she's not home. She's out shopping. A new outfit to go to this lobbying session, right? By the time I'd get ahold of her, she'd say, "Oh, minor detail!" (laughter) I'd be having a fit, you know—"What are we going to eat?" Caroline would assure me, "Oh, don't worry about it." Wouldn't you know it? When we arrived in Ottawa, there'd be no money for food, no place to stay. That happened to me twice, then I started saying to Caroline, "No. Either you get all the details and make sure we have the money, or I'm not going." (laughter) After that she got more diligent about getting the money.

When I think about it, our getting that Indian Act changed was pretty amazing. Especially when you think of the hundreds and thousands of dollars that went into lobbying *against* reinstatement. In comparison we got what? A few thousand dollars. Over all our years of lobbying perhaps not even $10,000. The Assembly of First Nations had all their big lawyers, their big budgets, their lobbying power, their 'old boys' network."

And we got status back for our kids too. On this reserve we can likely get them band membership, once we have our band membership code in place. We got status back for the first generation children, and then it's up to the bands to decide on whether they get onto band lists. Plus, the reinstated women can have their say as band members on those codes; they can work and vote to get their children back on.

If the bands try to write sexual inequality into those membership codes, when they are screened by Ottawa that inequality will have to be taken out. That's why we still need a strong sexual equality clause for Native women in the Canadian Constitution— so that the aboriginal rights clause can't be used to over-rule sexual equality. That's why we'll keep lobbying for that clause as long as we need to.

If the bands don't get their act together and develop their band membership codes by the summer of 1987, the very thing will happen the men are most afraid of; the Indian Affairs bureaucracy will impose a membership code on them. In other words, Indian Affairs will again be making policies for Indian people. See, the new Act puts pressure on bands to take control of their own affairs, and that's exactly what the chiefs *say* they want.

We got those changes for them, and that's what the chiefs never realized—we're on their side. Those Indian leaders never understood that. They think that we women are just one way; that we want women's rights and don't care about anything else. We've always been for Native rights and the good of *all* Native people, the First Nations. Now they have to realize that if they don't get off their asses, and start making policies for the bands *now*, Indian Affairs is going to keep right on dictating to us. Two years—the time the bands were given to make up their own membership codes—goes by damn fast.

You know, when the Indian Act was amended to eliminate sexual discrimination, those changes gave Indian people more *power* than they ever had before. When the Act states that the bands are to come up with the policies, the criteria to determine band membership, that is more power. But who is seeing it as more power?

The time has come for the men to stop fighting against the women and start listening to us and working with us. What Sandra said is true: If we all worked together we could get a lot accomplished. We could have Indian self-government, but first we have to work together and be equal.

CHRONOLOGY OF EVENTS

1869
— Canadian Indian reservation system defined in Constitution Act

1876
— Indian Act introduced which regulates reserve life and defines who is legally Indian

1951
— Indian Act amended, but major aspects remain unchanged

1960s
— Individual Indian women such as Mary Two-Axe Early of Quebec publically condemn the sexual discriminatory sections of the Indian Act

1971
— Jeannette Lavell challenges sexual discrimination in the Indian Act through the Canadian court system
— Yvonne Bedard takes a similar case to court

1973
— Supreme Court rules against Lavell and Bedard, holding that the Indian Act could not be superseded by the Canadian Bill of Rights

Autumn 1976
— Juanita Perley occupies public building on Tobique Reserve, New Brunswick

Late August 1977
— Women demonstrate in front of Tobique band office over housing

— Women from Tobique demonstrate in front of Indian Affairs building, Fredericton, New Brunswick

August 30, 1977
— Tobique women begin band office occupation

Early September 1977
— Women are served with court injunction from the chief ordering them out of band office; they disregard the injunction

Mid-September 1977
— Band administration moves office equipment and files out of band office; women remain

October 3, 1977
— In band election women's candidate, Vaughn Nicholas, defeats former chief, George Francis

October 4, 1977
— Fire set in band office; extinguished by the women

November 1977
— Women gradually move out of band office

December 29, 1977
—Complaint of Sandra Lovelace against the Canadian government is filed with the United Nations Human Rights Committee, Geneva, Switzerland

Summer 1978
— Vaughn Nicholas resigns; George Francis is re-elected chief in by-election

July 14-21, 1979
— Native Women's Walk to Ottawa to protest the housing conditions on reservations

July 21, 1979
— Native Women's Rally on Parliament Hill, Ottawa

Fall 1979
— George Francis re-elected chief

Late November 1979
— Women occupy band office over continuing housing problems
— Violence results in a number of women moving into Perth-Andover motel for three weeks

Winter 1979/80
—Several "mini-protests" at band office over women's housing problems

January 1980
— Federal Conservative government of Joe Clark is defeated by Pierre Elliot Trudeau and the Liberals

Mid-1980
— Tobique band office burned to ground by arson

December 1980
— Shirley Bear leads protest at Big Cove Reserve, New Brunswick

Spring 1981
— Tobique women organize New Brunswick Native Women's Conference, Fredericton
— Shirley Bear is appointed to New Brunswick Advisory Council on the Status of Women
— Caroline Ennis begins her association with National Action Committee on the Status of Women

July 30, 1981
— United Nations Human Rights Committee finds Canada in breach of the International Covenant on Civil and Political Rights over sexual discrimination in the Indian Act

Mid-1981
— Caroline Ennis and Shirley Bear produce "12(1)(b)" pamphlet

1982
— Tobique women begin the regular practice of attending conferences and assemblies to promote the 12(1)(b) issue

March 1983
— Several Tobique women lobby at First Ministers' Conference on Constitutional Aboriginal Matters, Ottawa

Spring 1983
— National telephone campaign by Tobique women from the national headquarters of The United Church of Canada

October 1983
— Women's candidate, Dave Perley, elected chief in Tobique band election
— Women occupy band office to support the new chief and press for an investigation of old administration

March 1984
— Tobique women lobby at second First Ministers' Conference, Ottawa

June 18, 1984
— First reading of *Bill C-47: An Act to amend the Indian Act*

June 29, 1984
— Bill C-47 "killed" in Senate moments before start of Parliament's summer recess

September 4, 1984
— Federal Liberal government of John Turner defeated by Brian Mulroney and the Conservatives

November 1984
— Tobique women silenced at the Native Women's Association of Canada annual assembly, Ottawa
— Aboriginal Women's Coalition formed to fight for reinstatement of Indian women and children

Early 1985
— Bill C-31 tabled: a bill to eliminate sexual discrimination from the Indian Act

March 1985
— Tobique women present brief on Bill C-31 to the Standing

Committee on Indian Affairs and Northern Development, Ottawa
— Several Tobique women attend the third First Ministers' Conference, Ottawa

April 1985
— Canadian Charter of Rights and Freedoms takes affect, including the Section 15.(1) equality clause

June 28, 1985
— Bill C-31 passes final hurdle to become law, eliminating sexual discrimination from the Indian Act and offering full reinstatement to all those born with Indian status

August 17, 1985
— Reinstatement Celebration on Tobique Reserve

PRINTED IN CANADA
ON RECYCLED PAPER